Oh My Goddess!

ああっ女神さまっ 30

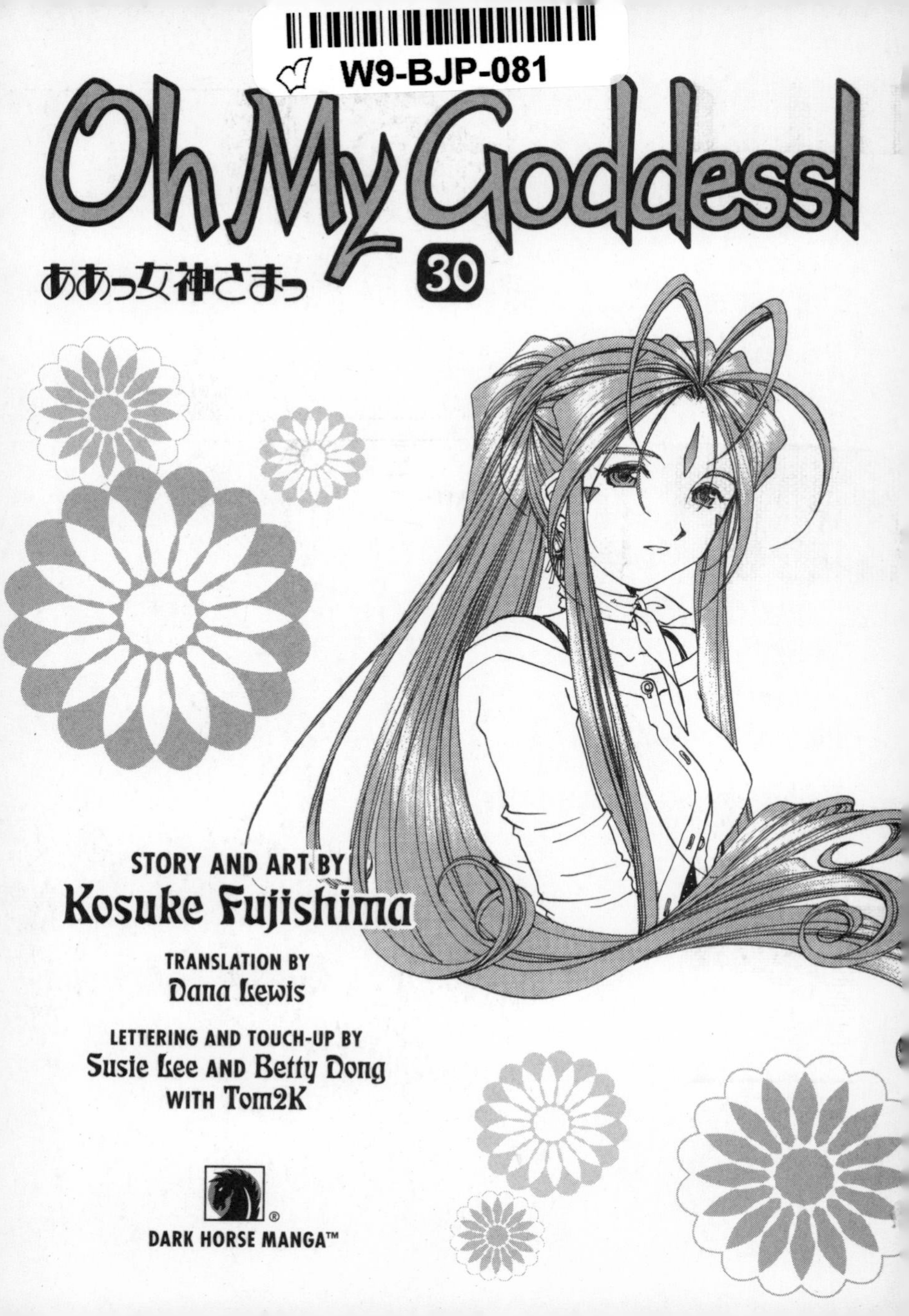

STORY AND ART BY
Kosuke Fujishima

TRANSLATION BY
Dana Lewis

LETTERING AND TOUCH-UP BY
Susie Lee AND Betty Dong
WITH Tom2K

DARK HORSE MANGA™

CHAPTER 189

Happy! Happy?

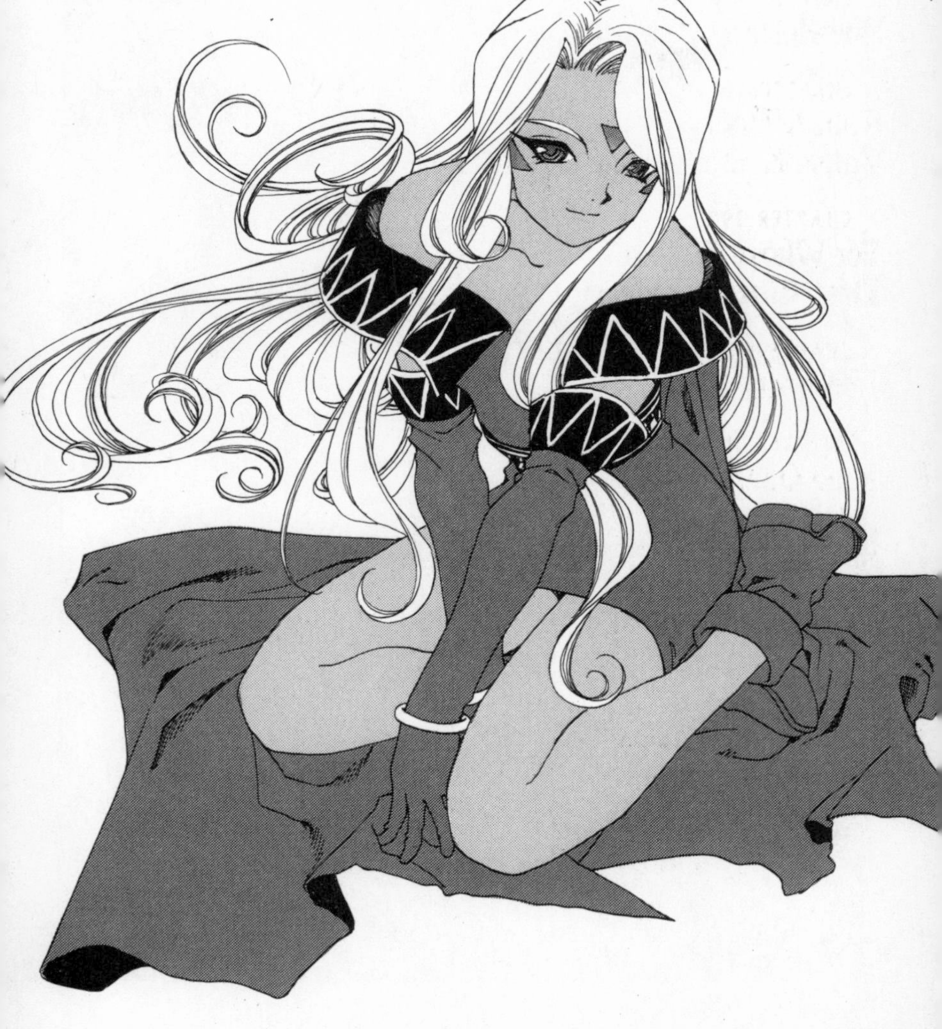

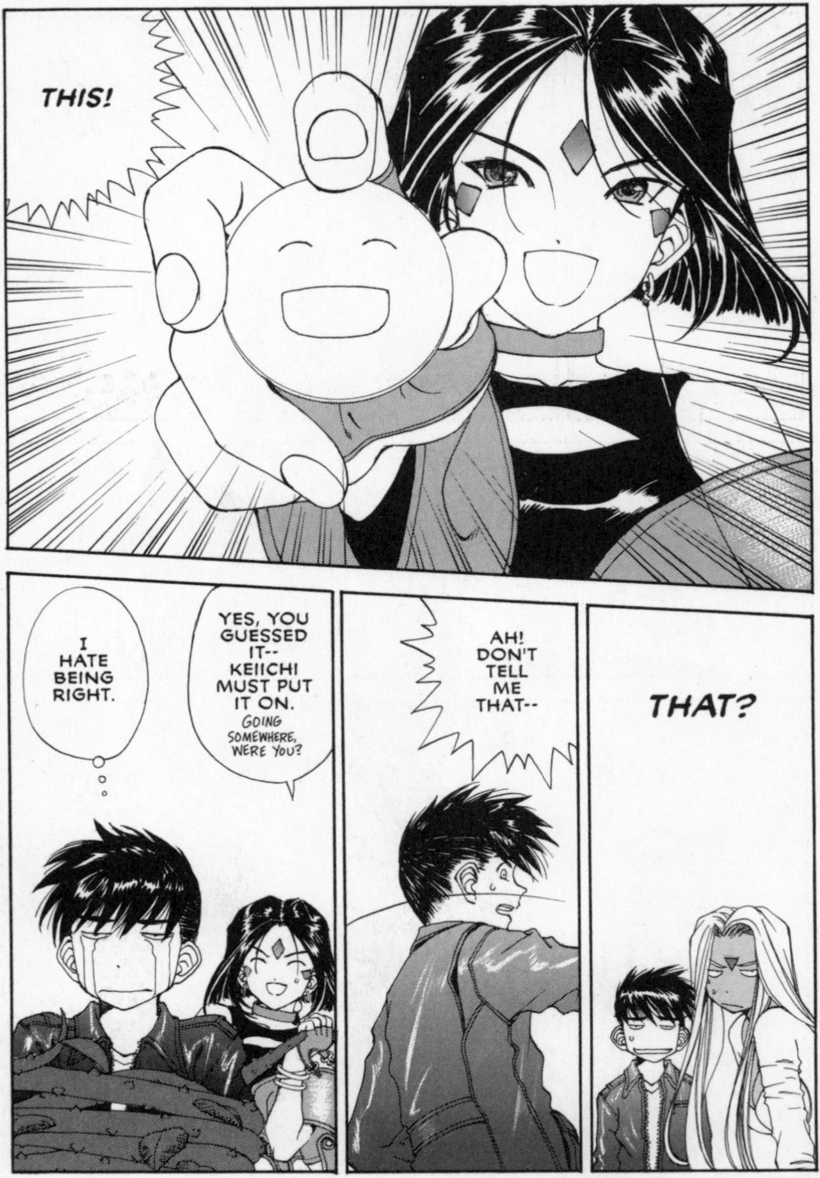
THIS!
THAT?
AH! DON'T TELL ME THAT--
YES, YOU GUESSED IT-- KEIICHI MUST PUT IT ON.
GOING SOMEWHERE, WERE YOU?
I HATE BEING RIGHT.

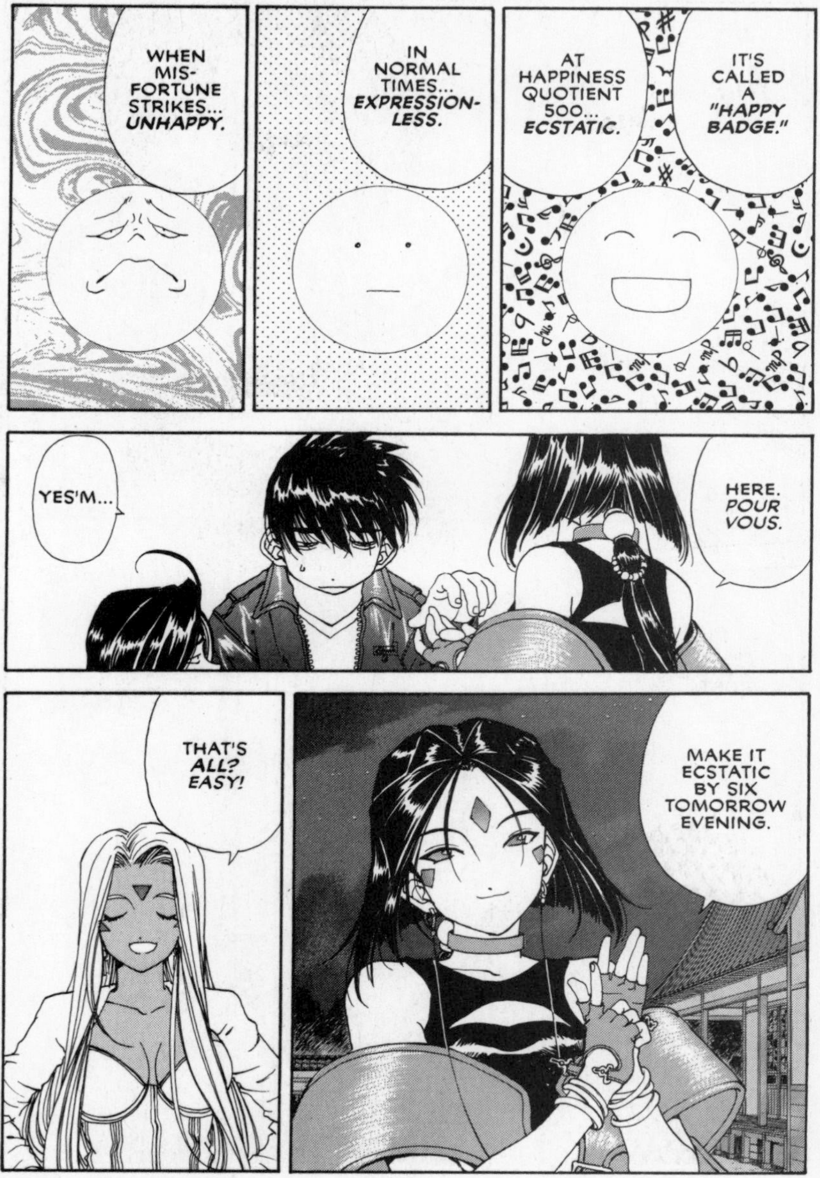
IT'S CALLED A "HAPPY BADGE."
AT HAPPINESS QUOTIENT 500... ECSTATIC.
IN NORMAL TIMES... EXPRESSIONLESS.
WHEN MISFORTUNE STRIKES... UNHAPPY.
HERE. POUR VOUS.
YES'M...
MAKE IT ECSTATIC BY SIX TOMORROW EVENING.
THAT'S ALL? EASY!

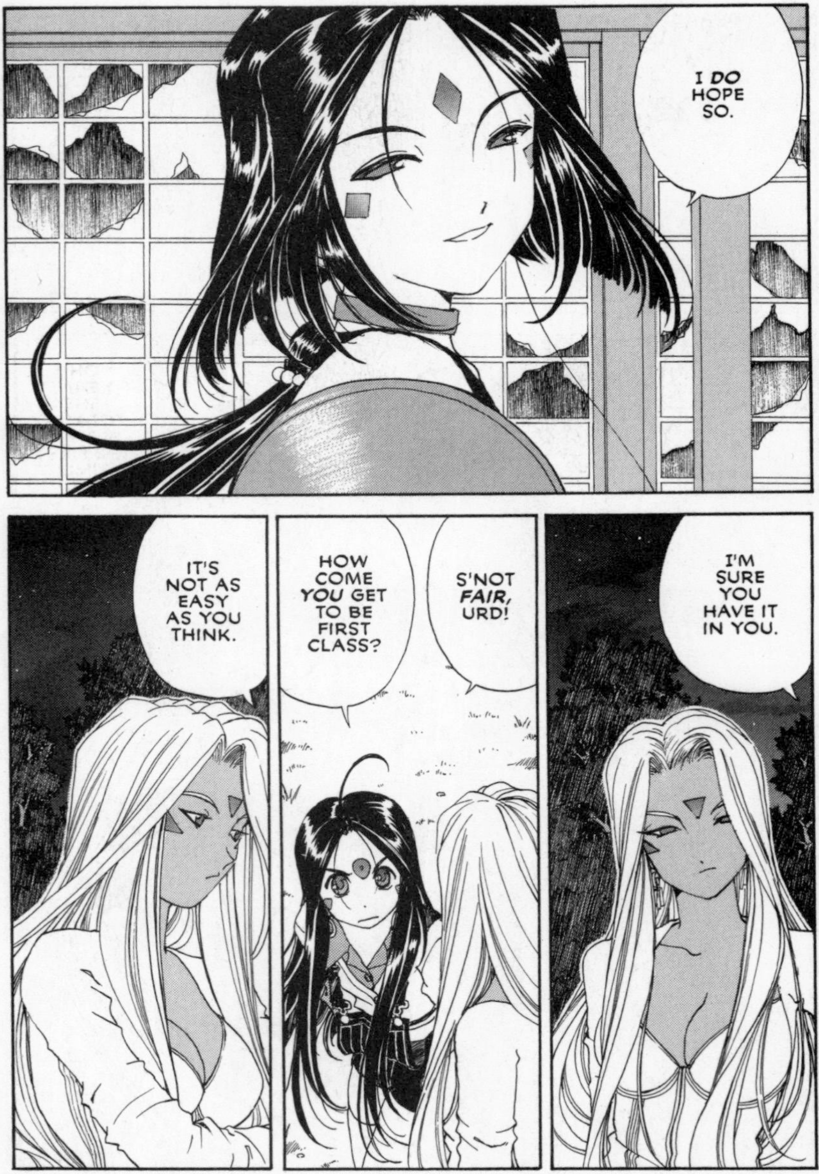
I DO HOPE SO.
I'M SURE YOU HAVE IT IN YOU.
S'NOT FAIR, URD!
HOW COME YOU GET TO BE FIRST CLASS?
IT'S NOT AS EASY AS YOU THINK.

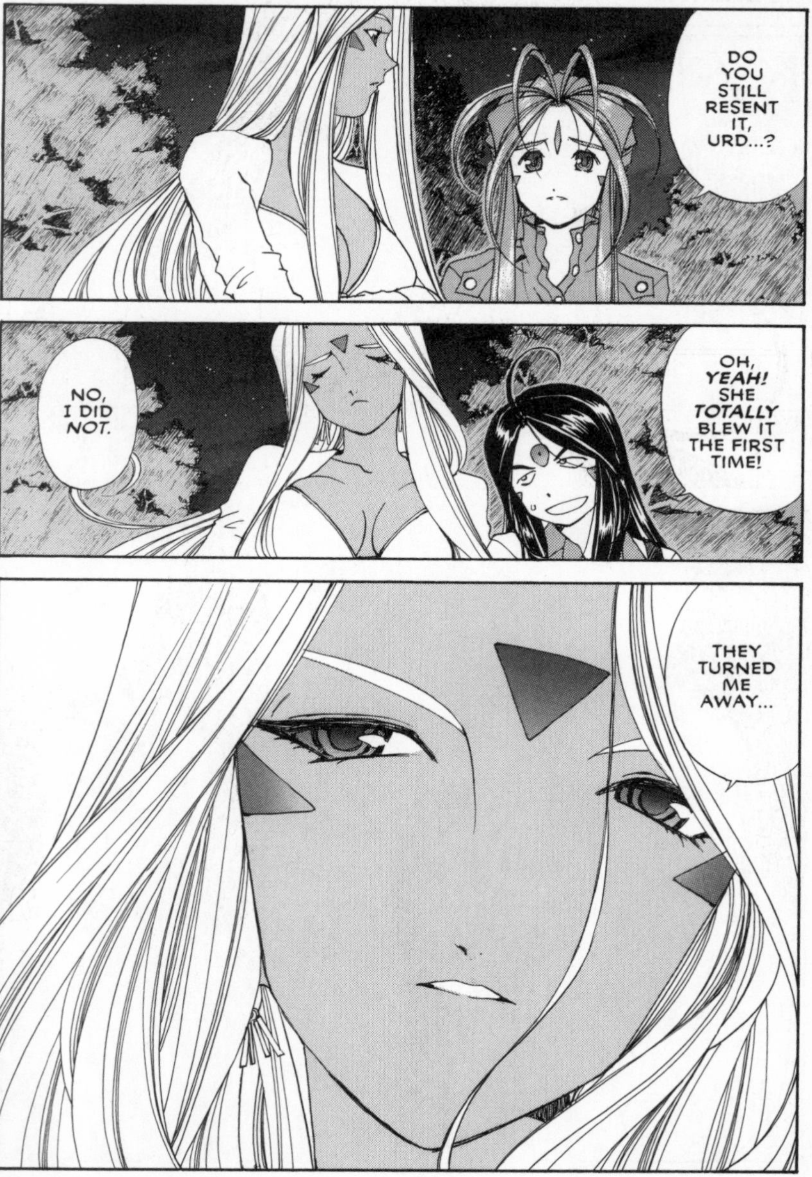
DO YOU STILL RESENT IT, URD...?
OH, *YEAH!* SHE *TOTALLY* BLEW IT THE FIRST TIME!
NO, I DID *NOT*.
THEY TURNED ME AWAY...

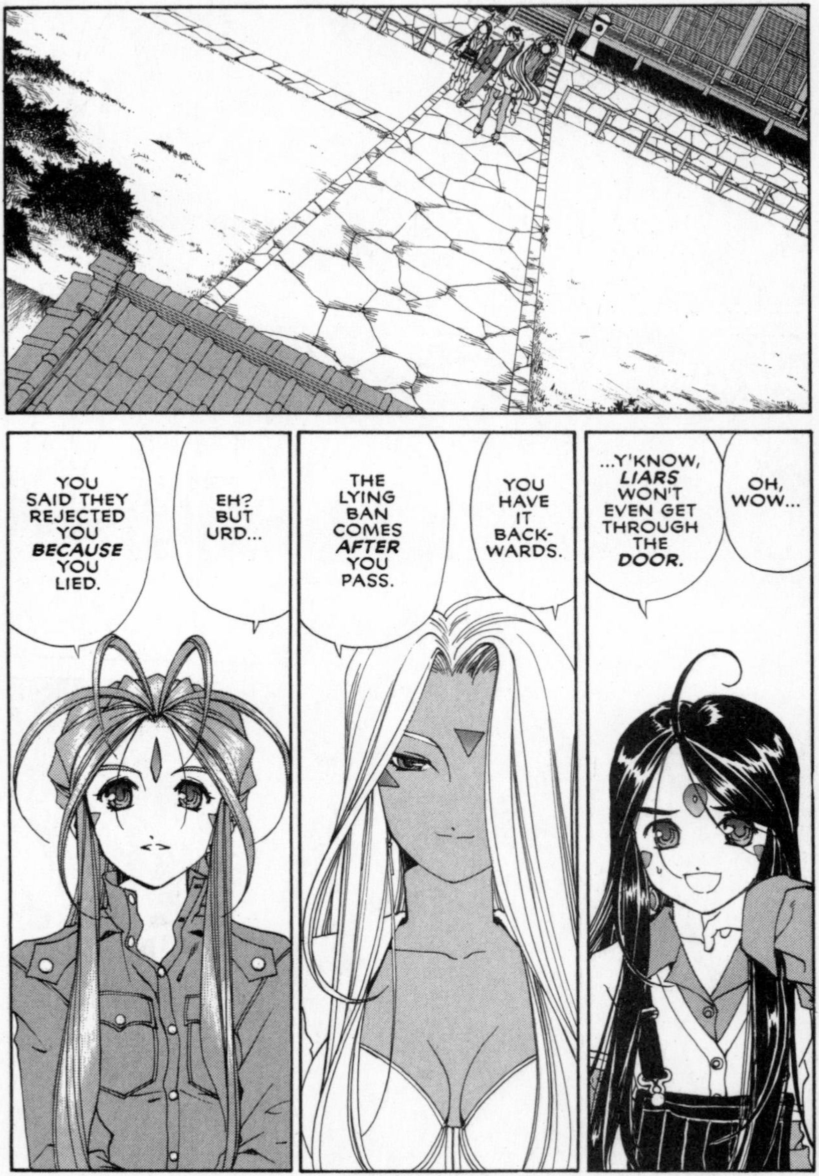
OH, WOW...
...Y'KNOW, LIARS WON'T EVEN GET THROUGH THE DOOR.
YOU HAVE IT BACK-WARDS.
THE LYING BAN COMES AFTER YOU PASS.
EH? BUT URD...
YOU SAID THEY REJECTED YOU BECAUSE YOU LIED.

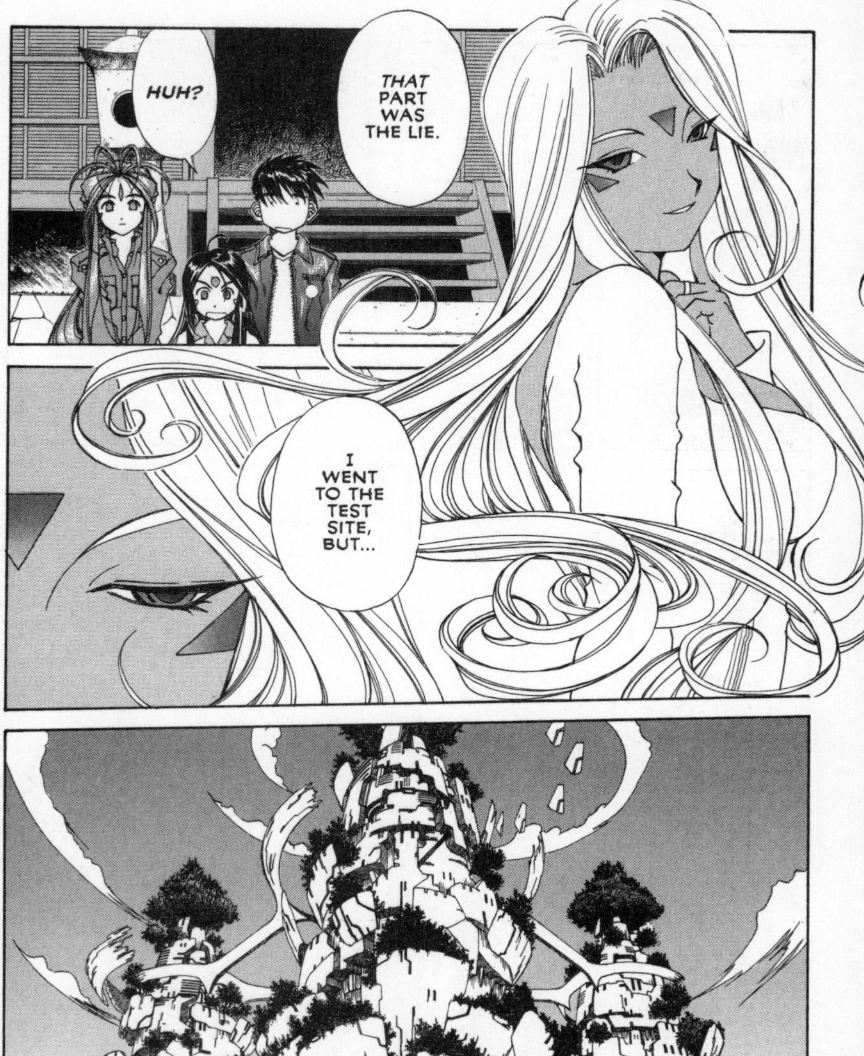
THAT PART WAS THE LIE.
HUH?
I WENT TO THE TEST SITE, BUT...

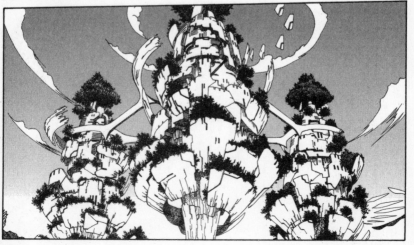

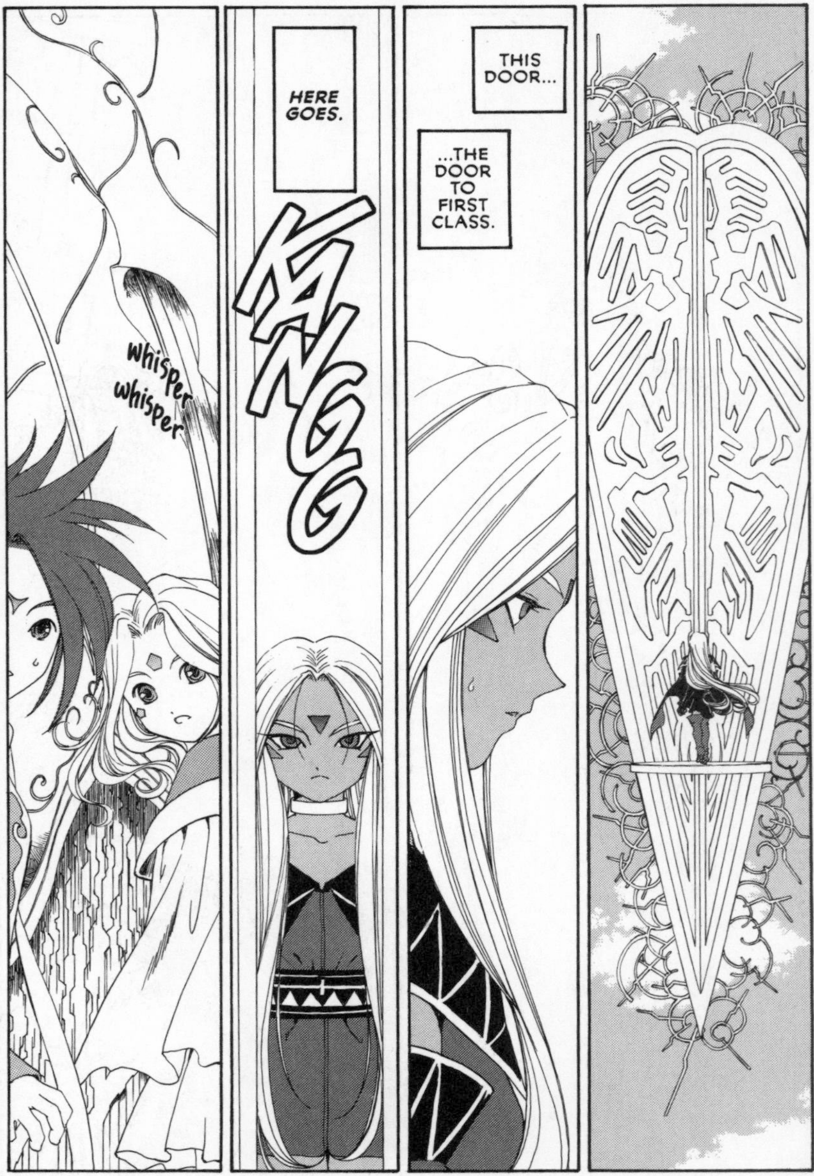
THIS DOOR...
...THE DOOR TO FIRST CLASS.
HERE GOES.
KANGG
whisper whisper

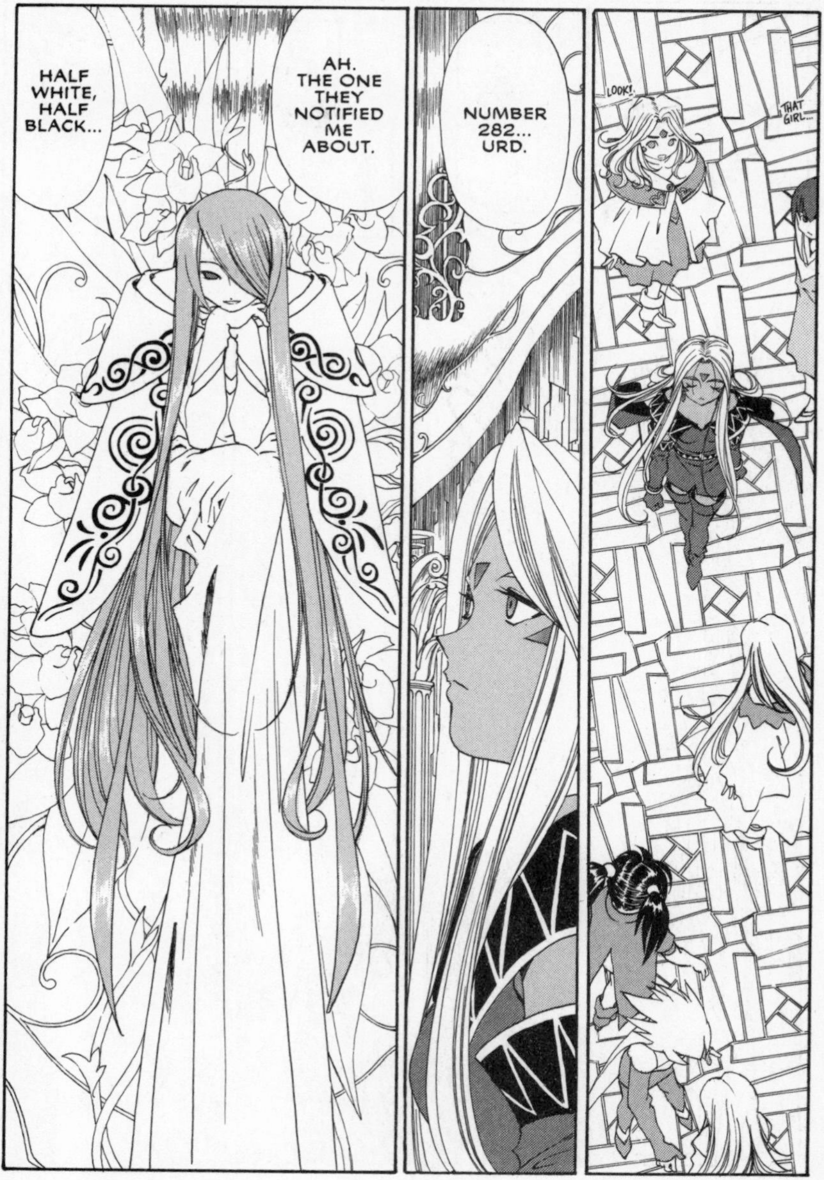
LOOK!
THAT GIRL...
NUMBER 282... URD.
AH. THE ONE THEY NOTIFIED ME ABOUT.
HALF WHITE, HALF BLACK...

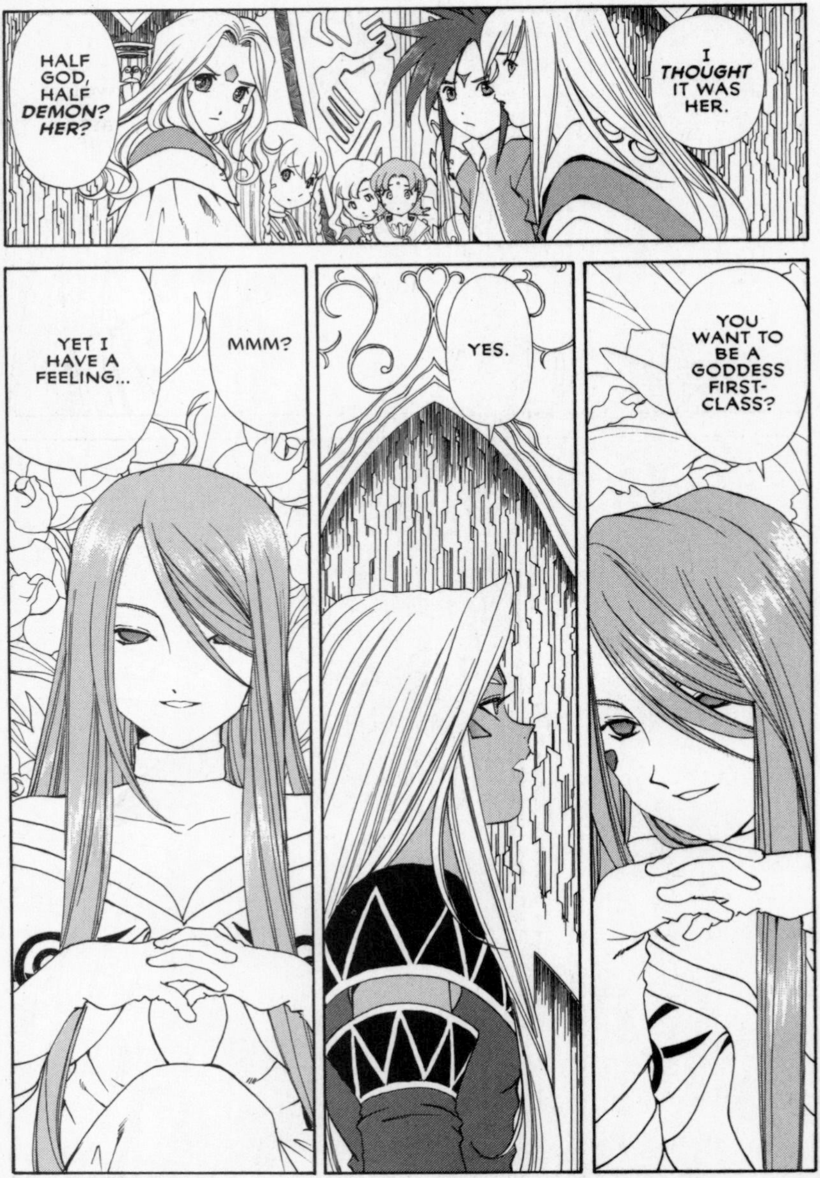
I THOUGHT IT WAS HER.
HALF GOD, HALF DEMON? HER?
YOU WANT TO BE A GODDESS FIRST-CLASS?
YES.
MMM?
YET I HAVE A FEELING...

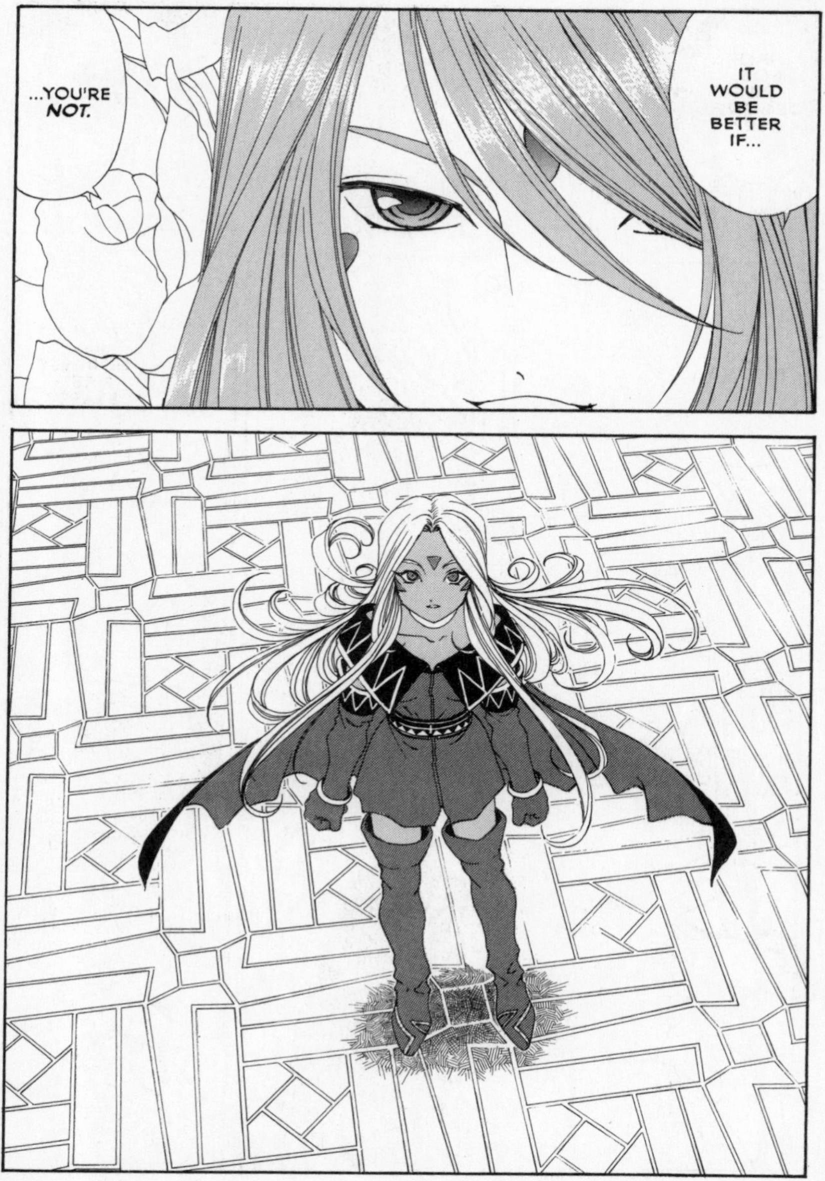
IT WOULD BE BETTER IF...
...YOU'RE *NOT.*

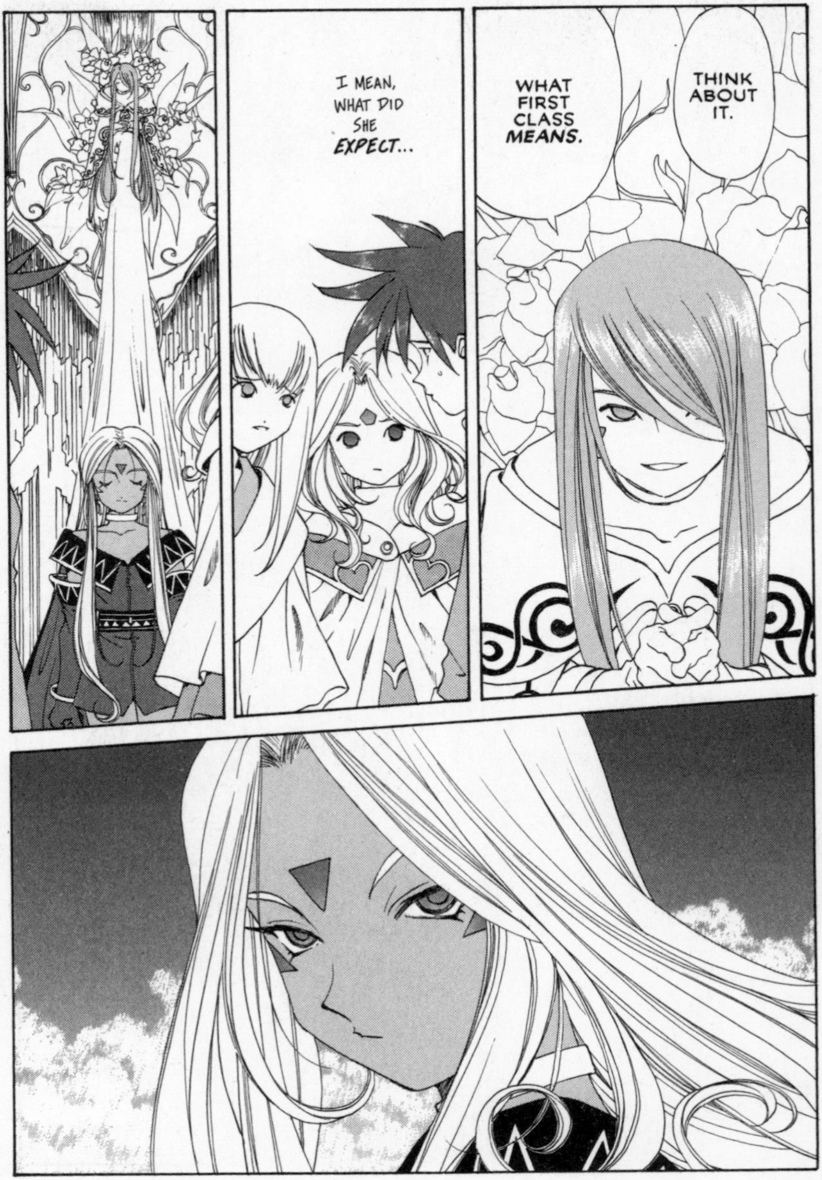
THINK ABOUT IT.
WHAT FIRST CLASS MEANS.
I MEAN, WHAT DID SHE EXPECT...

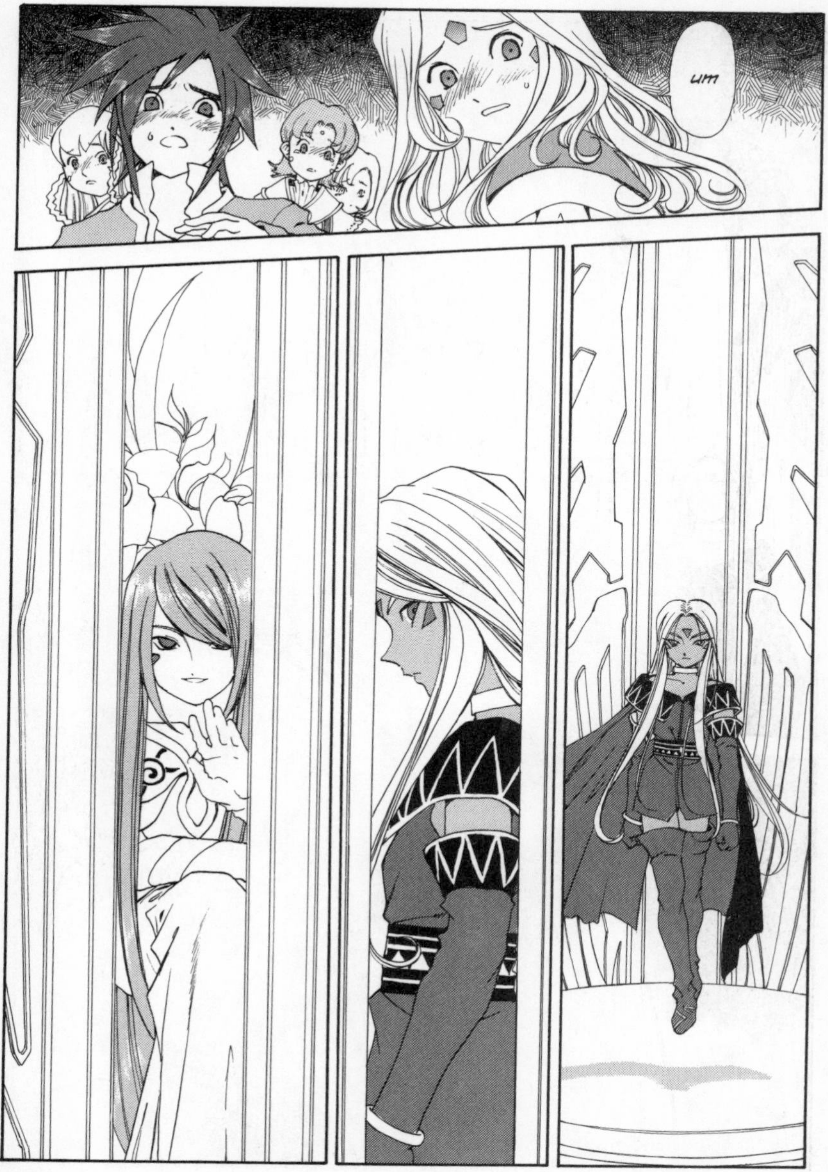
Um

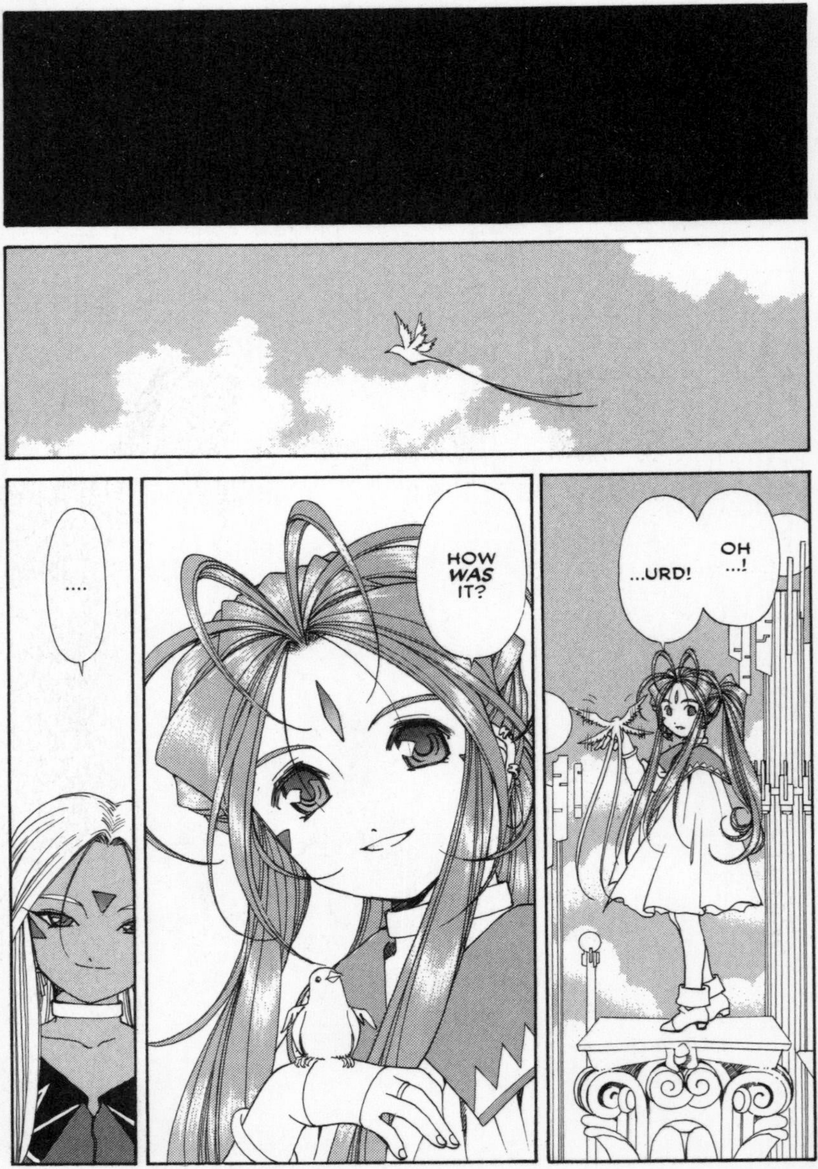
OH ...!
...URD!
HOW *WAS* IT?
....

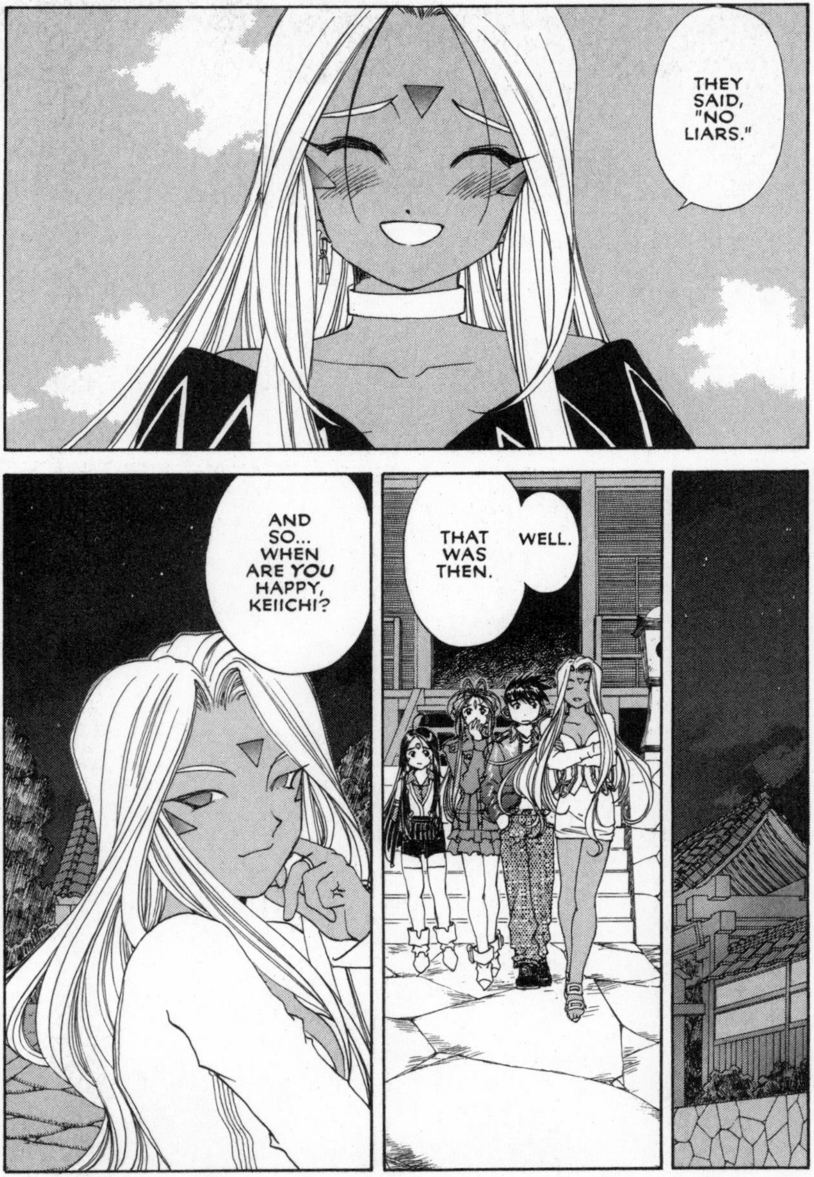
THEY SAID, "NO LIARS."
WELL.
THAT WAS THEN.
AND SO... WHEN ARE *YOU* HAPPY, KEIICHI?

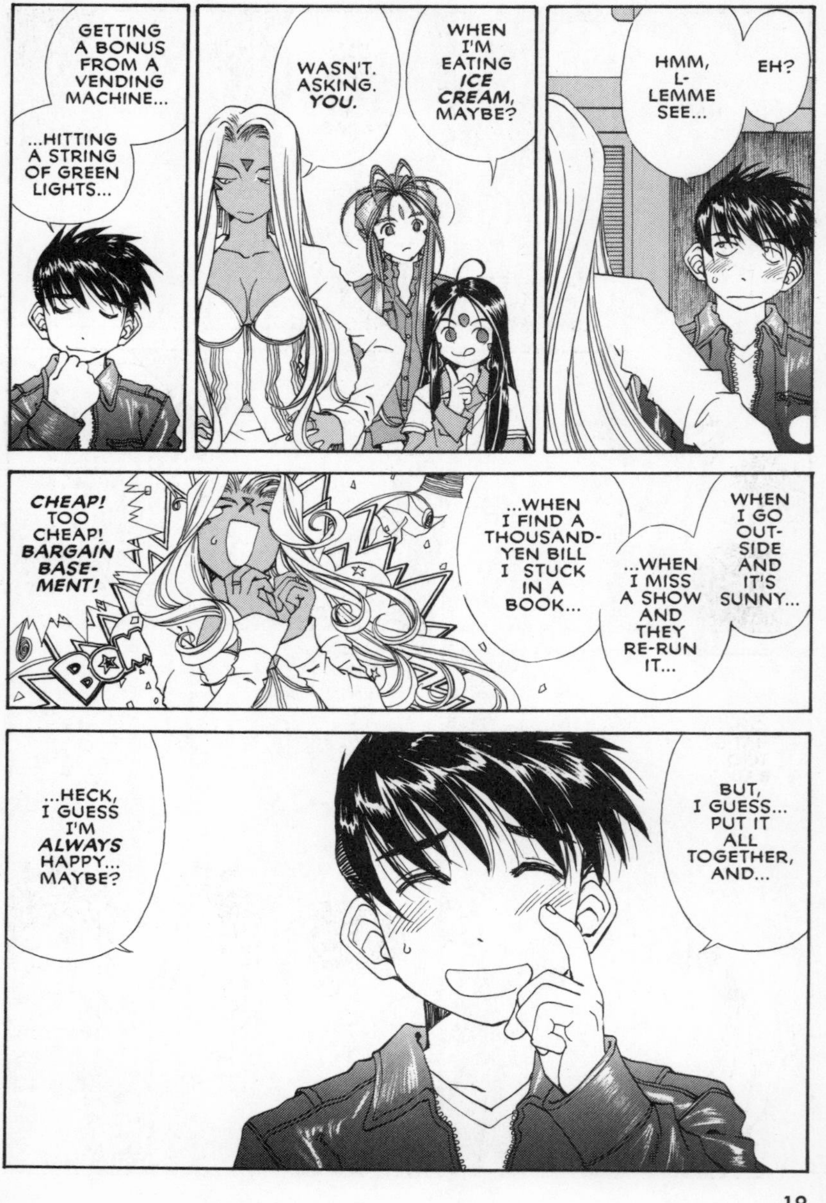
EH?
HMM, L-LEMME SEE...
WHEN I'M EATING *ICE CREAM,* MAYBE?
WASN'T. ASKING. *YOU.*
GETTING A BONUS FROM A VENDING MACHINE...
...HITTING A STRING OF GREEN LIGHTS...
WHEN I GO OUT-SIDE AND IT'S SUNNY...
...WHEN I MISS A SHOW AND THEY RE-RUN IT...
...WHEN I FIND A THOUSAND-YEN BILL I STUCK IN A BOOK...
CHEAP! TOO CHEAP! *BARGAIN BASE-MENT!*
BOM
BUT, I GUESS... PUT IT ALL TOGETHER, AND...
...HECK, I GUESS I'M *ALWAYS* HAPPY... MAYBE?

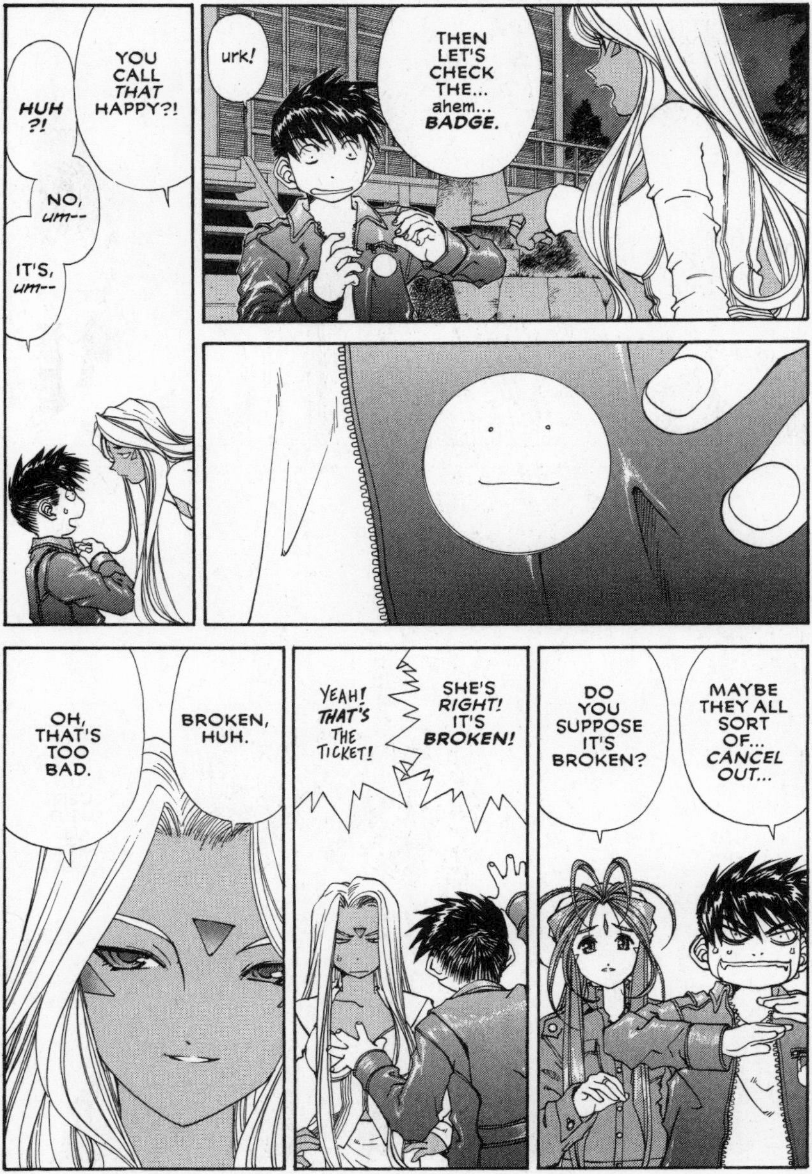
THEN LET'S CHECK THE... ahem... BADGE.
urk!
YOU CALL THAT HAPPY?!
HUH ?!
NO, um--
IT'S, um--
MAYBE THEY ALL SORT OF... CANCEL OUT...
DO YOU SUPPOSE IT'S BROKEN?
SHE'S RIGHT! IT'S BROKEN!
YEAH! THAT'S THE TICKET!
BROKEN, HUH.
OH, THAT'S TOO BAD.

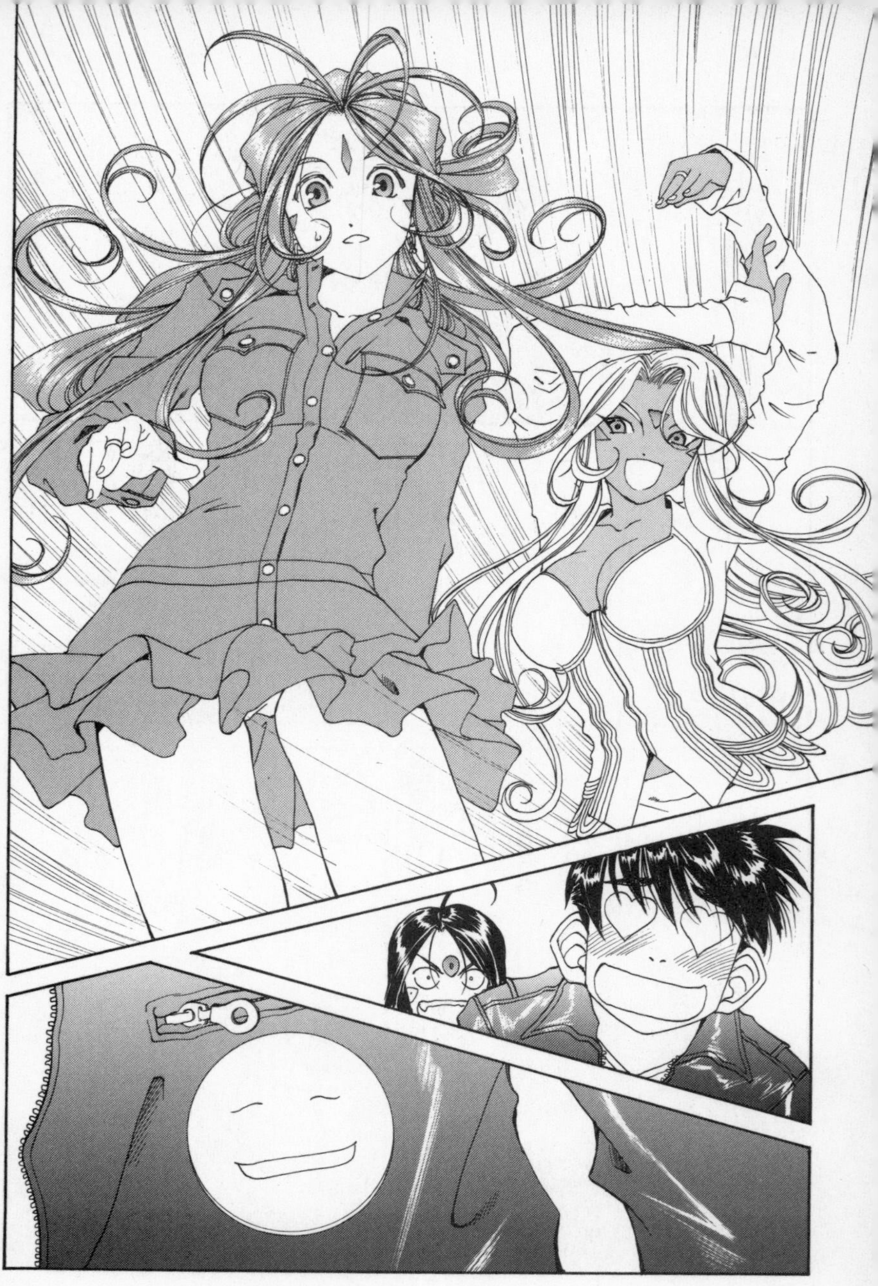

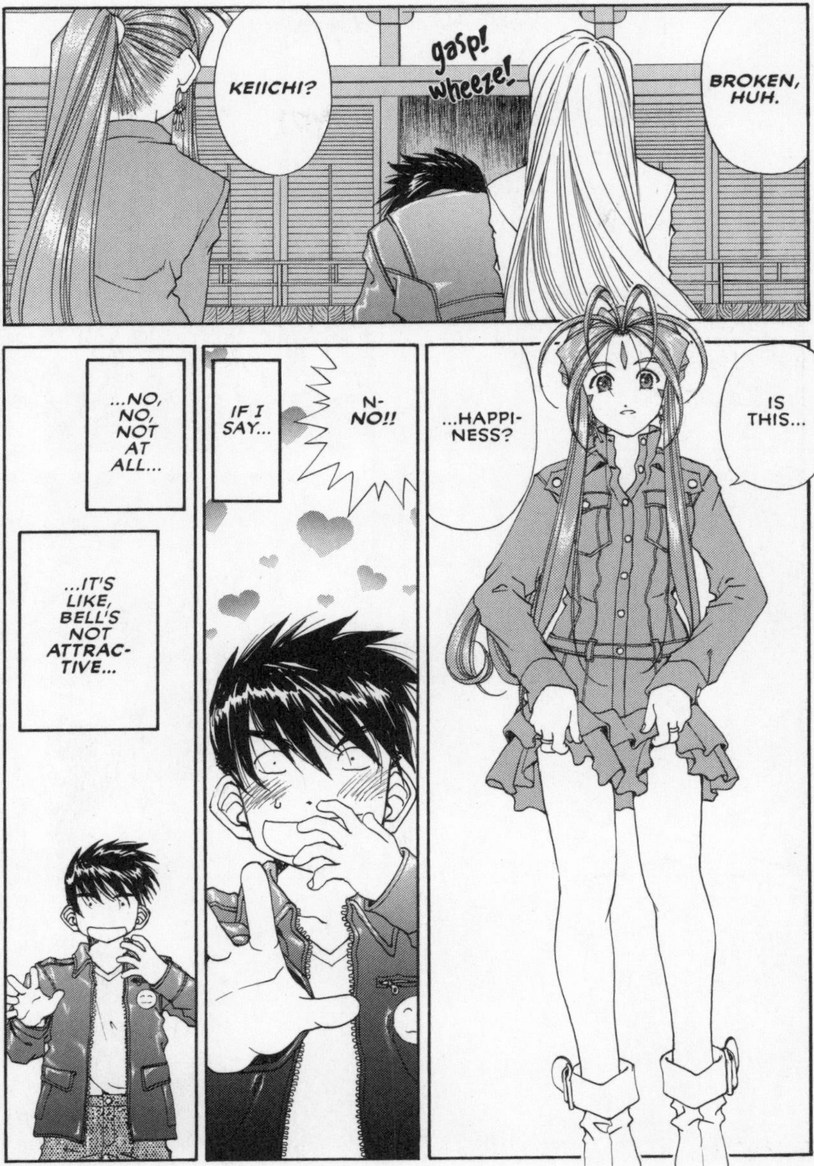
BROKEN, HUH.
gasp! wheeze!
KEIICHI?
IS THIS...
...HAPPINESS?
N-NO!!
IF I SAY...
...NO, NO, NOT AT ALL...
...IT'S LIKE, BELL'S NOT ATTRACTIVE...

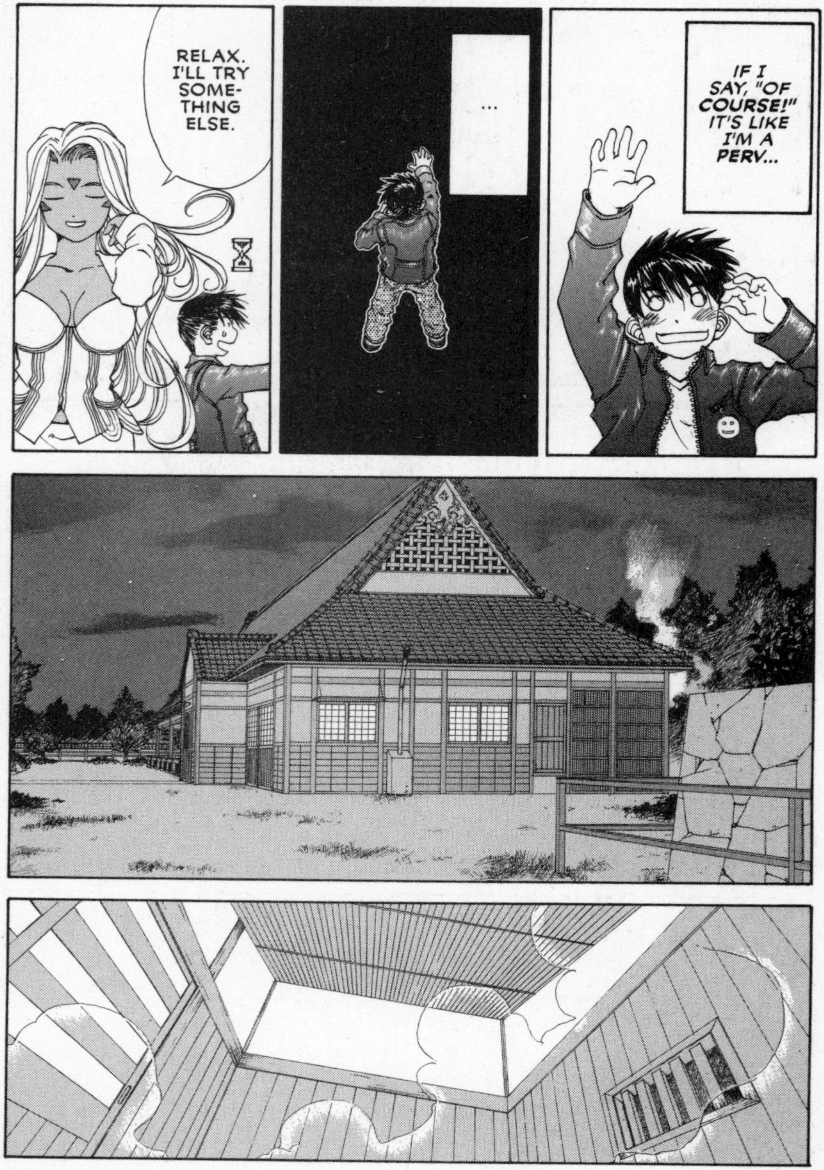
IF I SAY, "OF COURSE!" IT'S LIKE I'M A PERV...
...
RELAX. I'LL TRY SOME-THING ELSE.

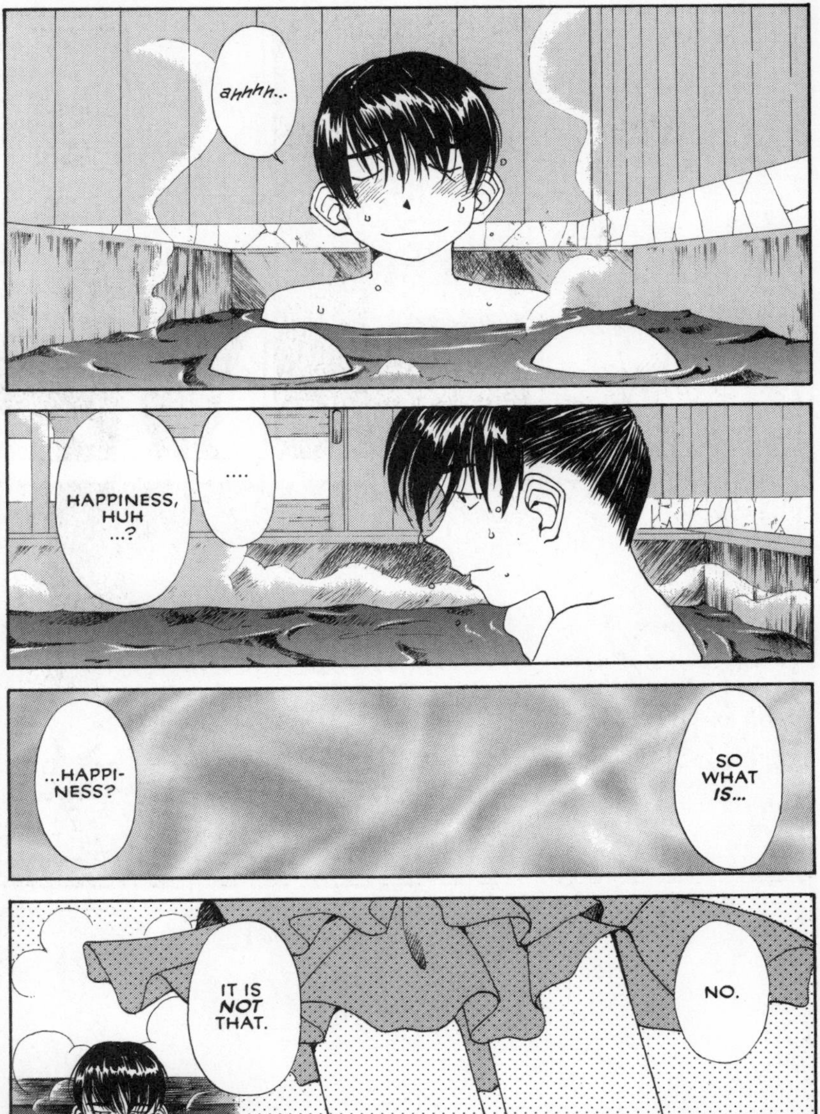
ahhhh...
....
HAPPINESS, HUH ...?
SO WHAT *IS*...
...HAPPINESS?
NO.
IT IS *NOT* THAT.

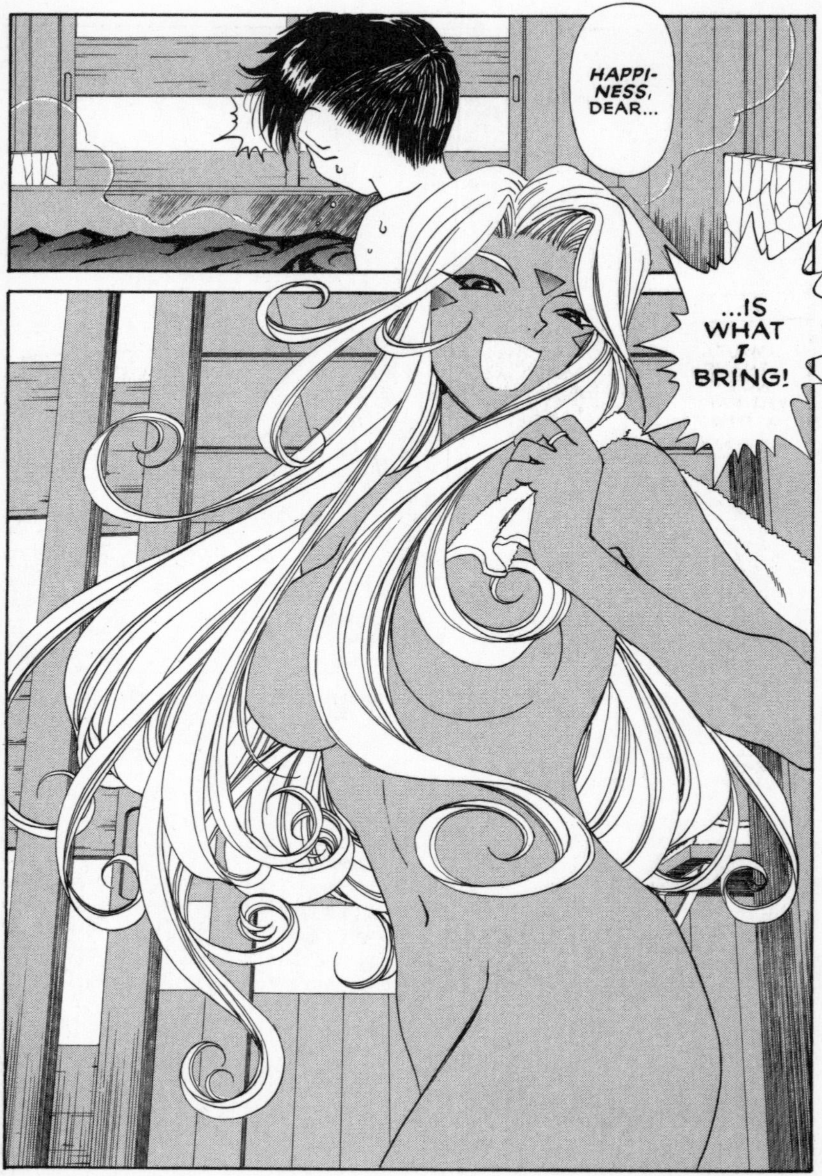
HAPPI-
NESS,
DEAR...
...IS
WHAT
I
BRING!

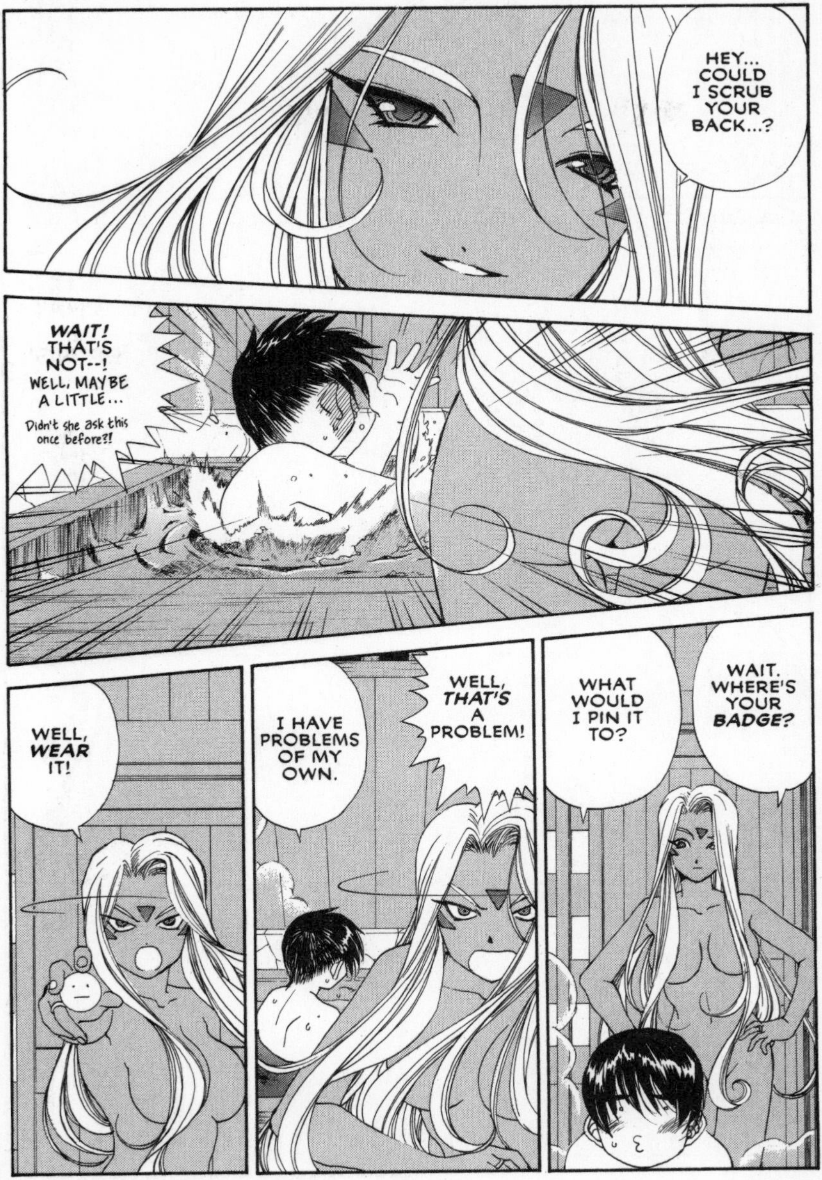
HEY... COULD I SCRUB YOUR BACK...?
WAIT! THAT'S NOT--! WELL, MAYBE A LITTLE...
Didn't she ask this once before?!
WAIT. WHERE'S YOUR BADGE?
WHAT WOULD I PIN IT TO?
WELL, THAT'S A PROBLEM!
I HAVE PROBLEMS OF MY OWN.
WELL, WEAR IT!

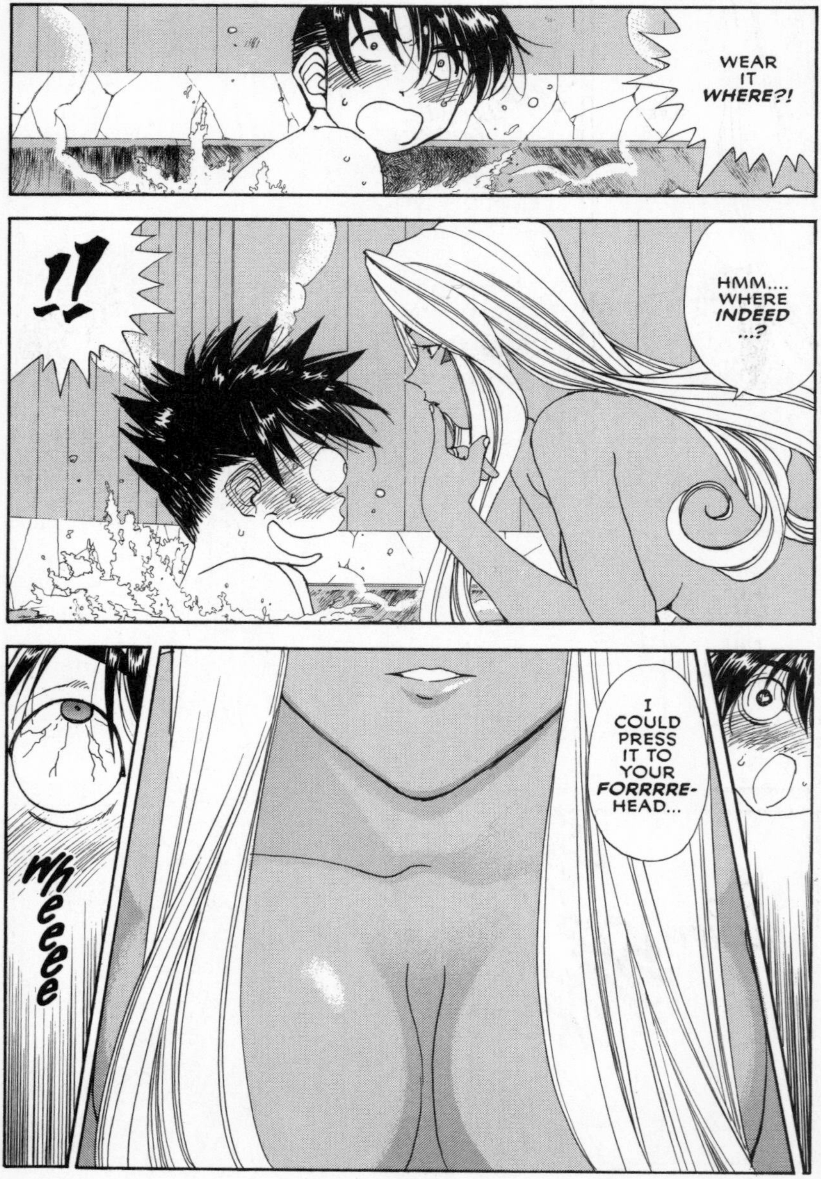
WEAR IT *WHERE?!*
HMM.... WHERE *INDEED* ...?
!!
I COULD PRESS IT TO YOUR *FORRRRE-* HEAD...
Wheeeee

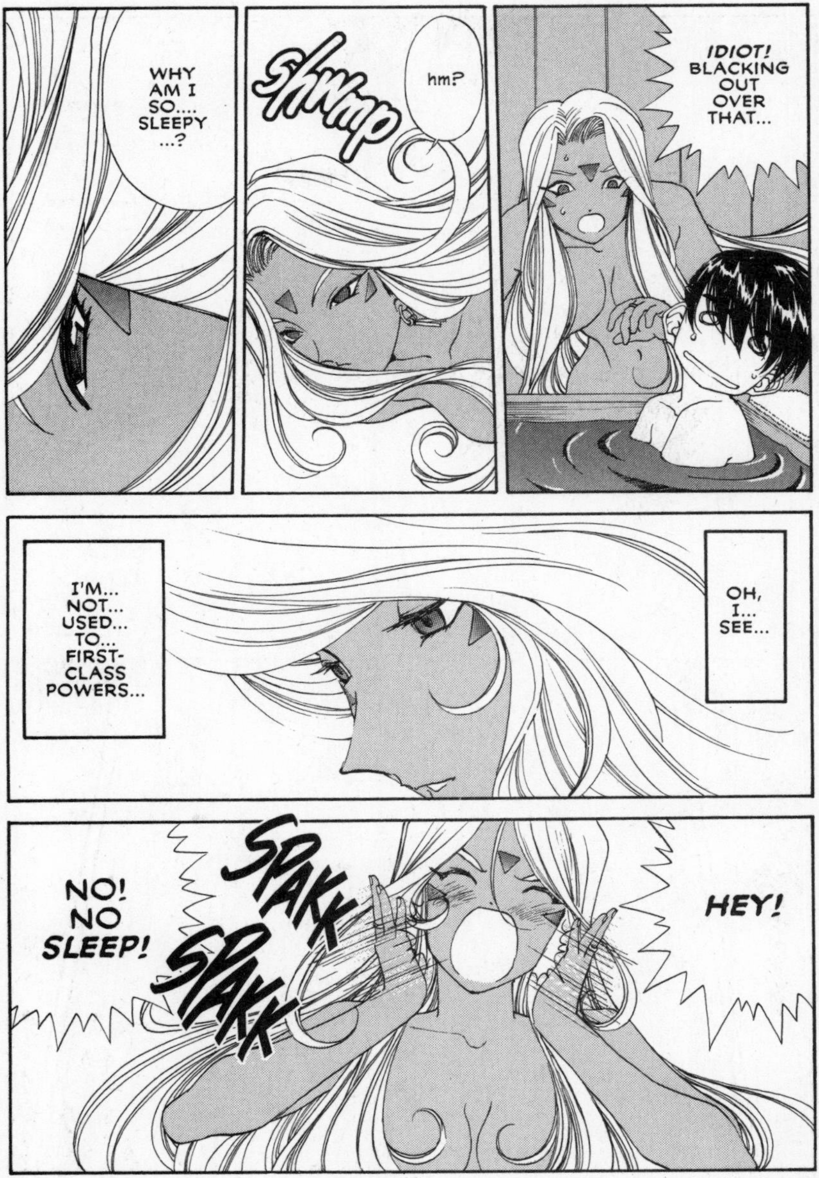

IDIOT! BLACKING OUT OVER THAT...
hm?
SHWMP
WHY AM I SO.... SLEEPY ...?
OH, I... SEE...
I'M... NOT... USED... TO... FIRST-CLASS POWERS...
HEY!
SPAKK SPAKK
NO! NO SLEEP!

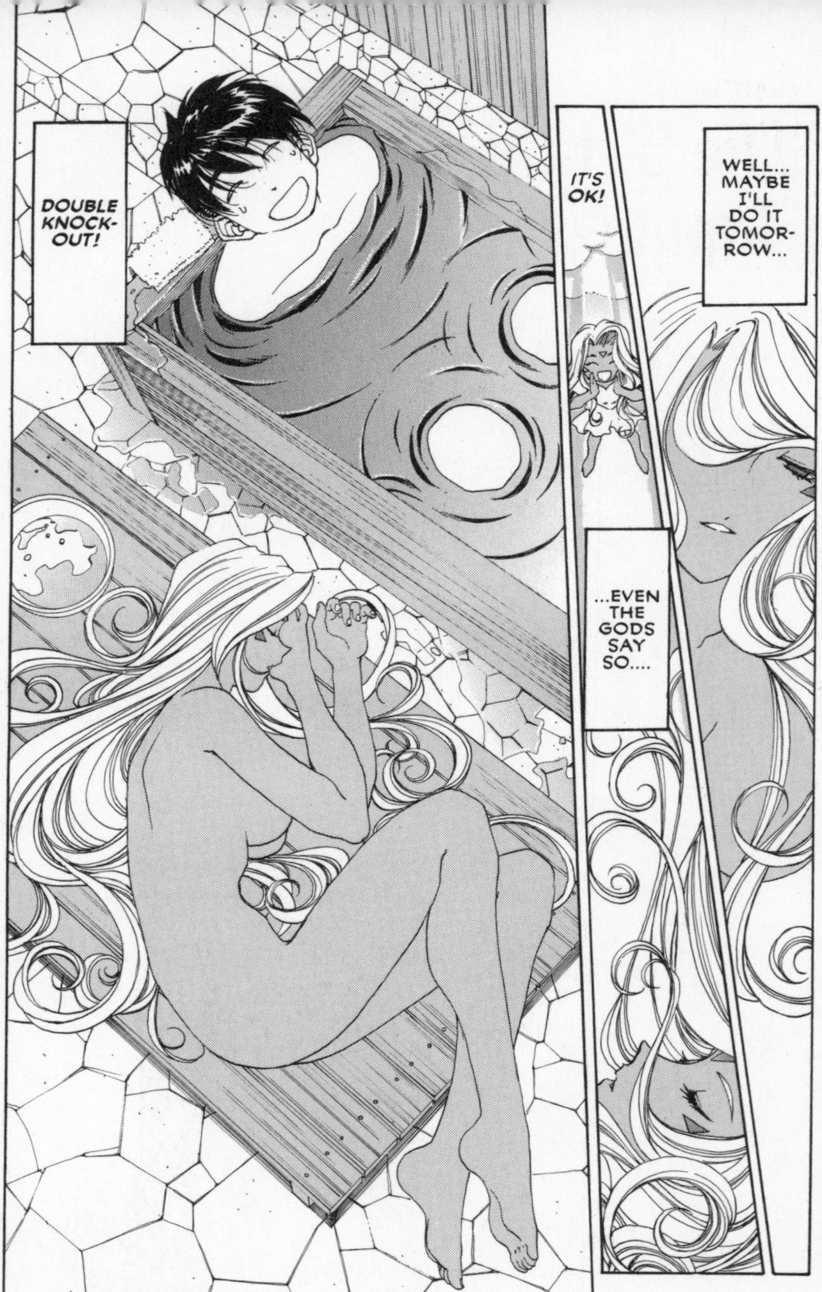
WELL... MAYBE I'LL DO IT TOMORROW...
IT'S OK!
...EVEN THE GODS SAY SO....
DOUBLE KNOCK-OUT!

CHAPTER 190

The Herald of Happiness

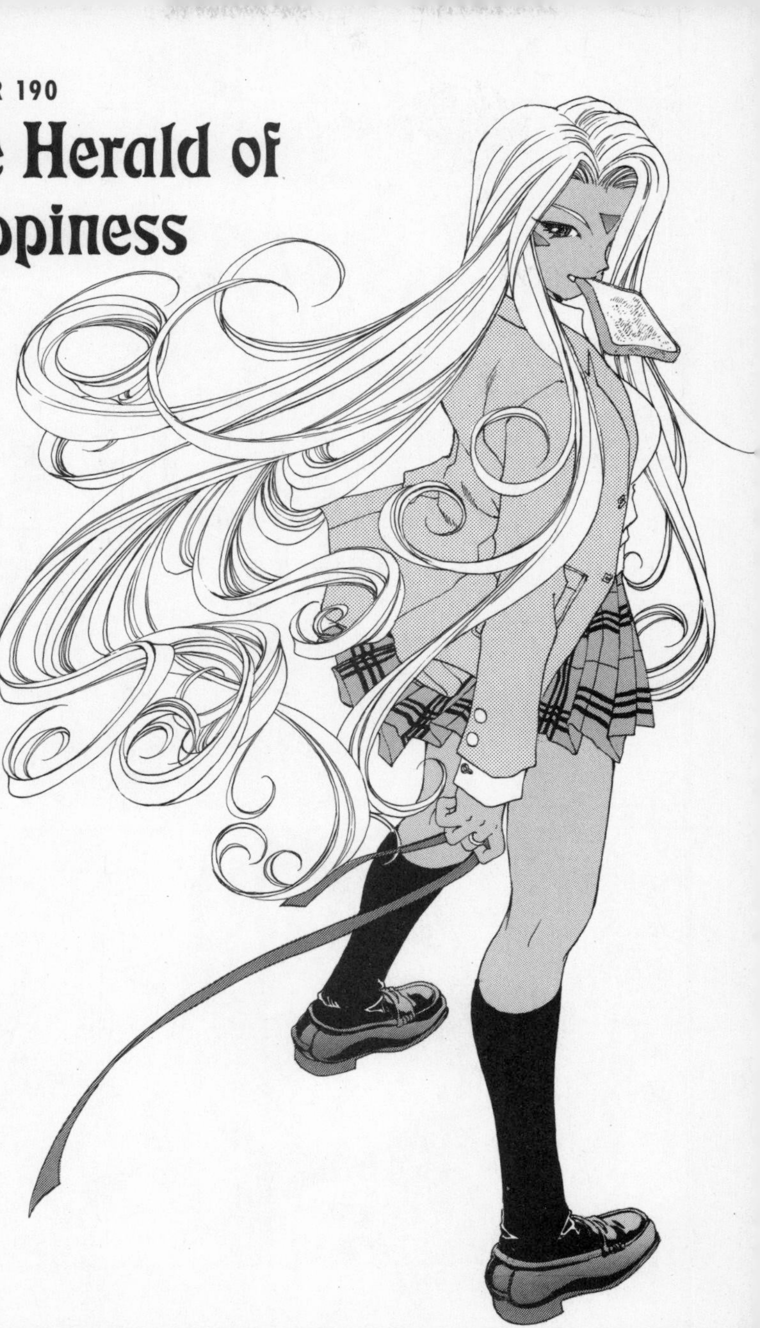

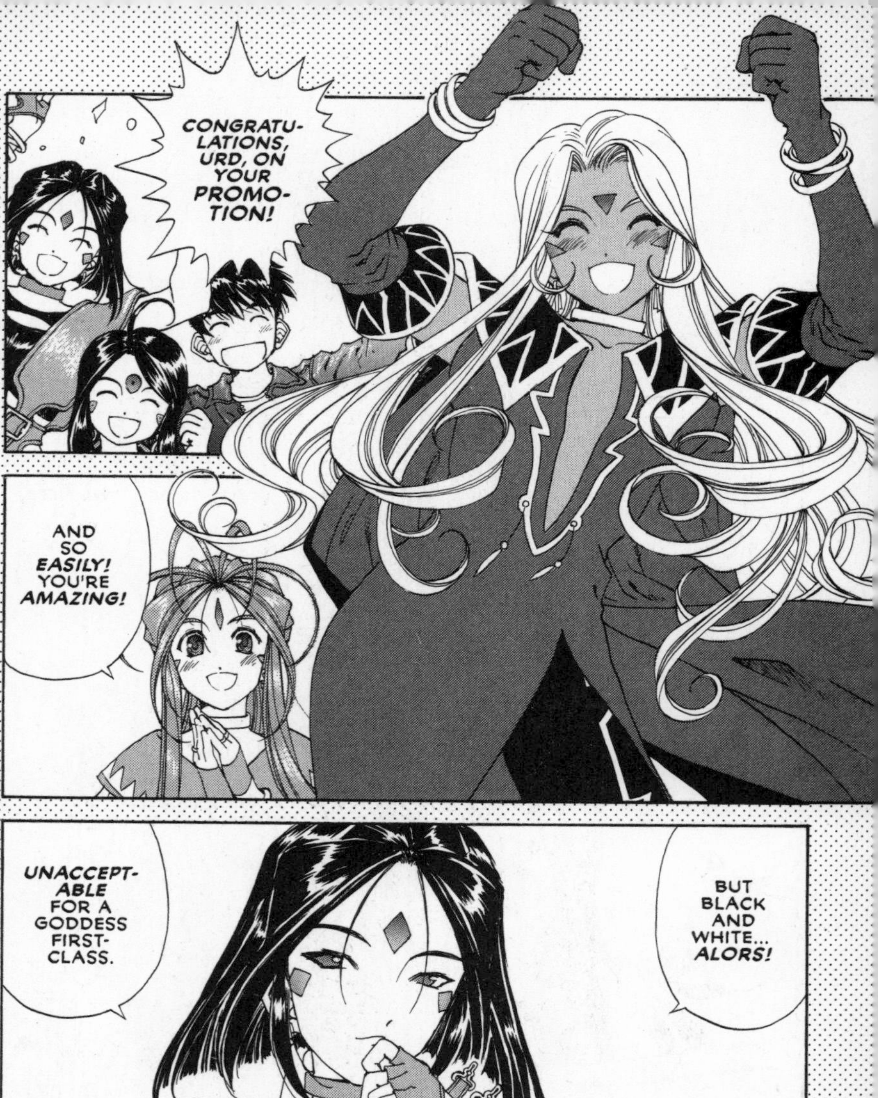
CONGRATU-LATIONS, URD, ON YOUR PROMO-TION!
AND SO EASILY! YOU'RE AMAZING!
BUT BLACK AND WHITE... ALORS!
UNACCEPT-ABLE FOR A GODDESS FIRST-CLASS.

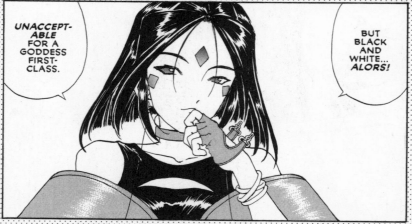

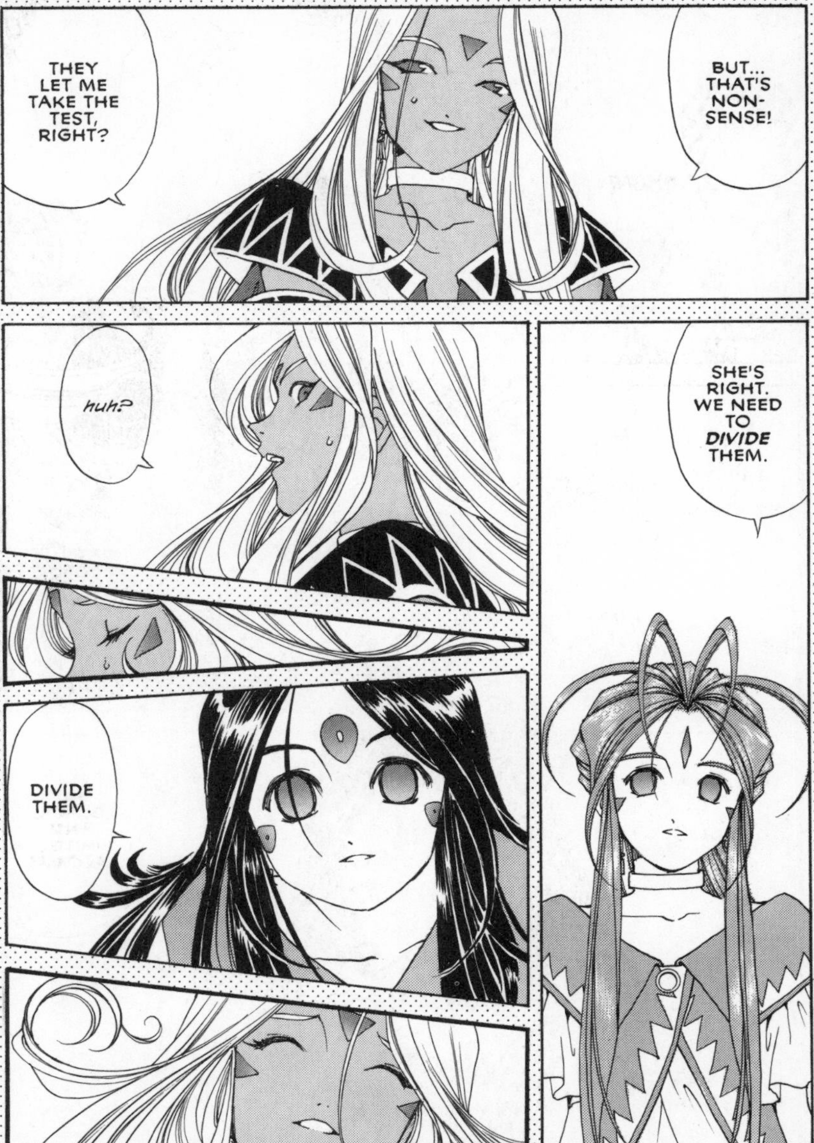
BUT... THAT'S NON-SENSE!
THEY LET ME TAKE THE TEST, RIGHT?
SHE'S RIGHT. WE NEED TO *DIVIDE* THEM.
huh?
DIVIDE THEM.

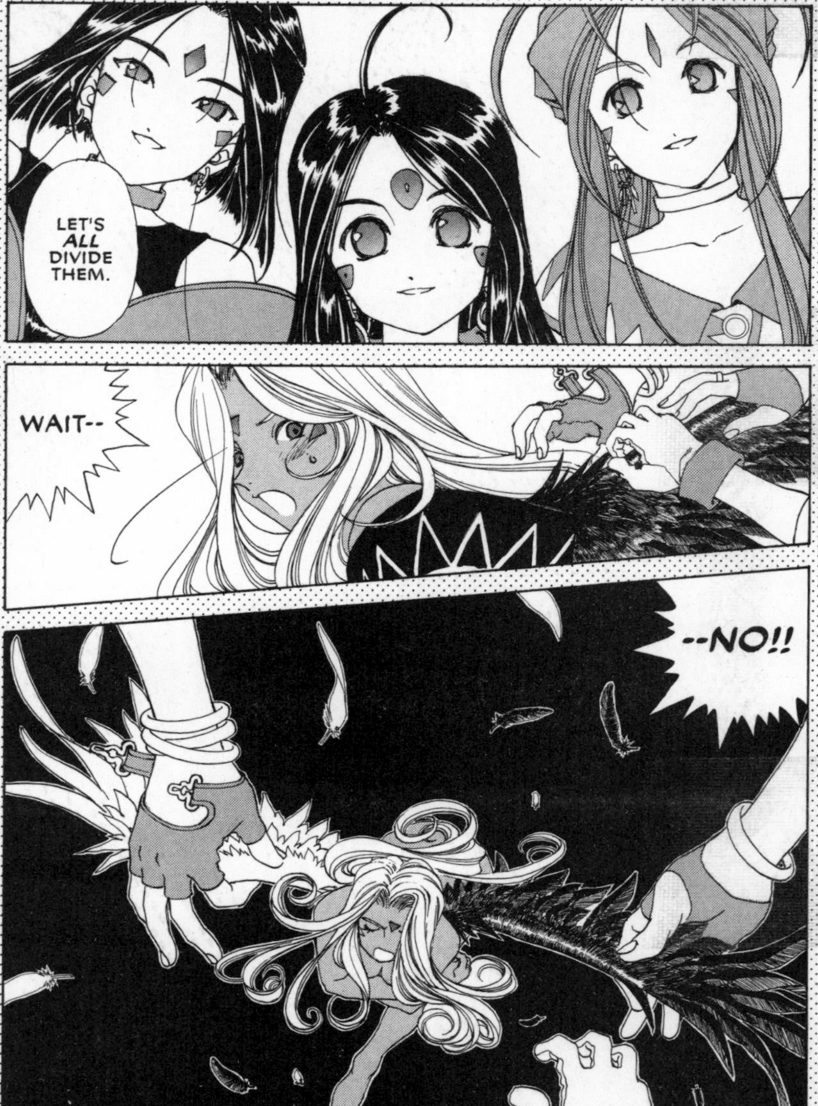
LET'S ALL DIVIDE THEM.
WAIT--
--NO!!

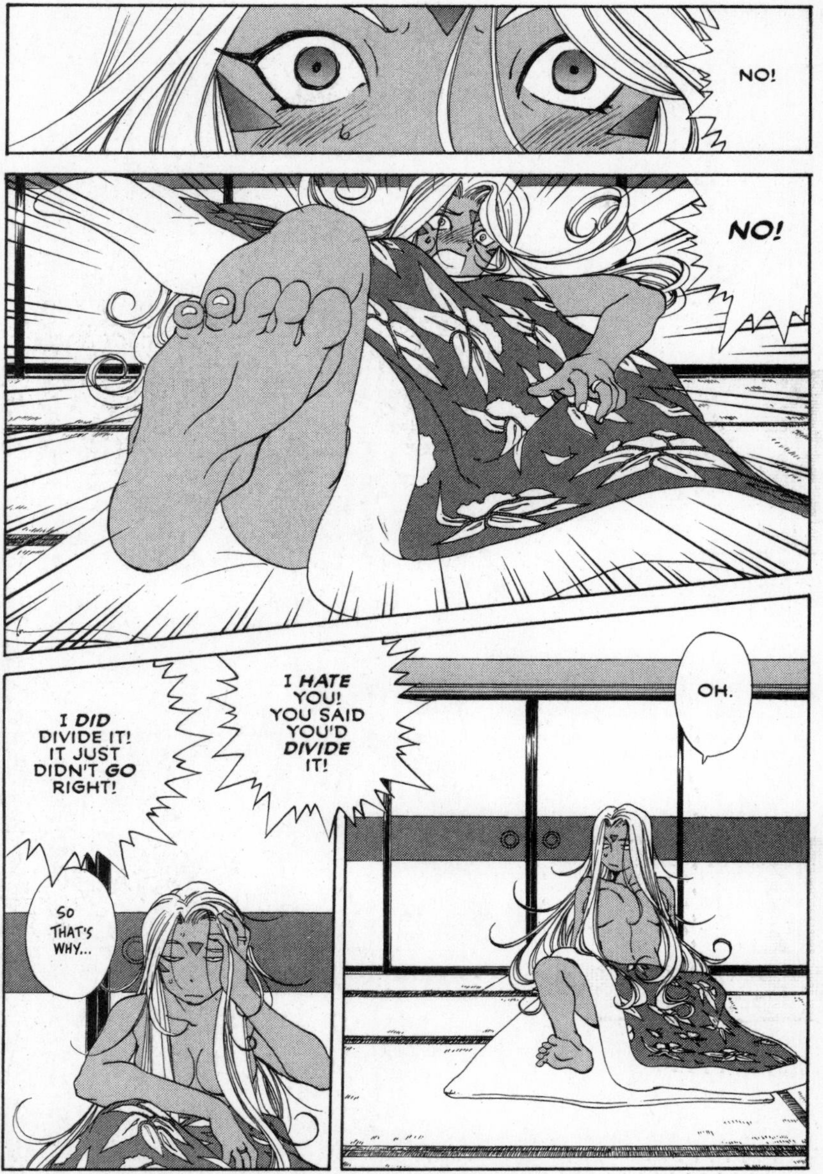
NO!
NO!
AAAH
OH.
I HATE YOU! YOU SAID YOU'D DIVIDE IT!
I DID DIVIDE IT! IT JUST DIDN'T GO RIGHT!
SO THAT'S WHY...

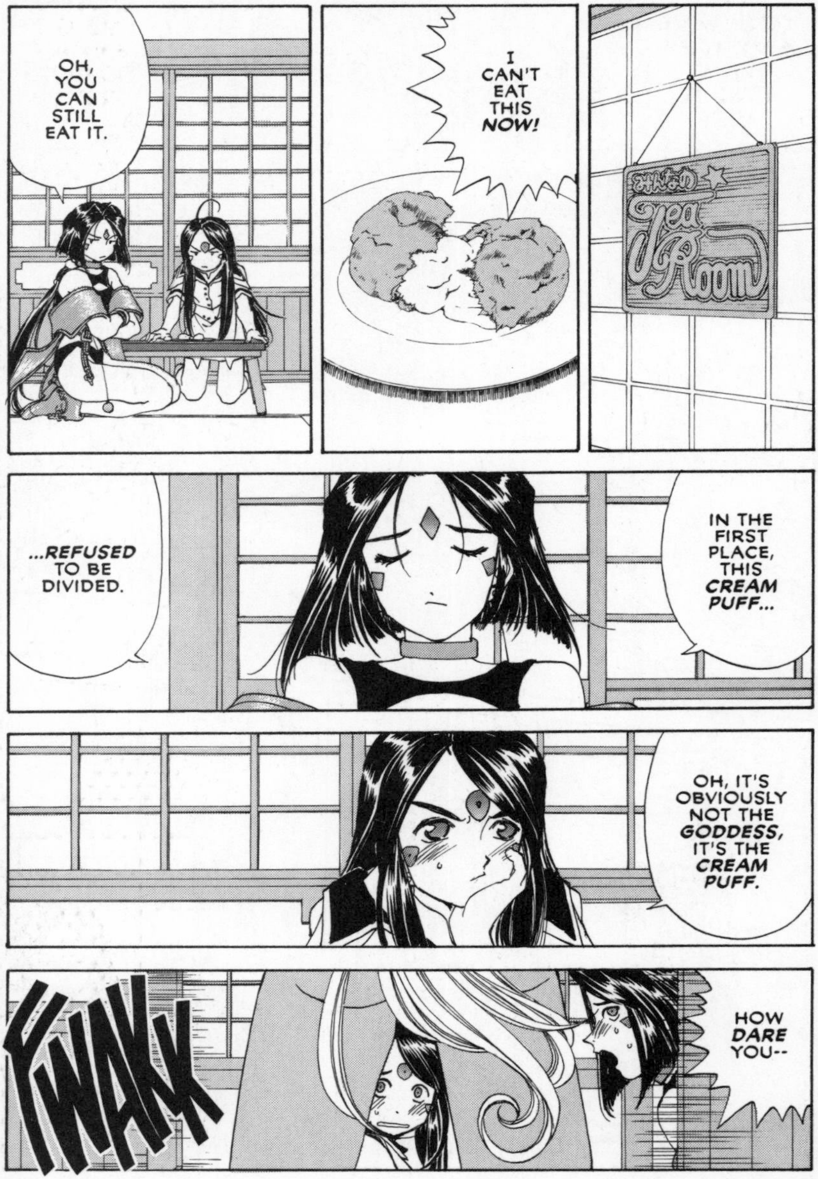
Tea Room
I CAN'T EAT THIS NOW!
OH, YOU CAN STILL EAT IT.
IN THE FIRST PLACE, THIS CREAM PUFF...
...REFUSED TO BE DIVIDED.
OH, IT'S OBVIOUSLY NOT THE GODDESS, IT'S THE CREAM PUFF.
HOW DARE YOU--
FWAK

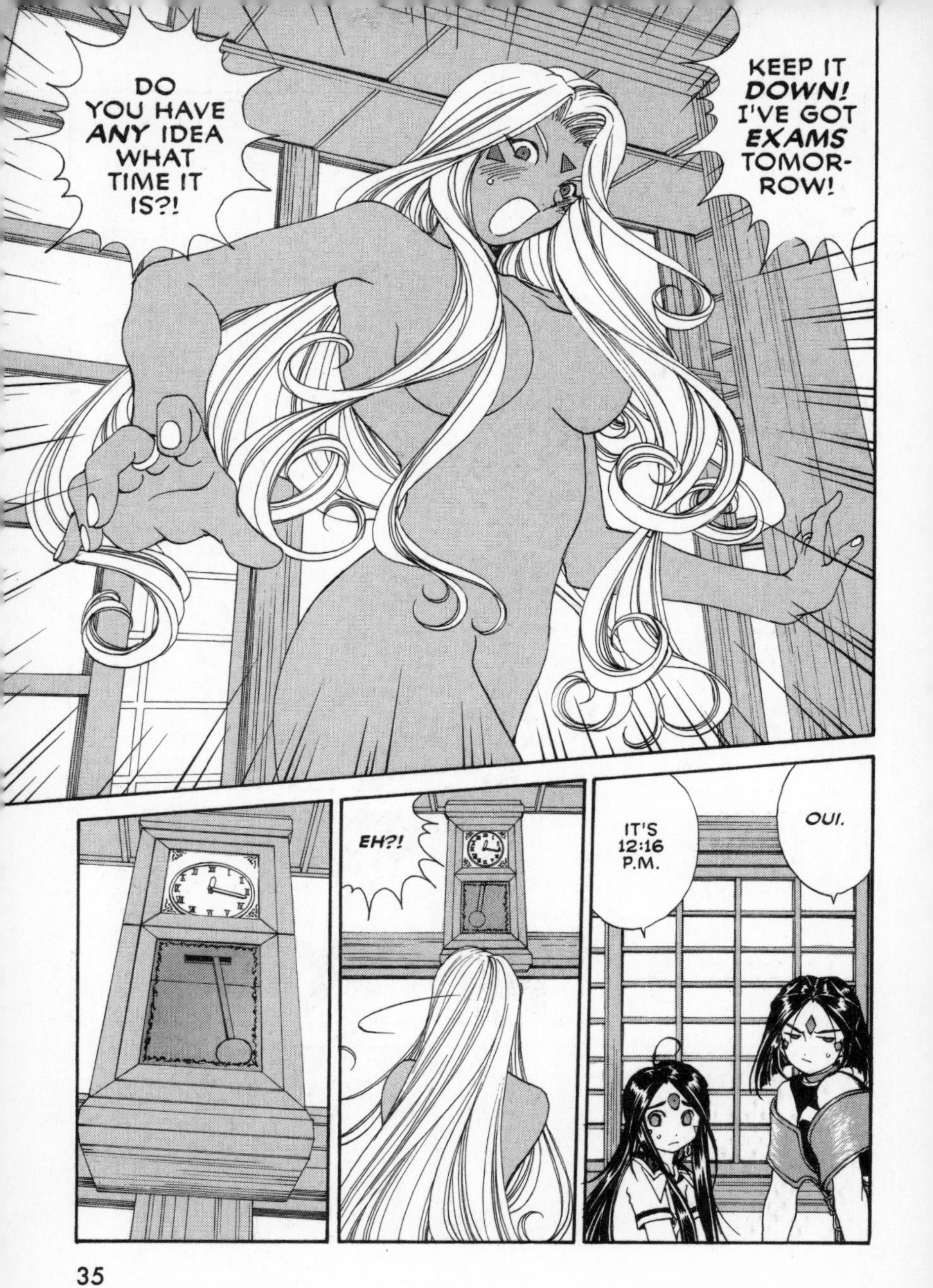
KEEP IT DOWN! I'VE GOT EXAMS TOMORROW!
DO YOU HAVE ANY IDEA WHAT TIME IT IS?!
OUI.
IT'S 12:16 P.M.
EH?!

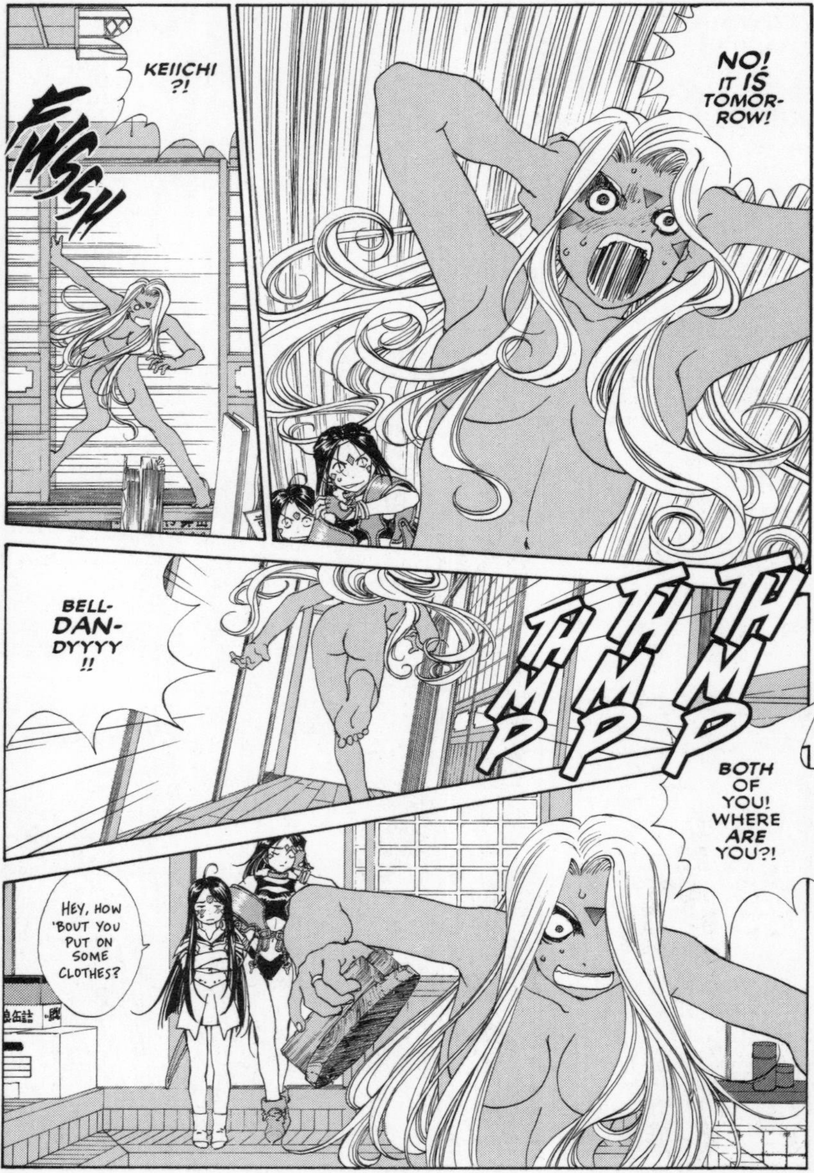
NO! IT IS TOMORROW!
KEIICHI ?!
FWSSH
THMP
THMP
THMP
BELL-DANDYYYY !!
BOTH OF YOU! WHERE ARE YOU?!
HEY, HOW 'BOUT YOU PUT ON SOME CLOTHES?

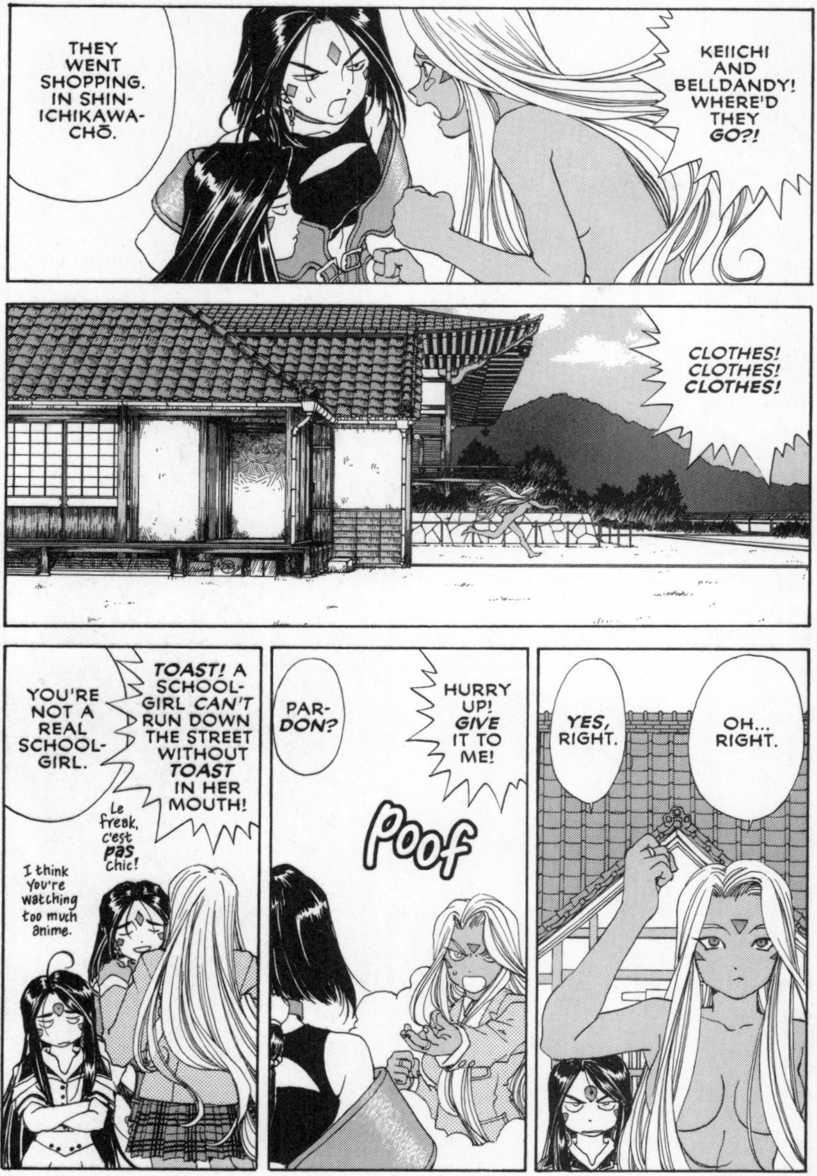
KEIICHI AND BELLDANDY! WHERE'D THEY GO?!
THEY WENT SHOPPING. IN SHIN-ICHIKAWA-CHŌ.
CLOTHES! CLOTHES! CLOTHES!
OH... RIGHT.
YES, RIGHT.
HURRY UP! GIVE IT TO ME!
PAR-DON?
poof
TOAST! A SCHOOL-GIRL CAN'T RUN DOWN THE STREET WITHOUT TOAST IN HER MOUTH!
YOU'RE NOT A REAL SCHOOL-GIRL.
Le freak, c'est pas chic!
I think you're watching too much anime.

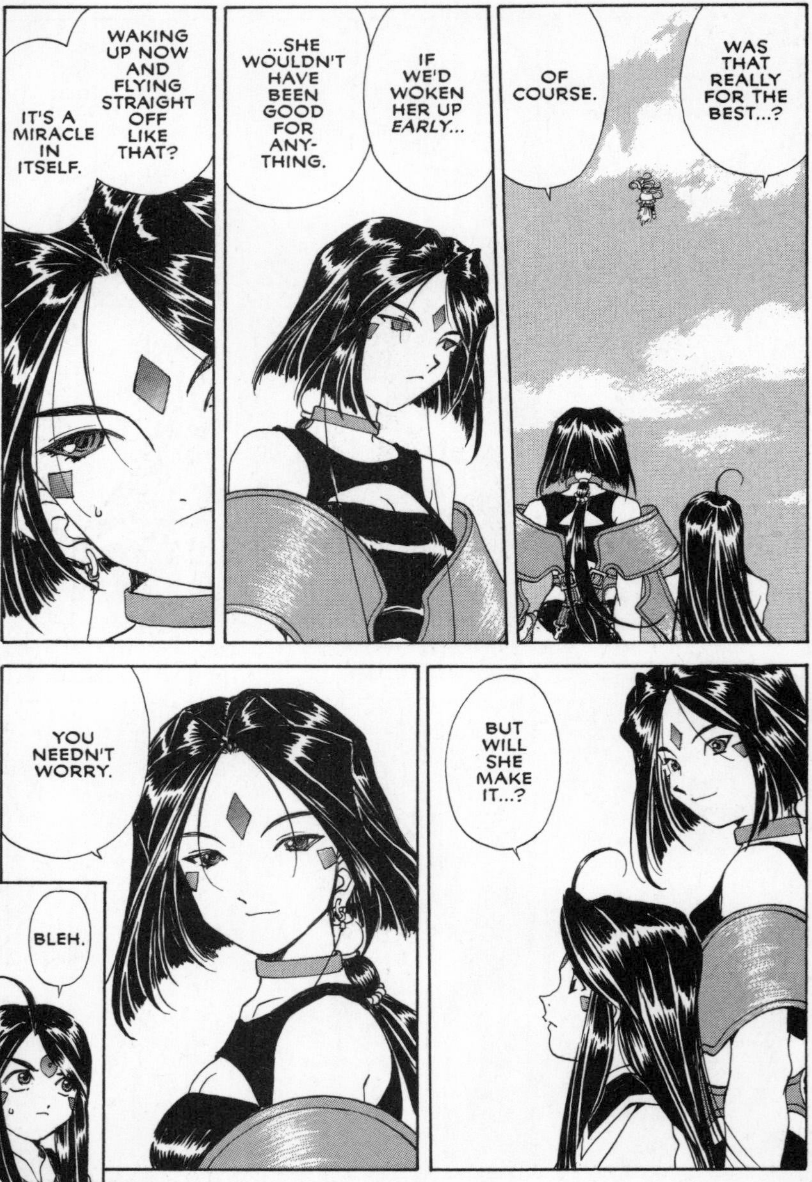
WAS THAT REALLY FOR THE BEST...?
OF COURSE.
IF WE'D WOKEN HER UP *EARLY*...
...SHE WOULDN'T HAVE BEEN GOOD FOR ANY-THING.
WAKING UP NOW AND FLYING STRAIGHT OFF LIKE THAT?
IT'S A MIRACLE IN ITSELF.
BUT WILL SHE MAKE IT...?
YOU NEEDN'T WORRY.
BLEH.

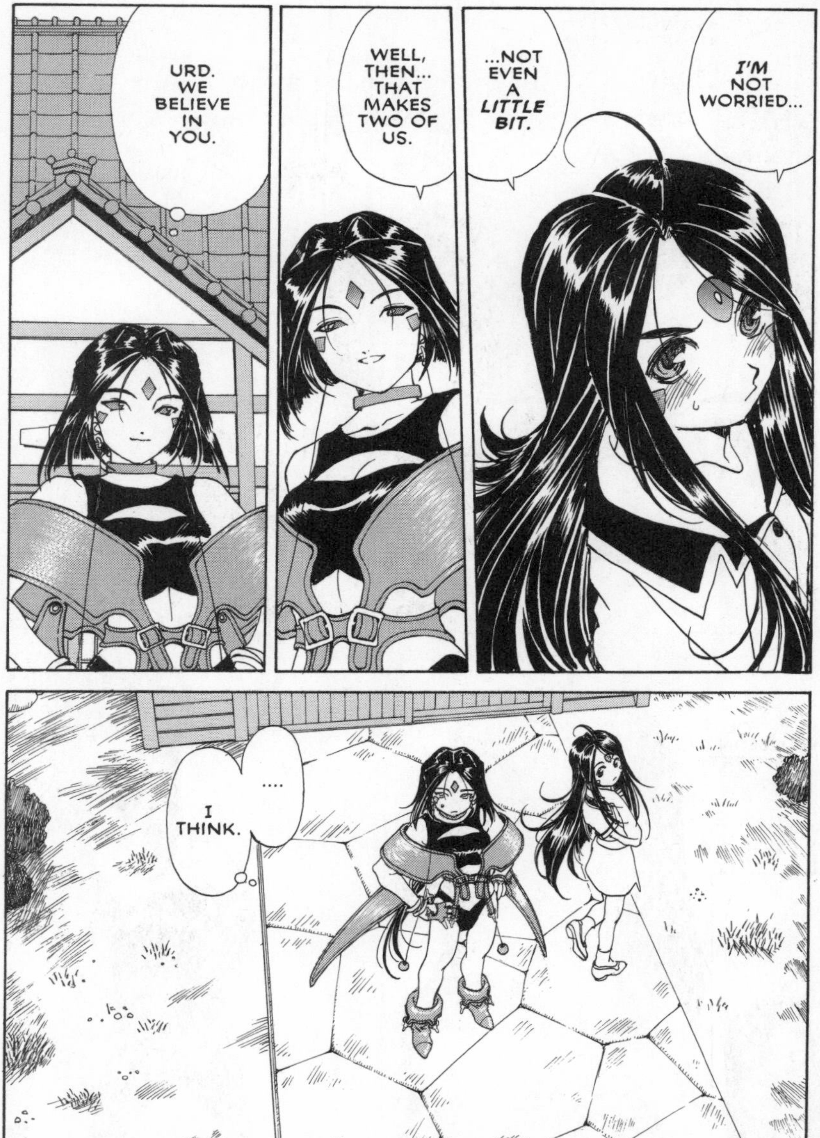
I'M NOT WORRIED...
...NOT EVEN A LITTLE BIT.
WELL, THEN... THAT MAKES TWO OF US.
URD. WE BELIEVE IN YOU.
....
I THINK.

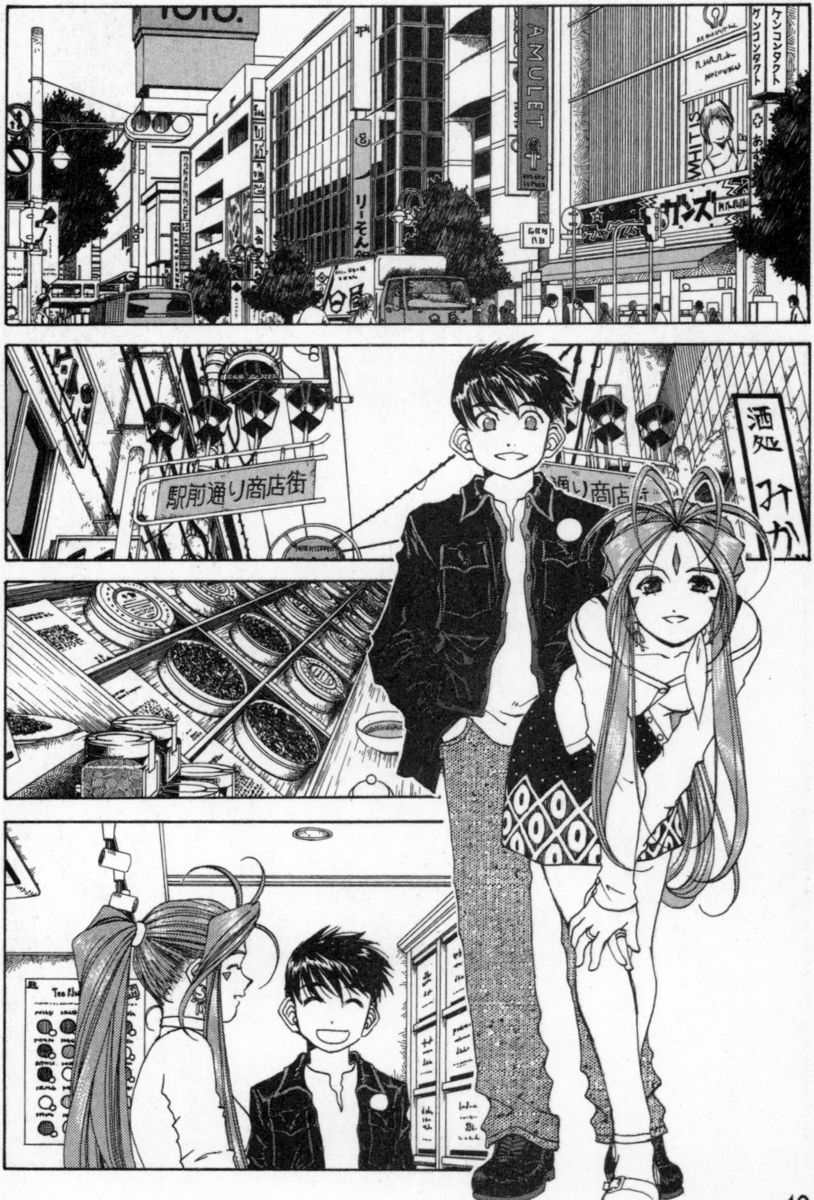
ケンコンタクト
ケンコンタクト
ガンズ
AMULET
酒処
みか
通り商店街
駅前通り商店街

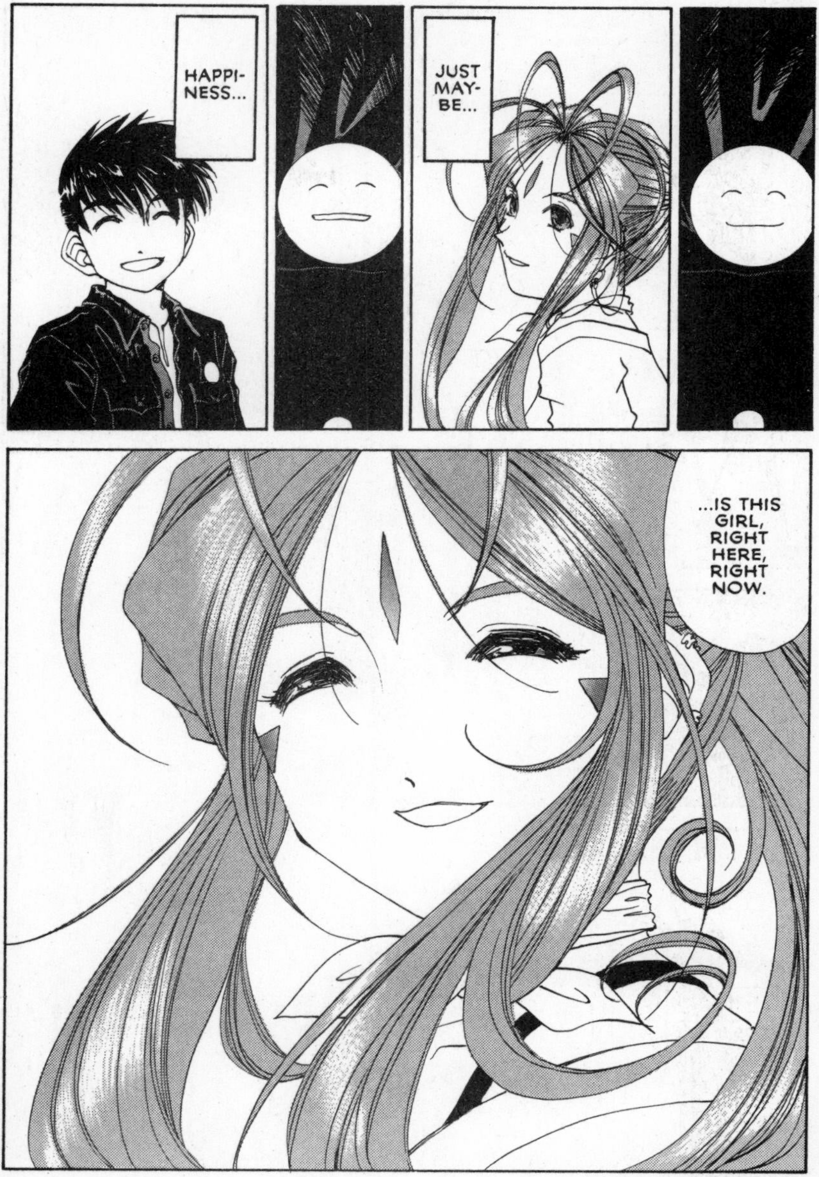
JUST MAY- BE...
HAPPI- NESS...
...IS THIS GIRL, RIGHT HERE, RIGHT NOW.

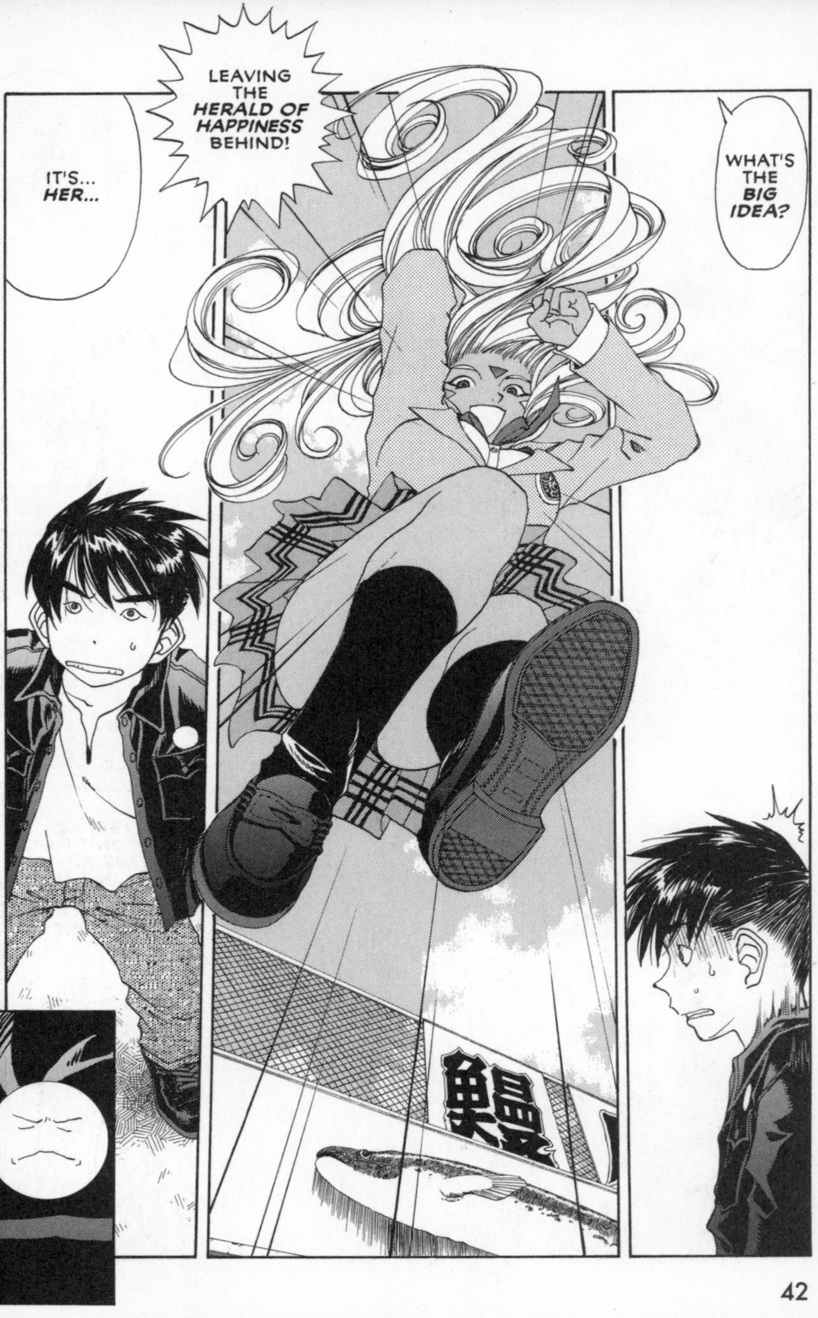
WHAT'S THE *BIG IDEA?*
LEAVING THE *HERALD OF HAPPINESS* BEHIND!
鰻
IT'S... *HER...*

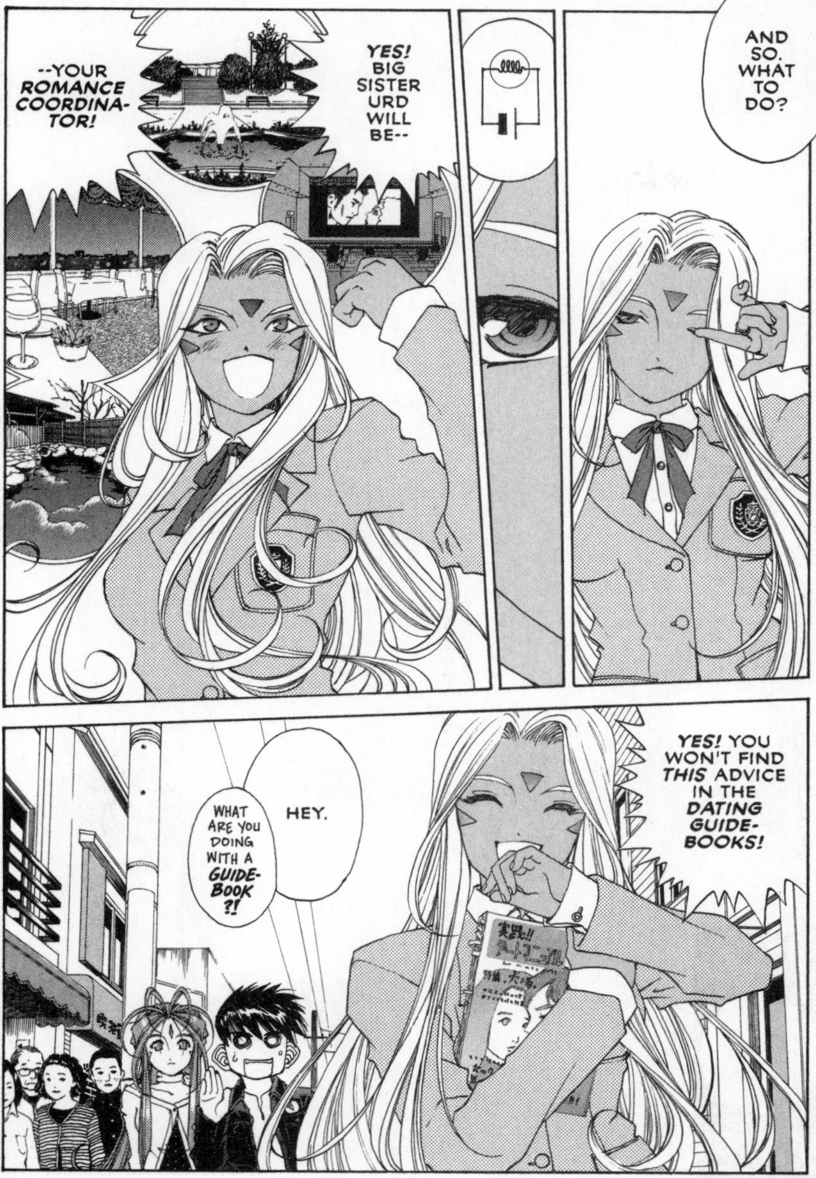
AND SO. WHAT TO DO?
YES! BIG SISTER URD WILL BE--
--YOUR ROMANCE COORDINATOR!
YES! YOU WON'T FIND THIS ADVICE IN THE DATING GUIDE-BOOKS!
HEY.
WHAT ARE YOU DOING WITH A GUIDE-BOOK?!

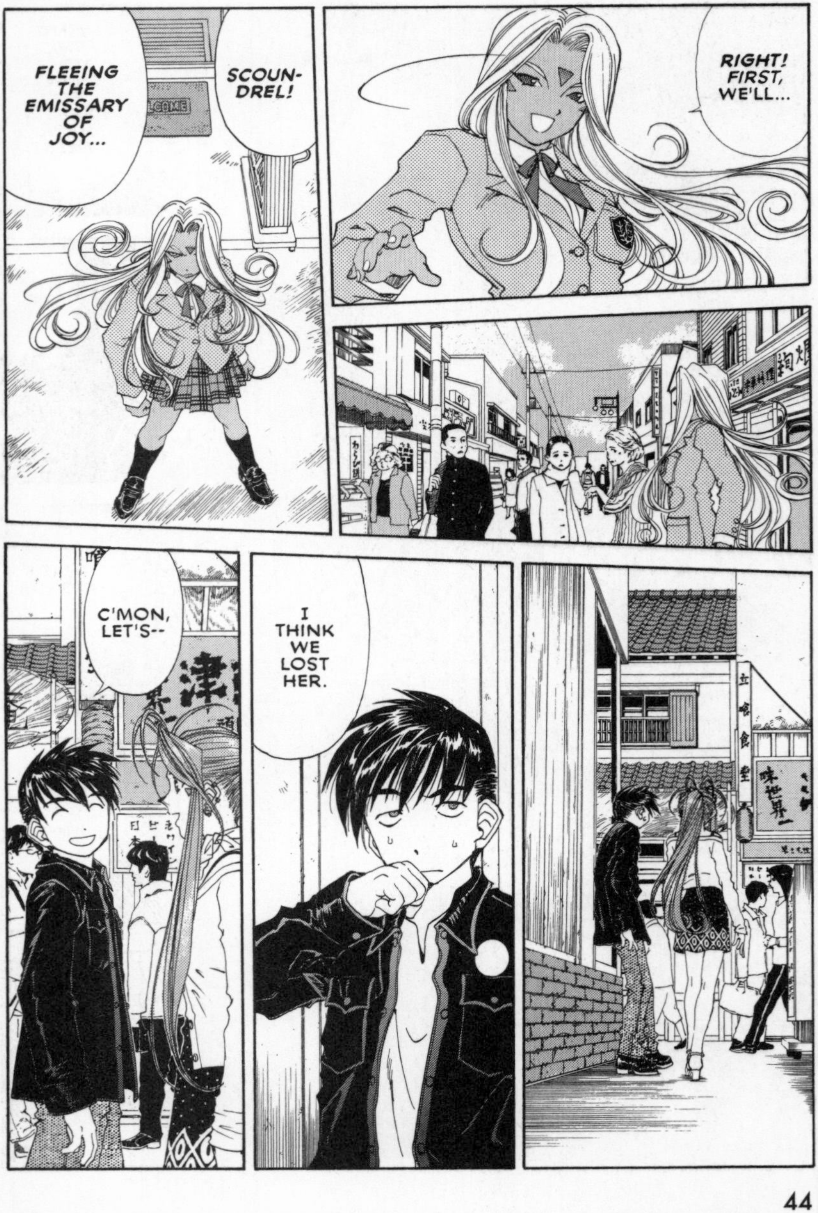
RIGHT! FIRST, WE'LL...
SCOUN-DREL!
FLEEING THE EMISSARY OF JOY...
I THINK WE LOST HER.
C'MON, LET'S--

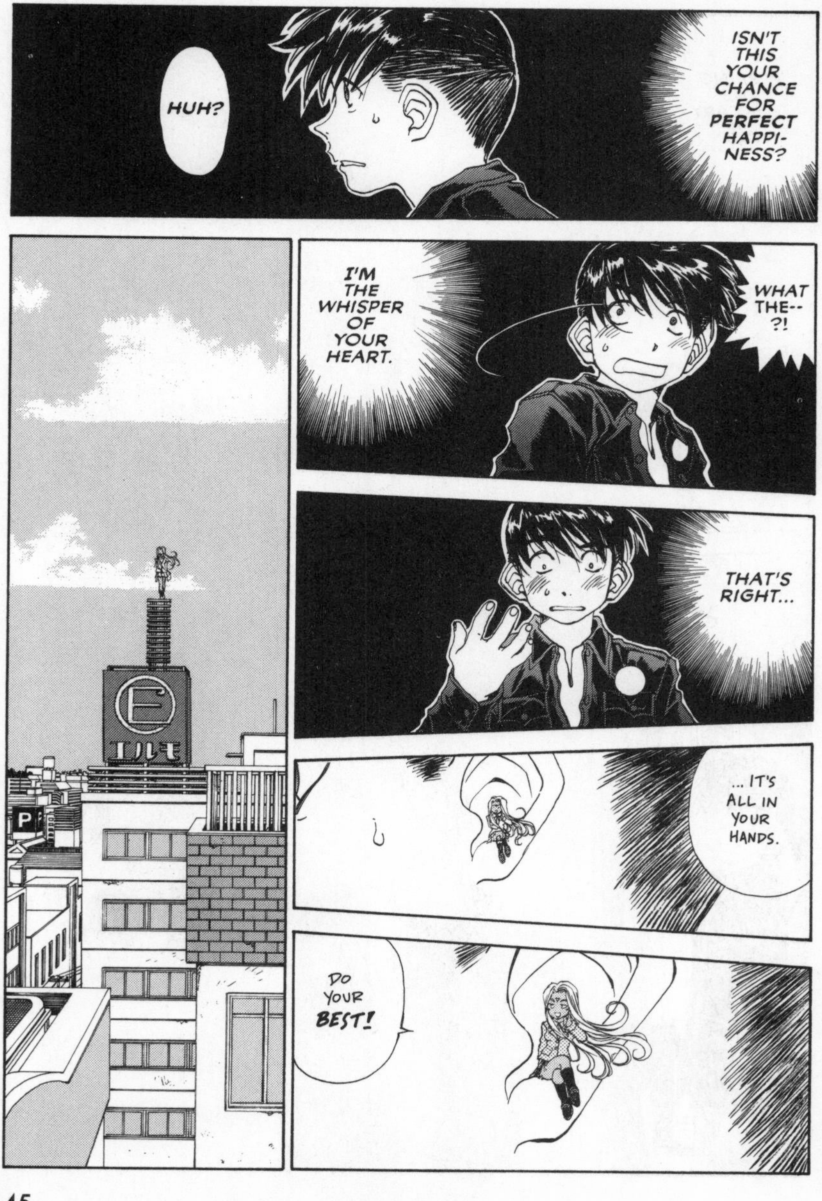

ISN'T THIS YOUR CHANCE FOR PERFECT HAPPINESS?
HUH?
WHAT THE--?!
I'M THE WHISPER OF YOUR HEART.
THAT'S RIGHT...
...IT'S ALL IN YOUR HANDS.
DO YOUR BEST!
エルモ

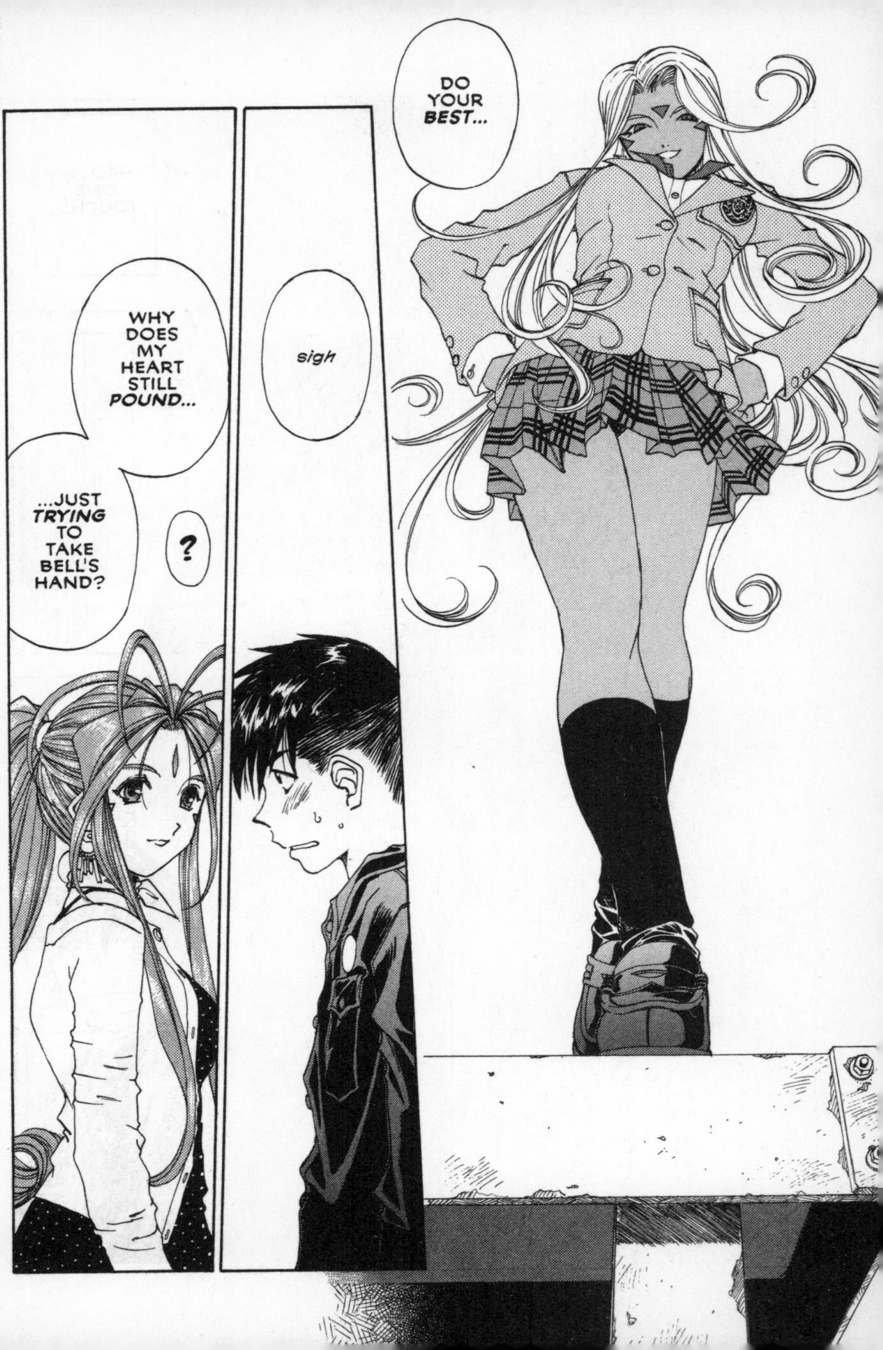
DO YOUR BEST...
sigh
WHY DOES MY HEART STILL POUND...
...JUST TRYING TO TAKE BELL'S HAND?
?

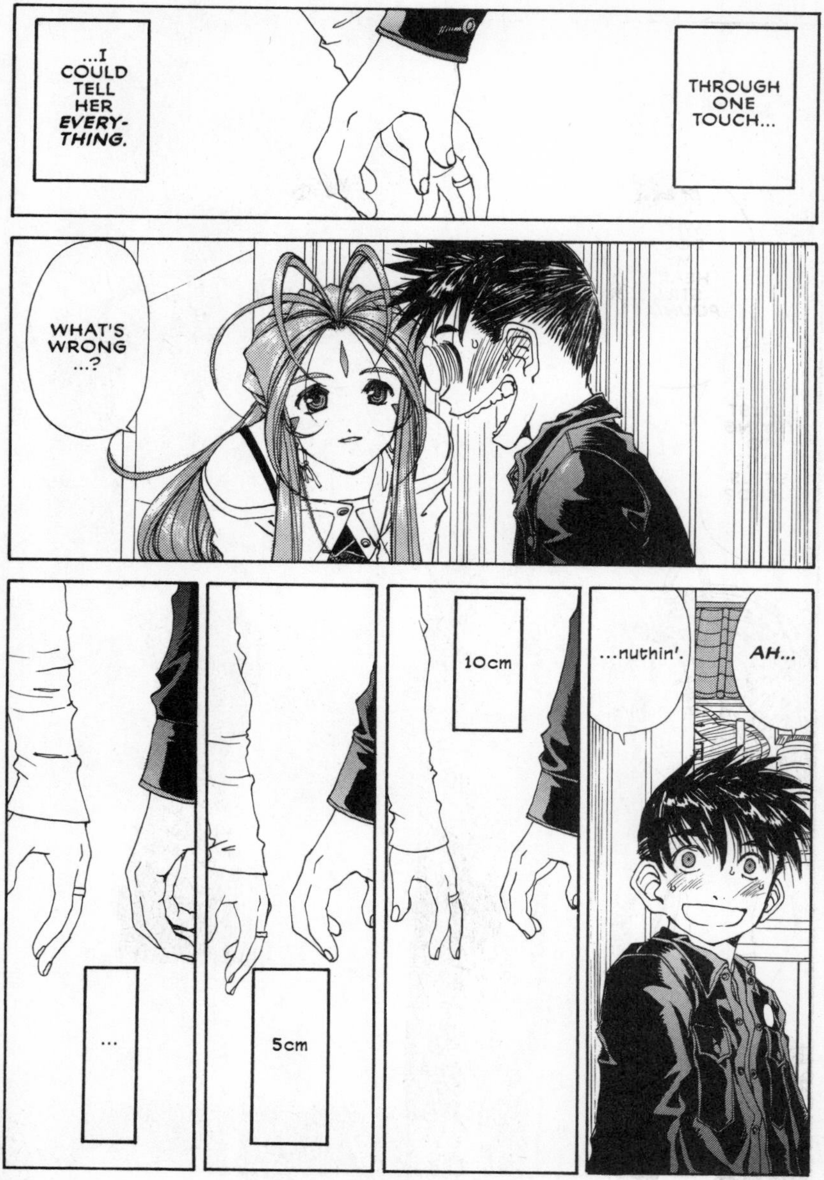
THROUGH ONE TOUCH...
...I COULD TELL HER *EVERY-THING.*
WHAT'S WRONG ...?
AH...
...nuthin'.
10cm
5cm
...

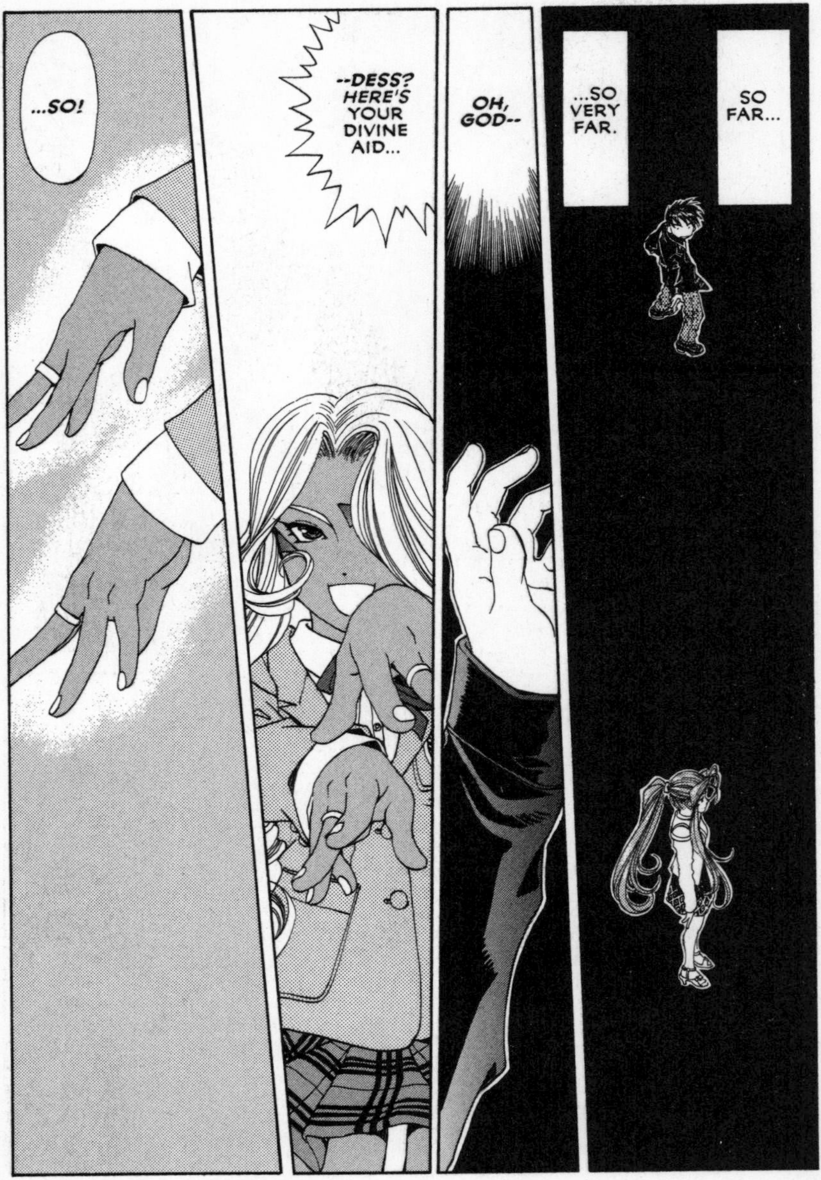
SO FAR...
...SO VERY FAR.
OH, GOD--
--DESS? HERE'S YOUR DIVINE AID...
...SO!

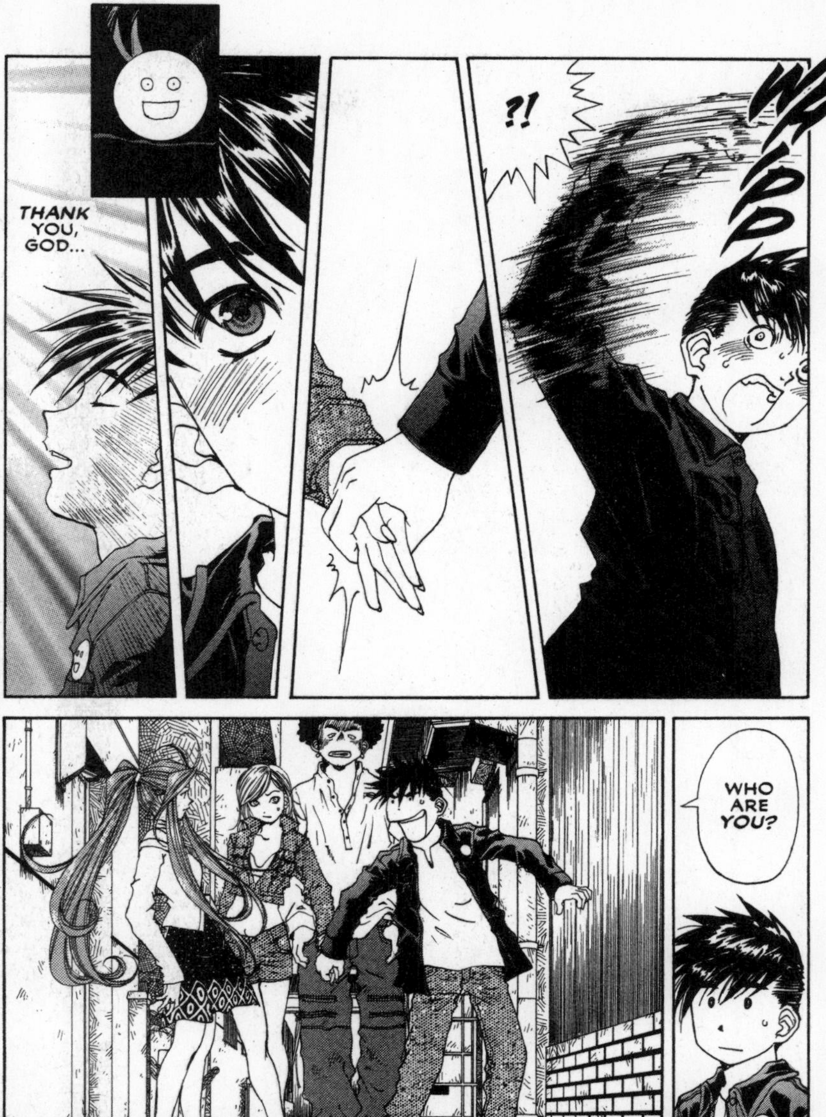
WHIPP
?!
THANK YOU, GOD...
WHO ARE YOU?

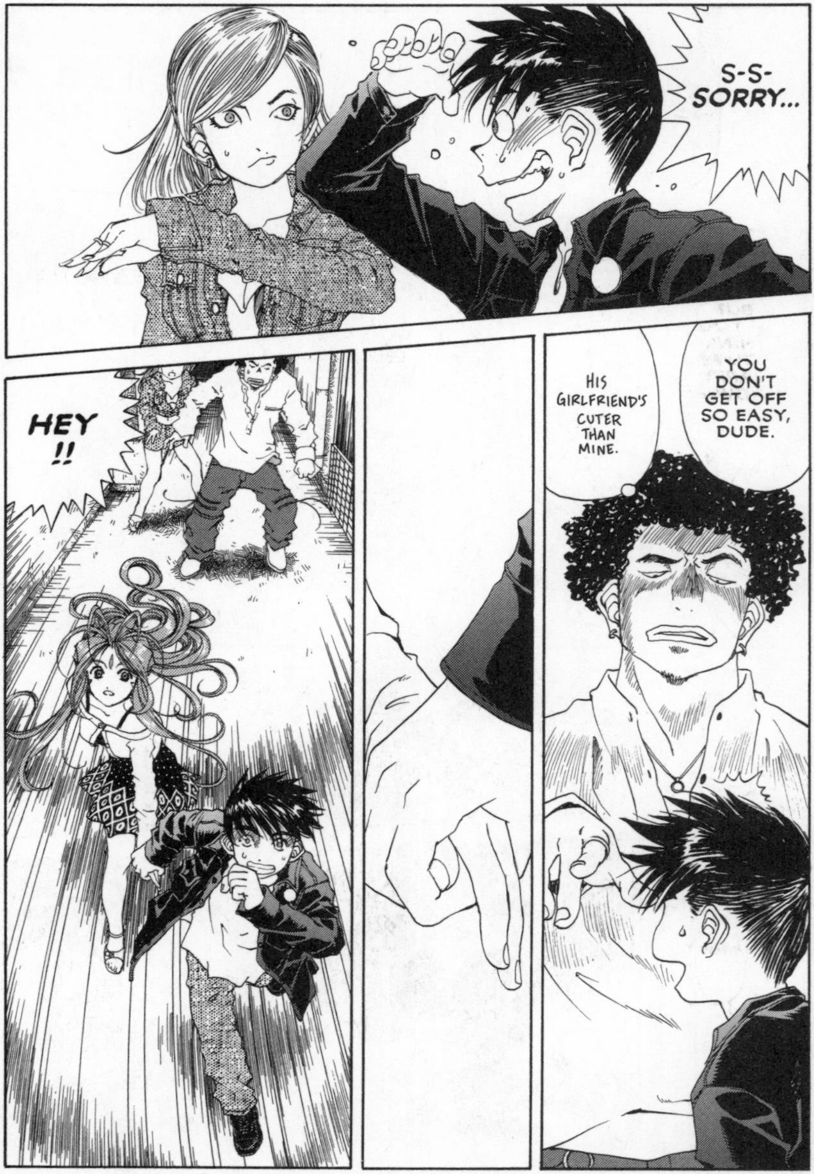
S-S-SORRY...
YOU DON'T GET OFF SO EASY, DUDE.
HIS GIRLFRIEND'S CUTER THAN MINE.
HEY !!

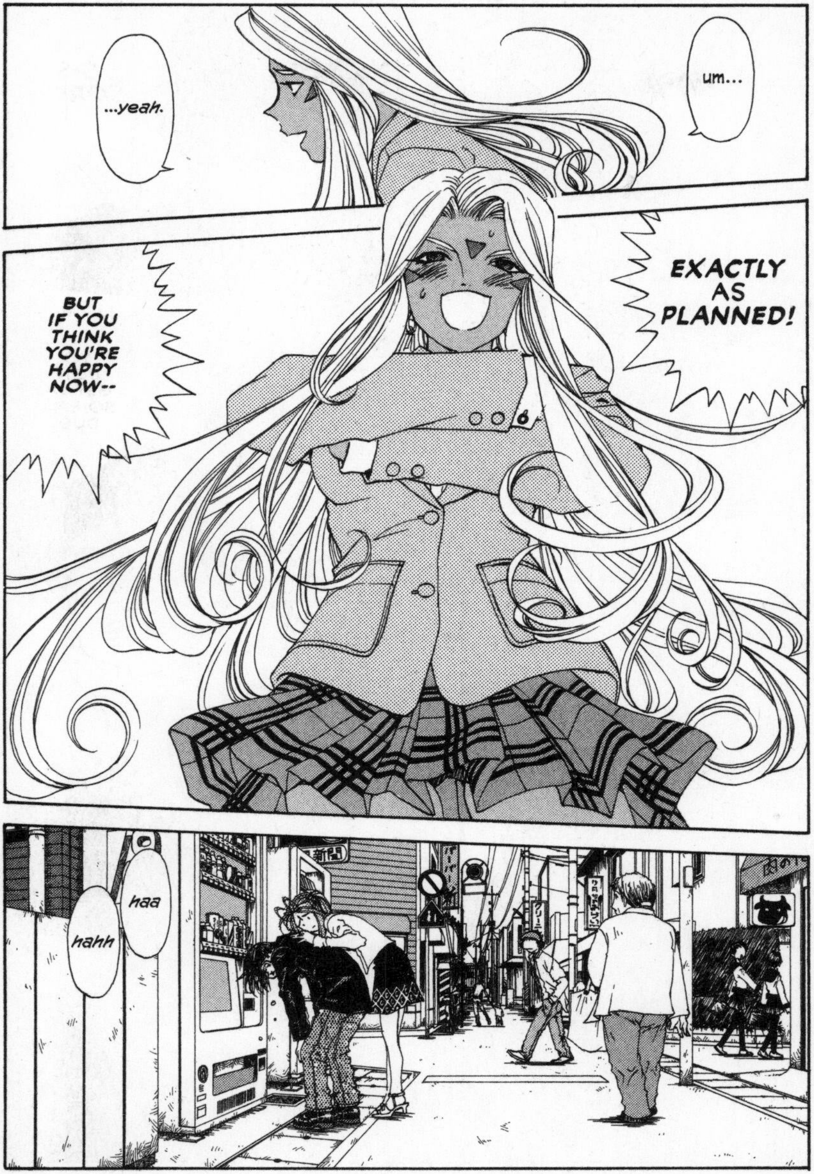
um...
...yeah.
EXACTLY AS PLANNED!
BUT IF YOU THINK YOU'RE HAPPY NOW--
haa
hahh

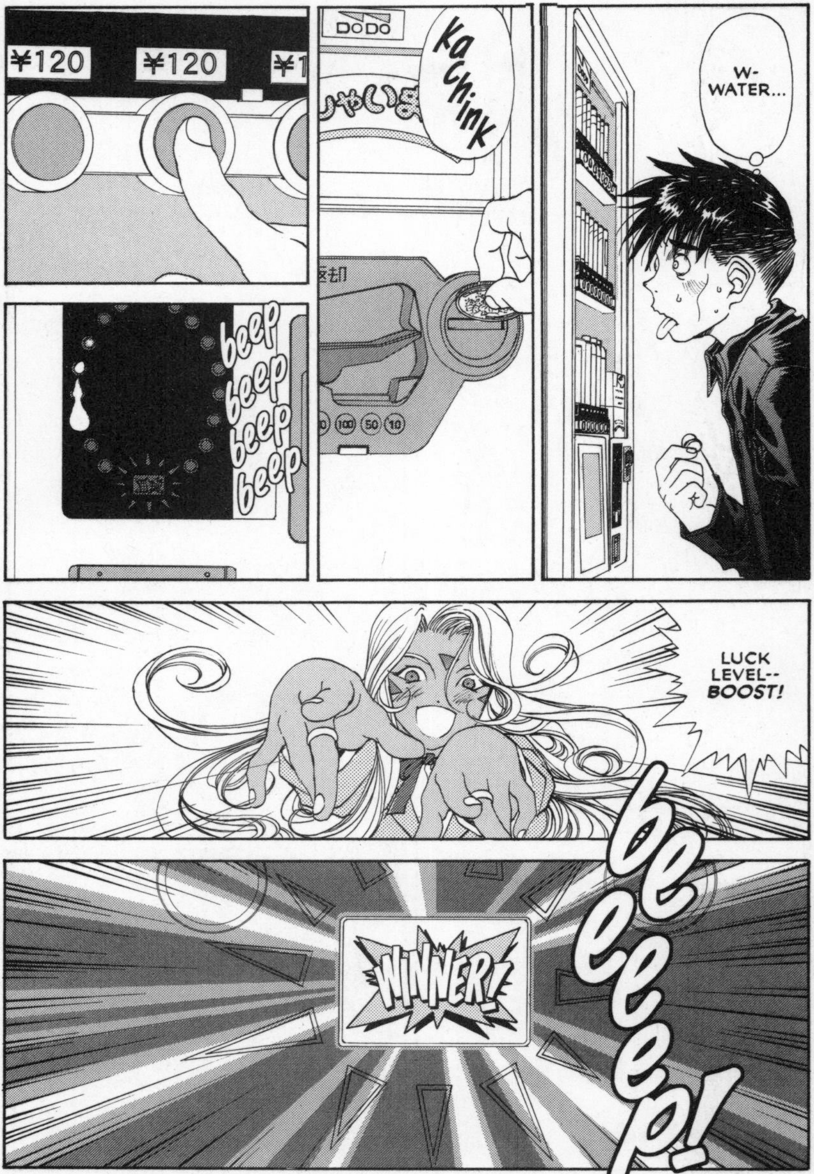
W-WATER...
DoDo
kachink
¥120 ¥120
beep beep beep beep
LUCK LEVEL--BOOST!
WINNER!
beeeep!

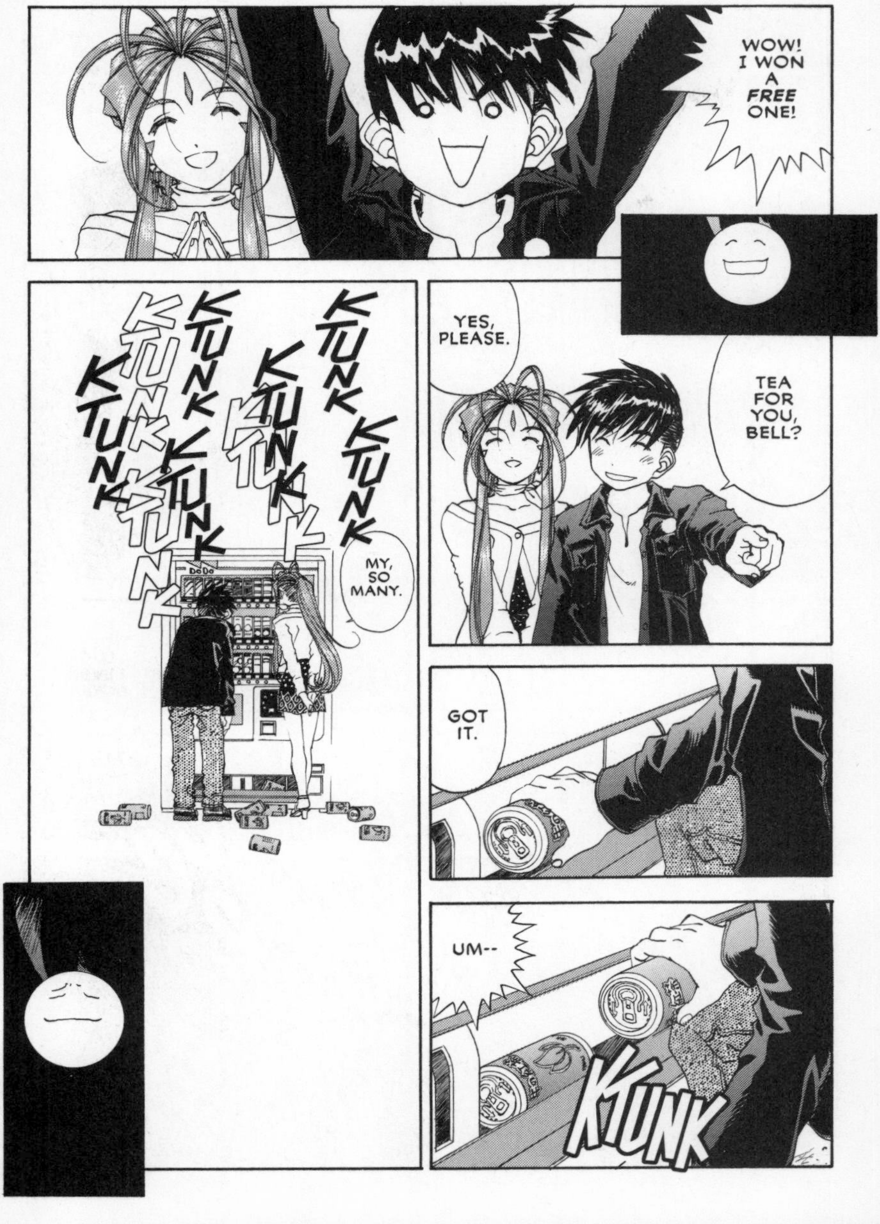
WOW! I WON A *FREE* ONE!
TEA FOR YOU, BELL?
YES, PLEASE.
GOT IT.
UM--
KTUNK
KTUNK KTUNK KTUNK KTUNK KTUNK KTUNK KTUNK KTUNK
MY, SO MANY.

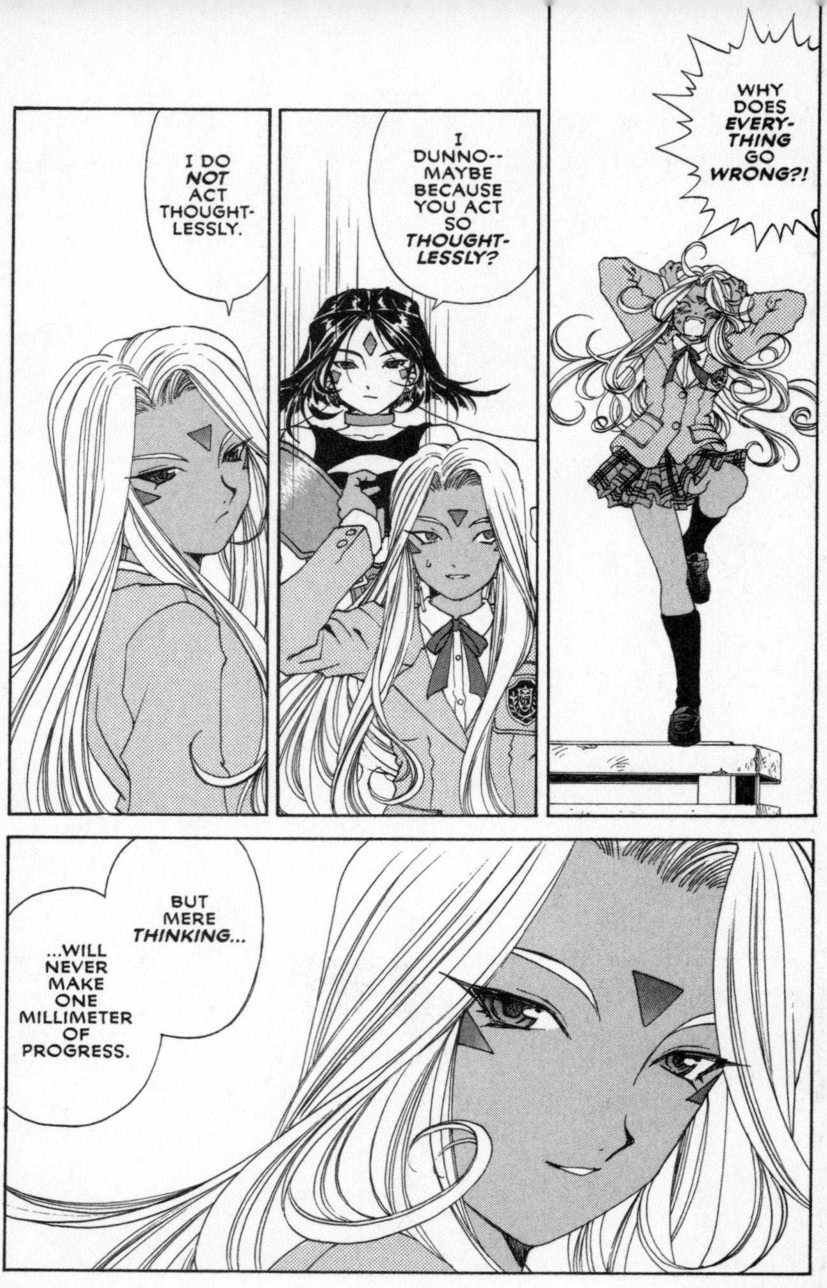
WHY DOES *EVERYTHING* GO *WRONG?!*
I DUNNO-- MAYBE BECAUSE YOU ACT SO *THOUGHTLESSLY?*
I DO *NOT* ACT THOUGHTLESSLY.
BUT MERE *THINKING...*
...WILL NEVER MAKE ONE MILLIMETER OF PROGRESS.

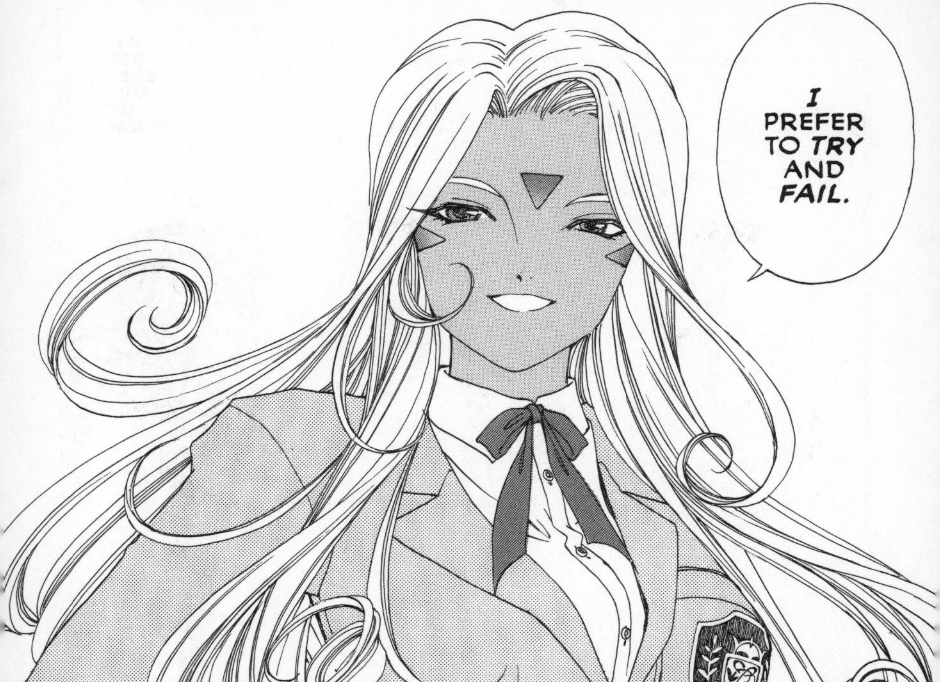
I PREFER TO *TRY* AND *FAIL*.

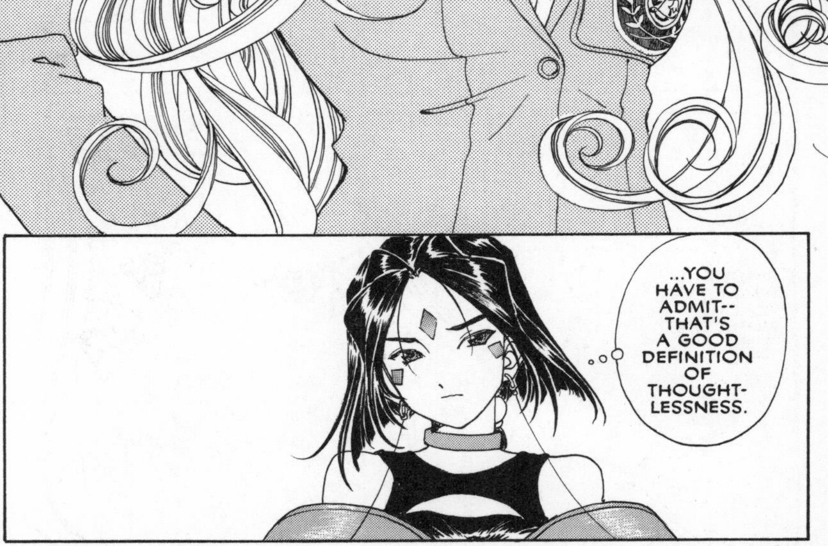
...YOU HAVE TO ADMIT-- THAT'S A GOOD DEFINITION OF THOUGHT-LESSNESS.

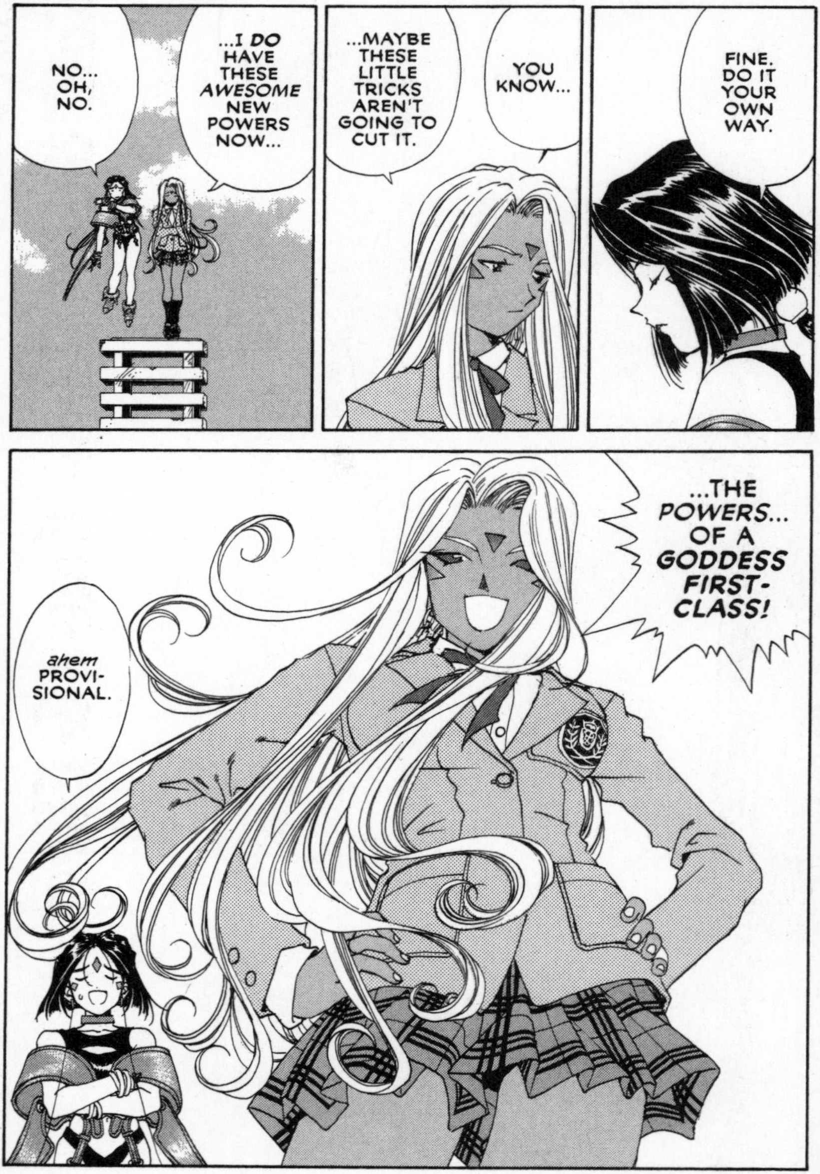
FINE. DO IT YOUR OWN WAY.
YOU KNOW...
...MAYBE THESE LITTLE TRICKS AREN'T GOING TO CUT IT.
...I *DO* HAVE THESE *AWESOME* NEW POWERS NOW...
NO... OH, NO.
...THE *POWERS...* OF A *GODDESS FIRST-CLASS!*
ahem PROVISIONAL.

Chapter 191
Rain & Happiness, Cause & Effect

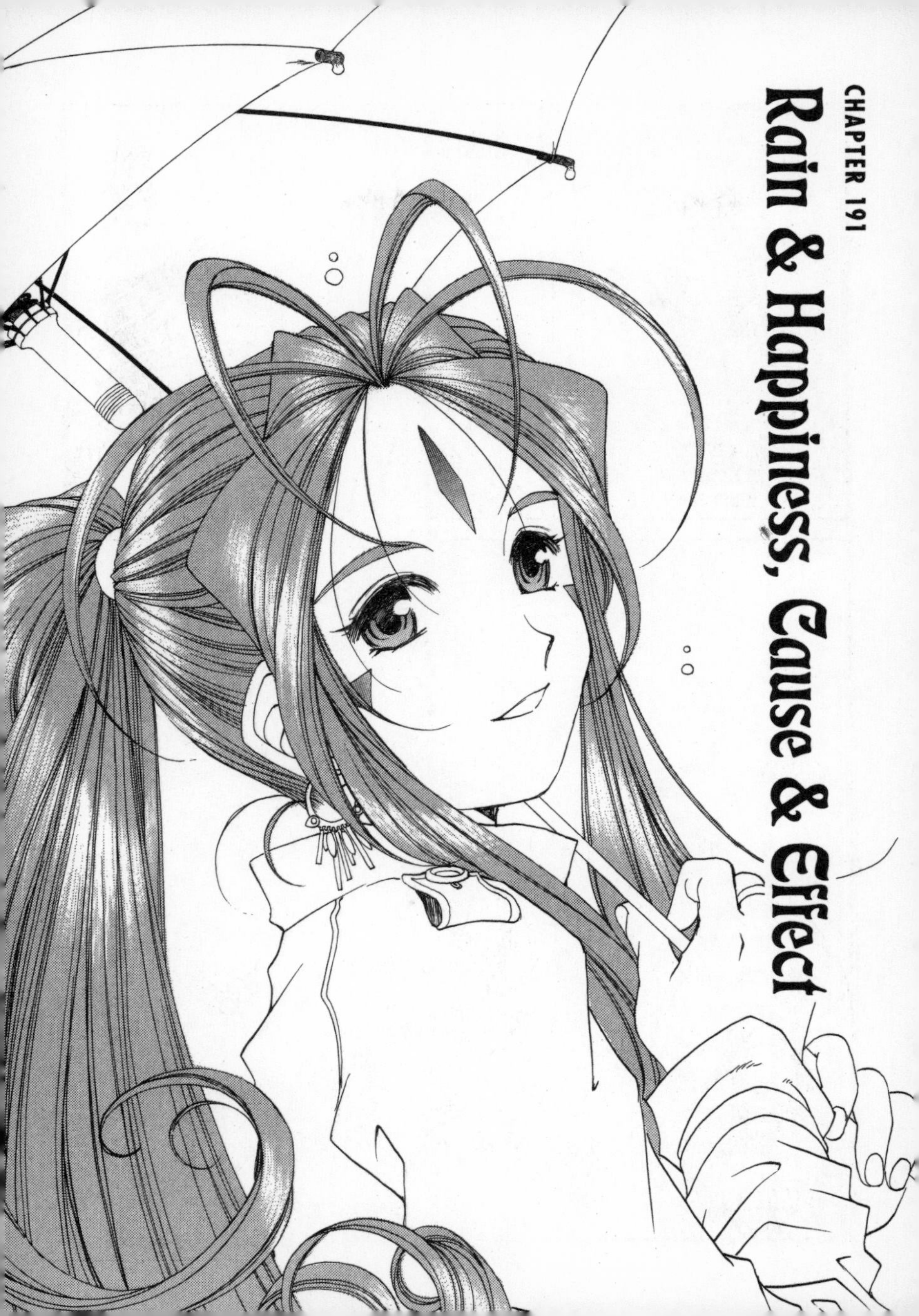

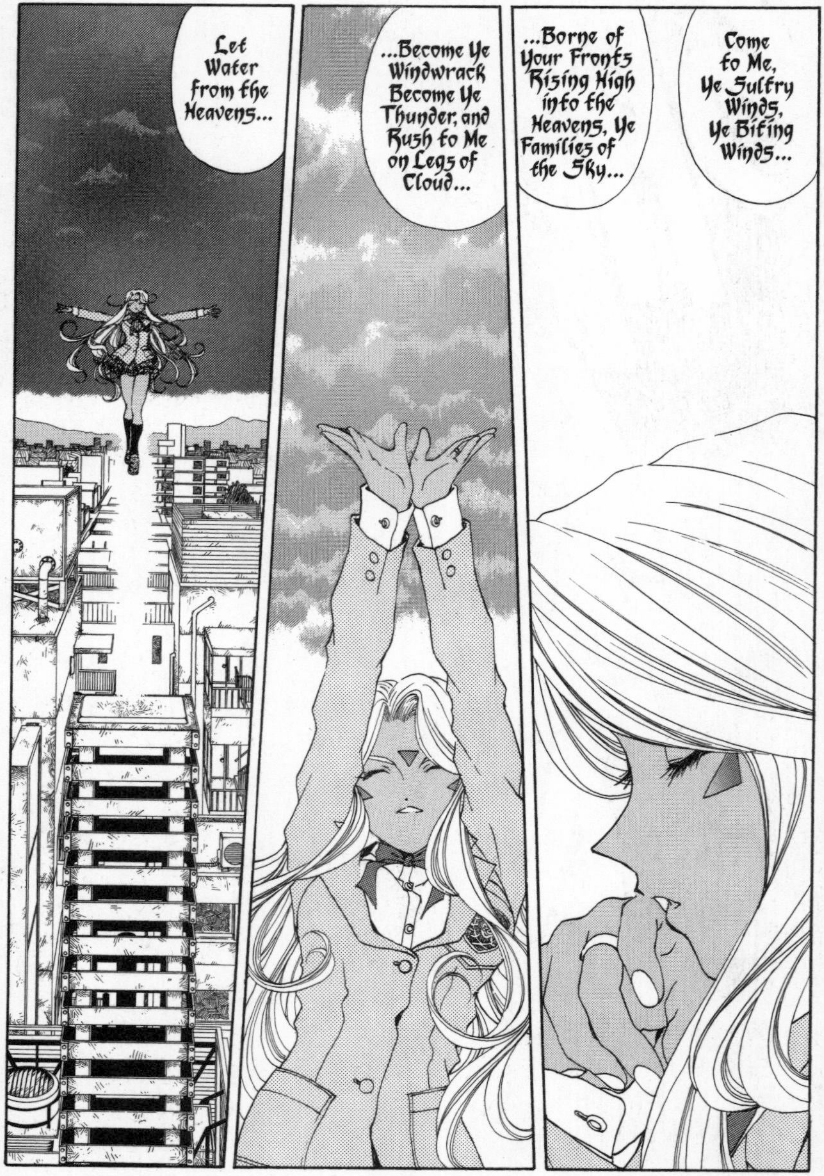
Come to Me, Ye Sultry Winds, Ye Biting Winds...
...Borne of Your Fronts Rising High into the Heavens, Ye Families of the Sky...
...Become Ye Windwrack Become Ye Thunder, and Rush to Me on Legs of Cloud...
Let Water from the Heavens...

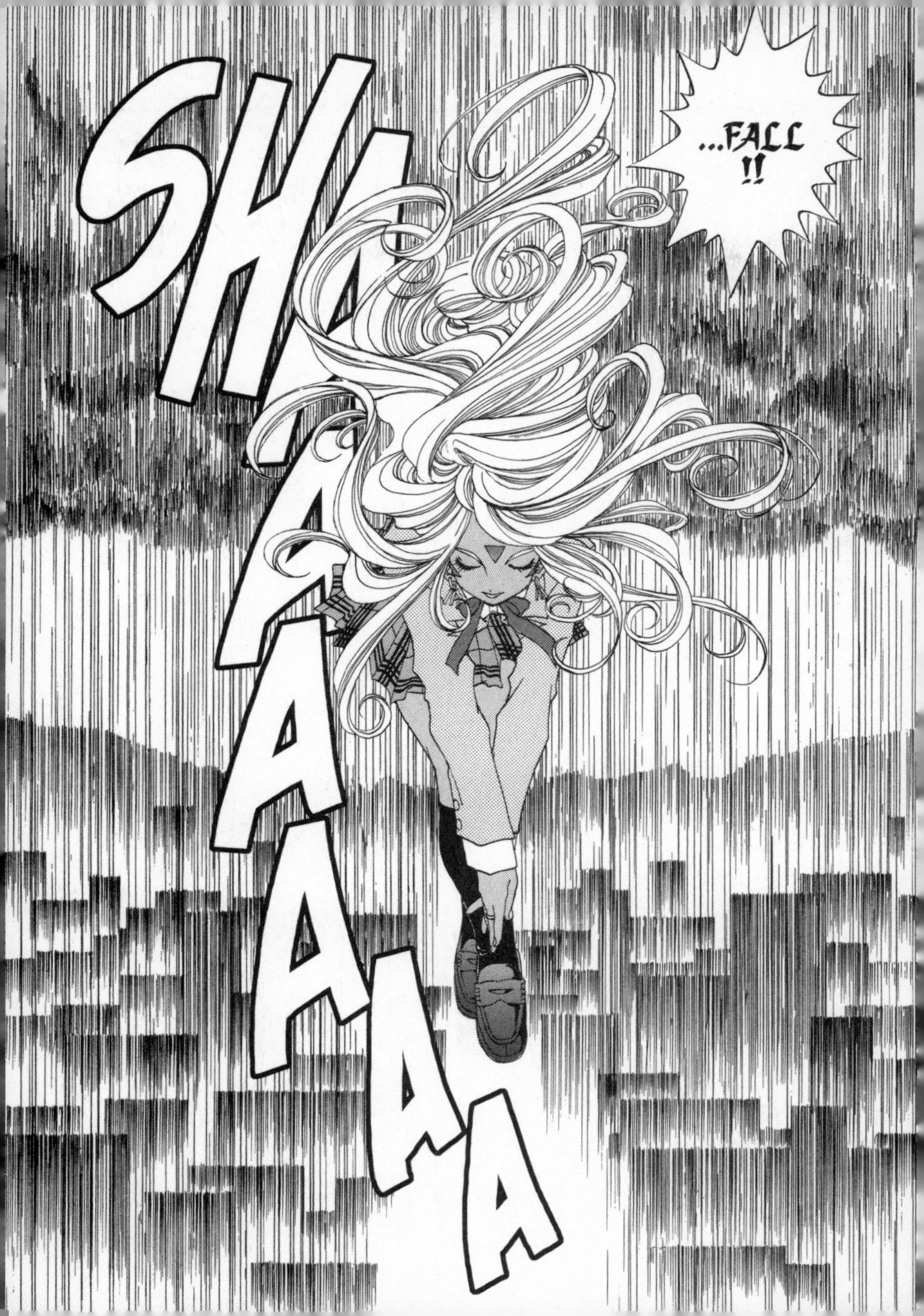
...FALL !!
SHAAAAAAA

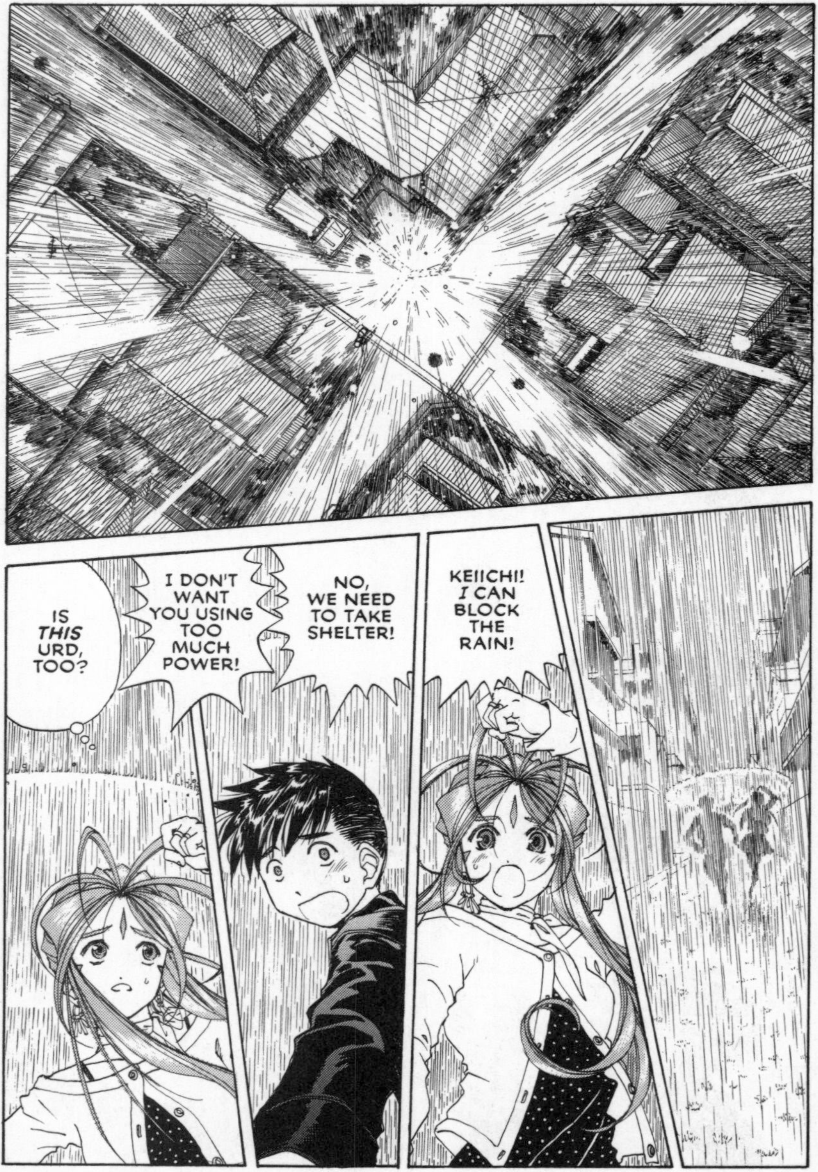
KEIICHI! *I* CAN BLOCK THE RAIN!
NO, WE NEED TO TAKE SHELTER!
I DON'T WANT YOU USING TOO MUCH POWER!
IS *THIS* URD, TOO?

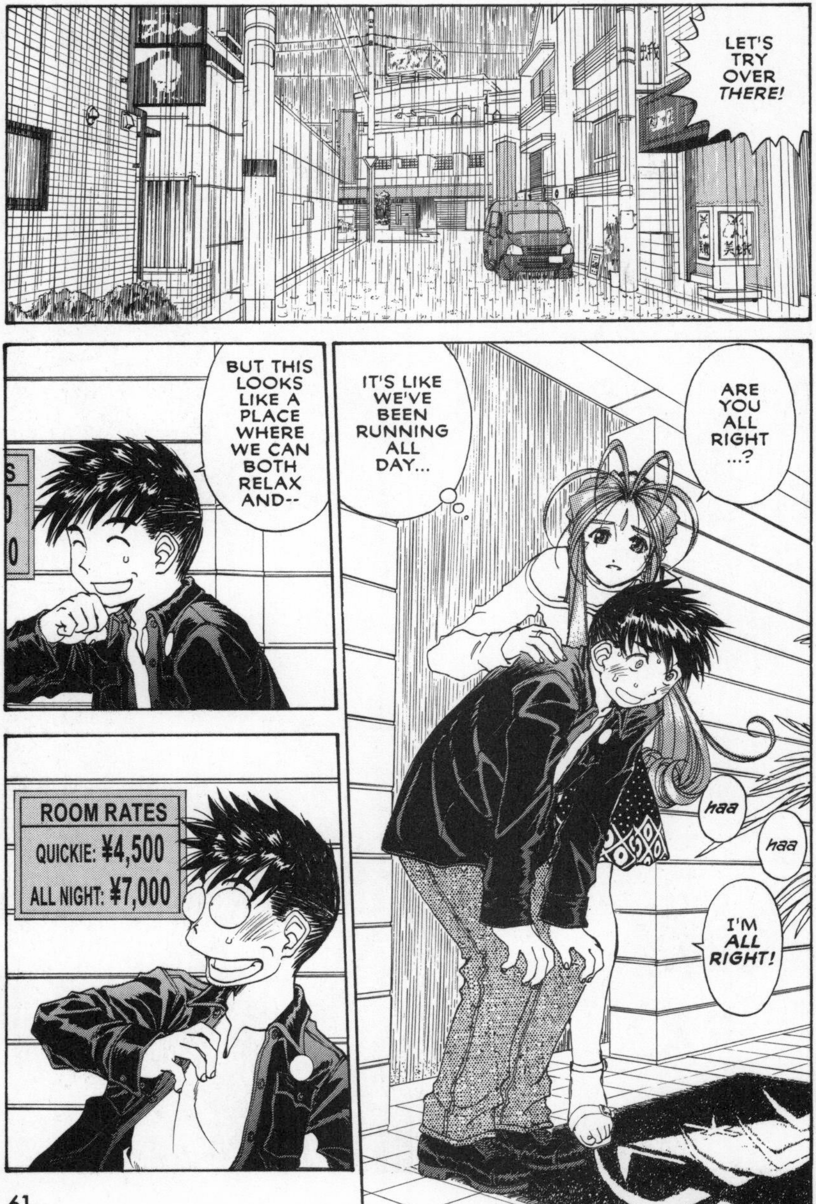
LET'S TRY OVER THERE!
ARE YOU ALL RIGHT ...?
IT'S LIKE WE'VE BEEN RUNNING ALL DAY...
haa
haa
I'M ALL RIGHT!
BUT THIS LOOKS LIKE A PLACE WHERE WE CAN BOTH RELAX AND--
ROOM RATES
QUICKIE: ¥4,500
ALL NIGHT: ¥7,000

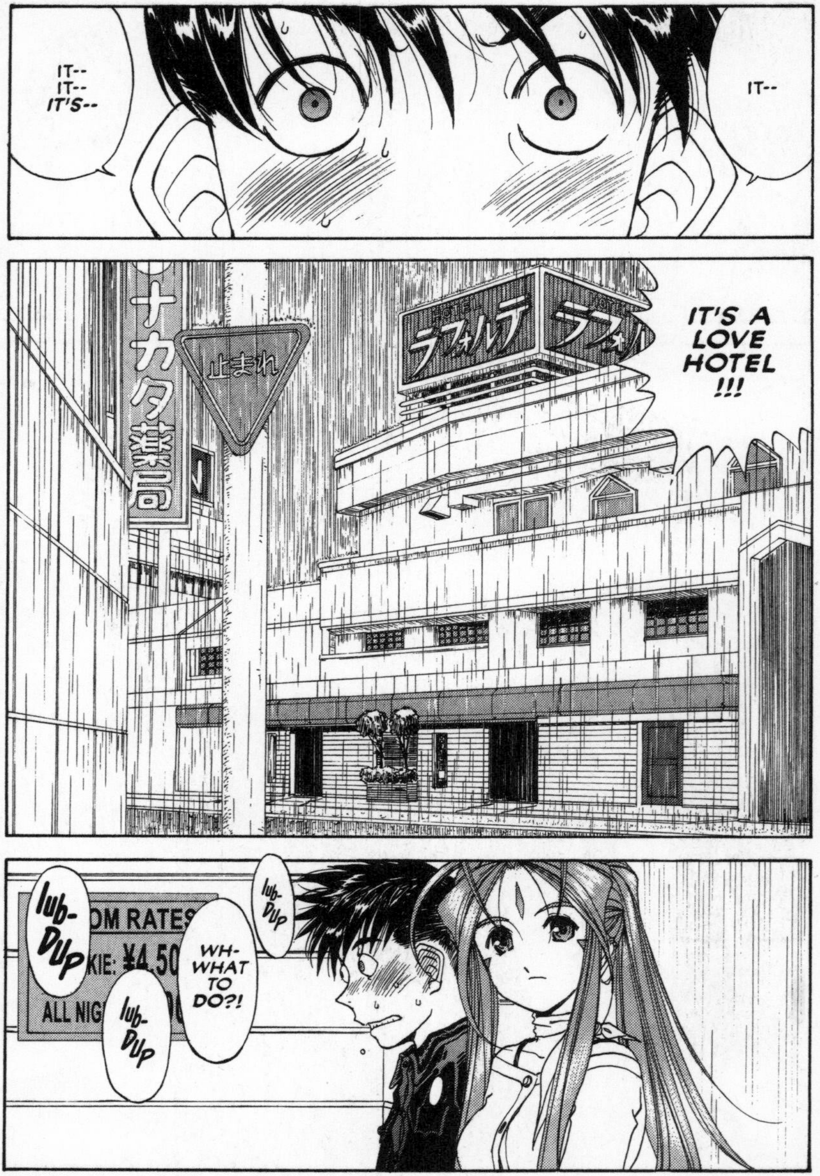
IT--
IT--
IT--
IT'S--
HOTEL
ラフォルテ
止まれ
ナカタ薬局
IT'S A LOVE HOTEL !!!
lub-DUP
WH- WHAT TO DO?!
lub-DUP
lub-DUP
OM RATES
KIE: ¥4.50
ALL NIG

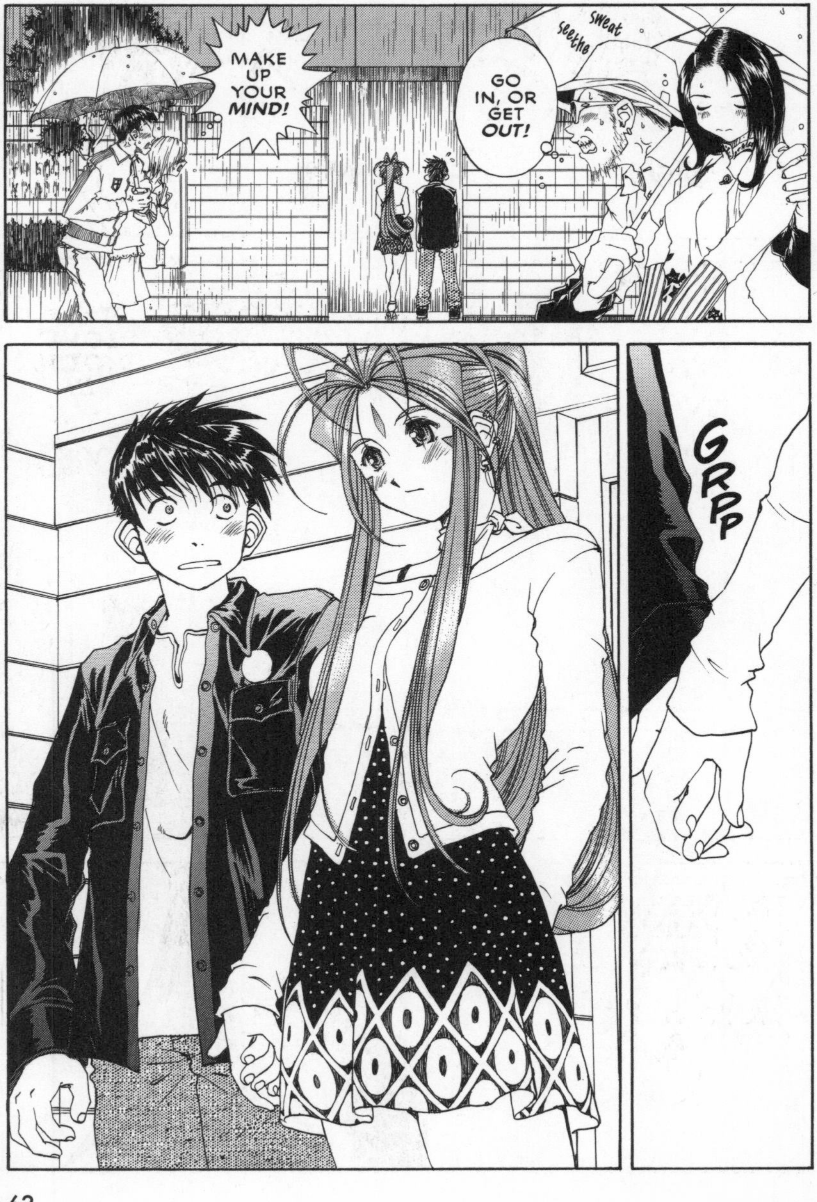
sweat
seethe
GO IN, OR GET OUT!
MAKE UP YOUR MIND!
GRPP

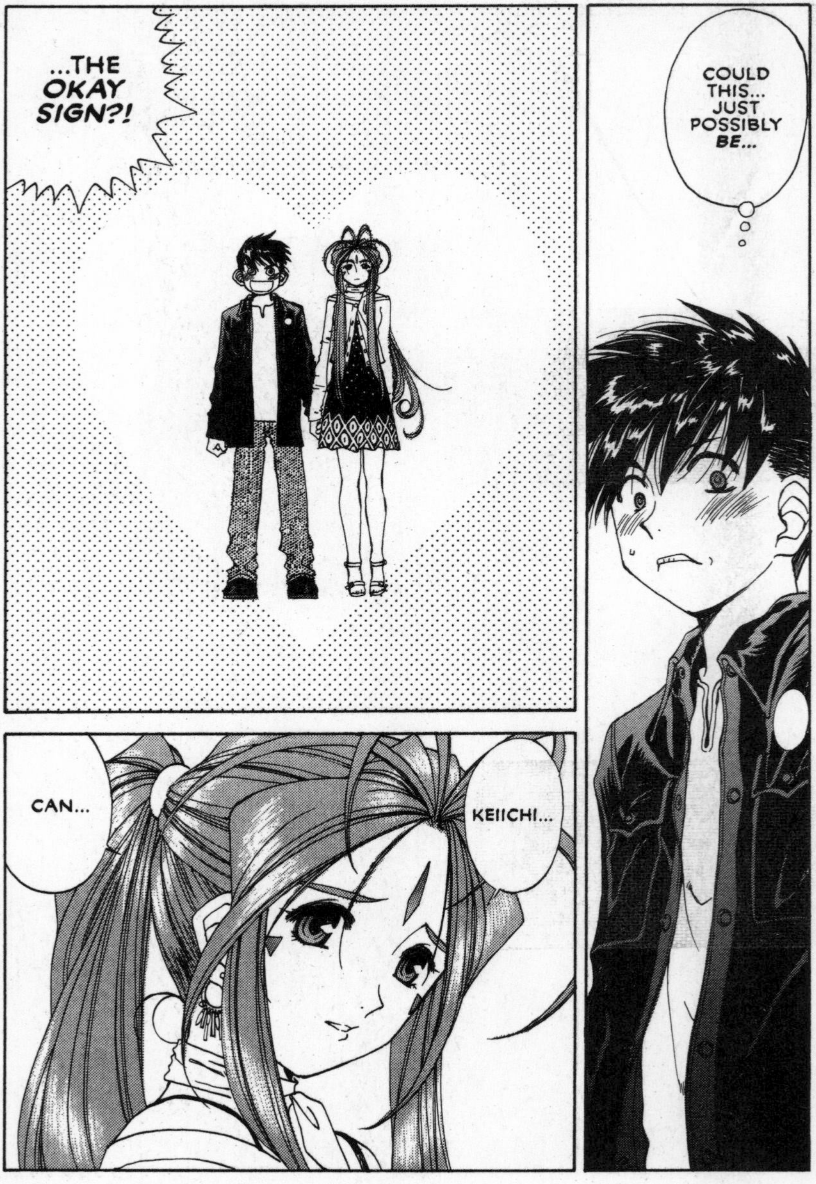
COULD THIS... JUST POSSIBLY BE...
...THE OKAY SIGN?!
KEIICHI...
CAN...

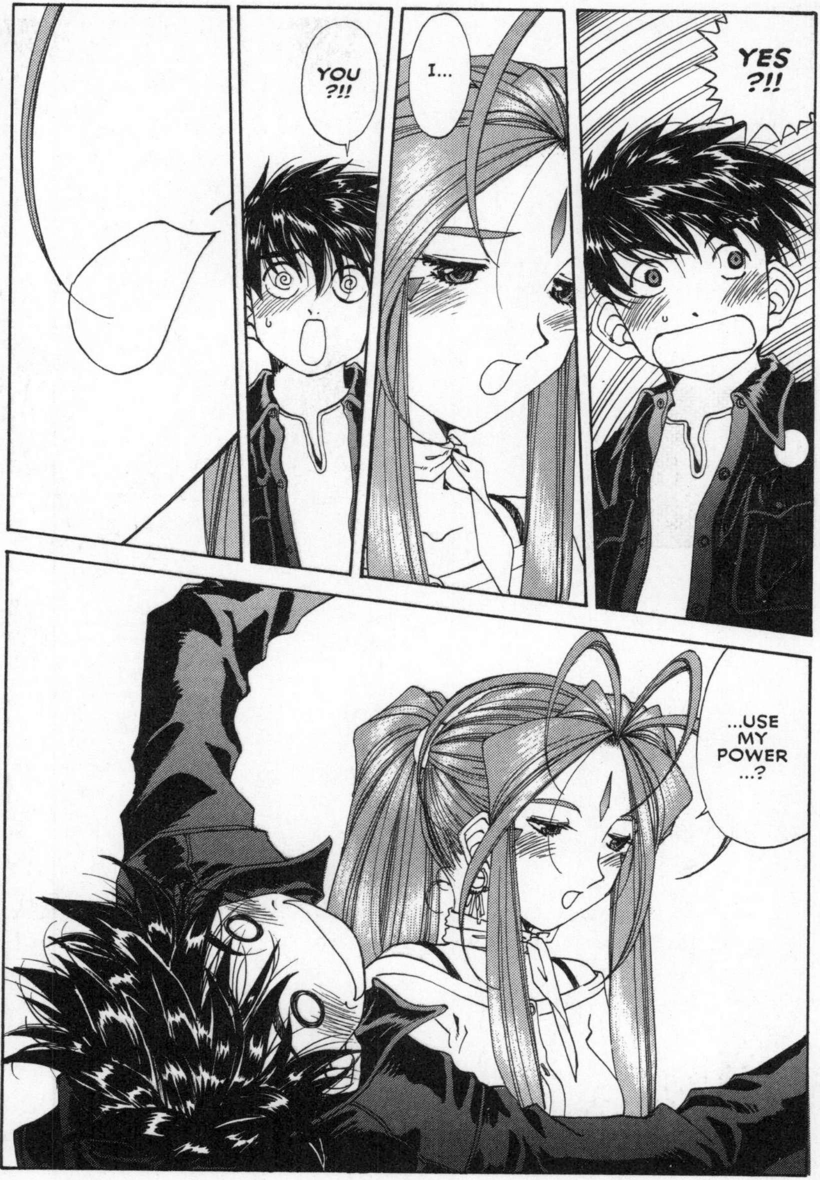
YES ?!!
I...
YOU ?!!
...USE MY POWER ...?

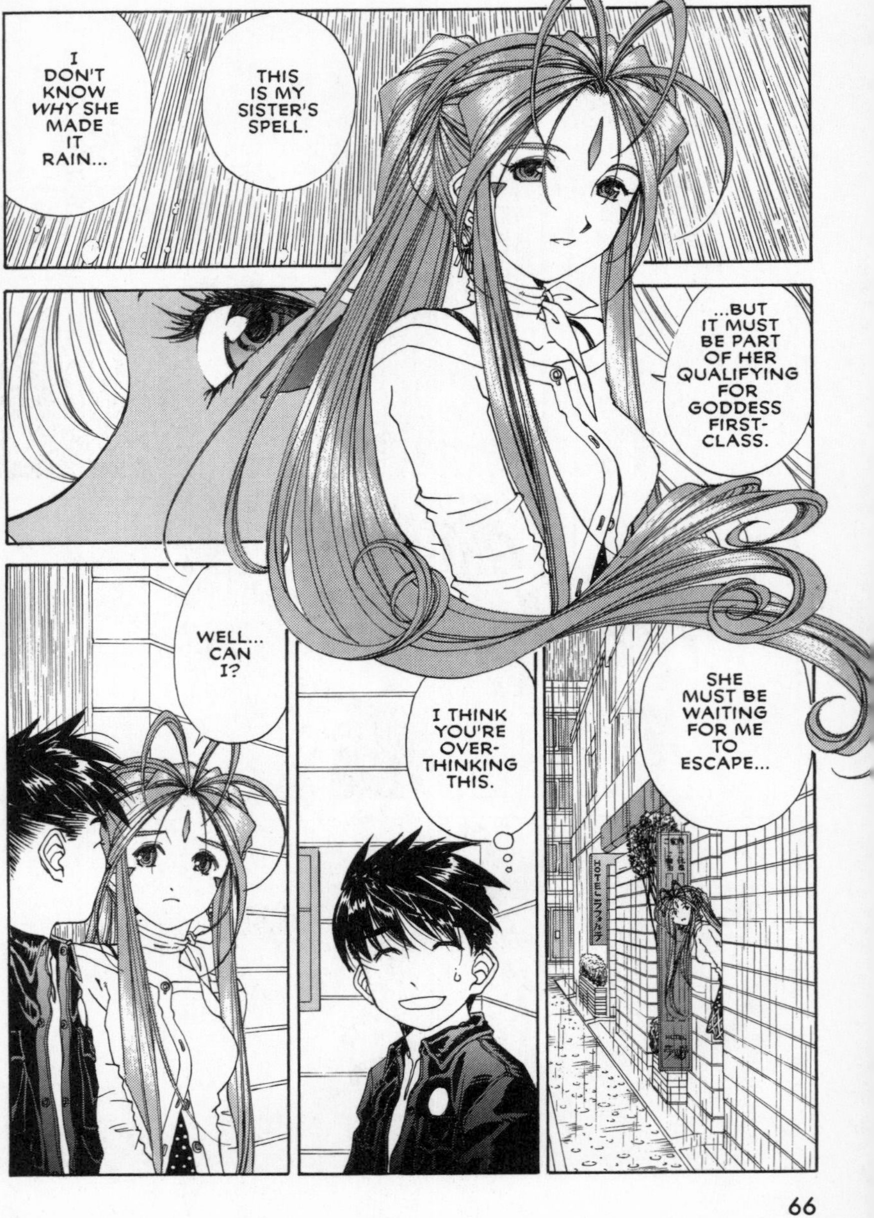
THIS IS MY SISTER'S SPELL.
I DON'T KNOW *WHY* SHE MADE IT RAIN...
...BUT IT MUST BE PART OF HER QUALIFYING FOR GODDESS FIRST-CLASS.
SHE MUST BE WAITING FOR ME TO ESCAPE...
I THINK YOU'RE OVER-THINKING THIS.
WELL... CAN I?

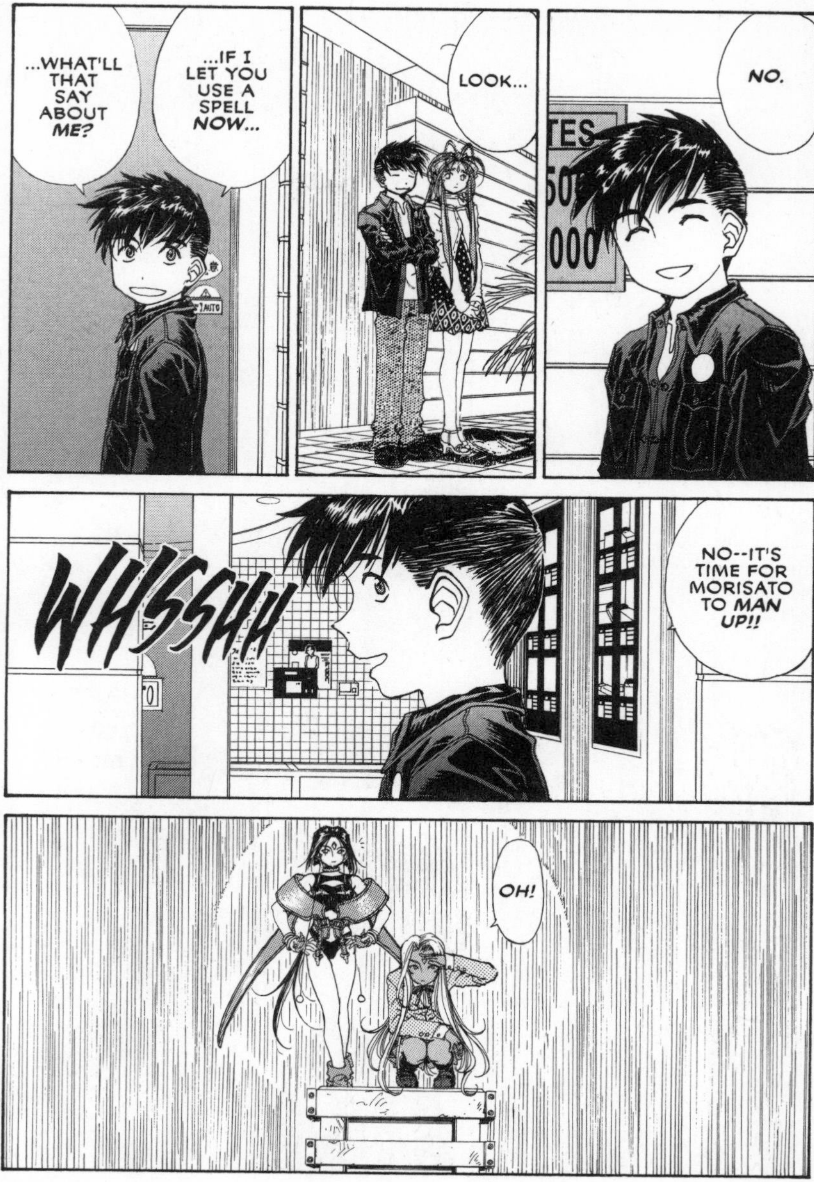
NO.
LOOK...
...IF I LET YOU USE A SPELL NOW...
...WHAT'LL THAT SAY ABOUT ME?
NO--IT'S TIME FOR MORISATO TO MAN UP!!
WHSSHH
OH!

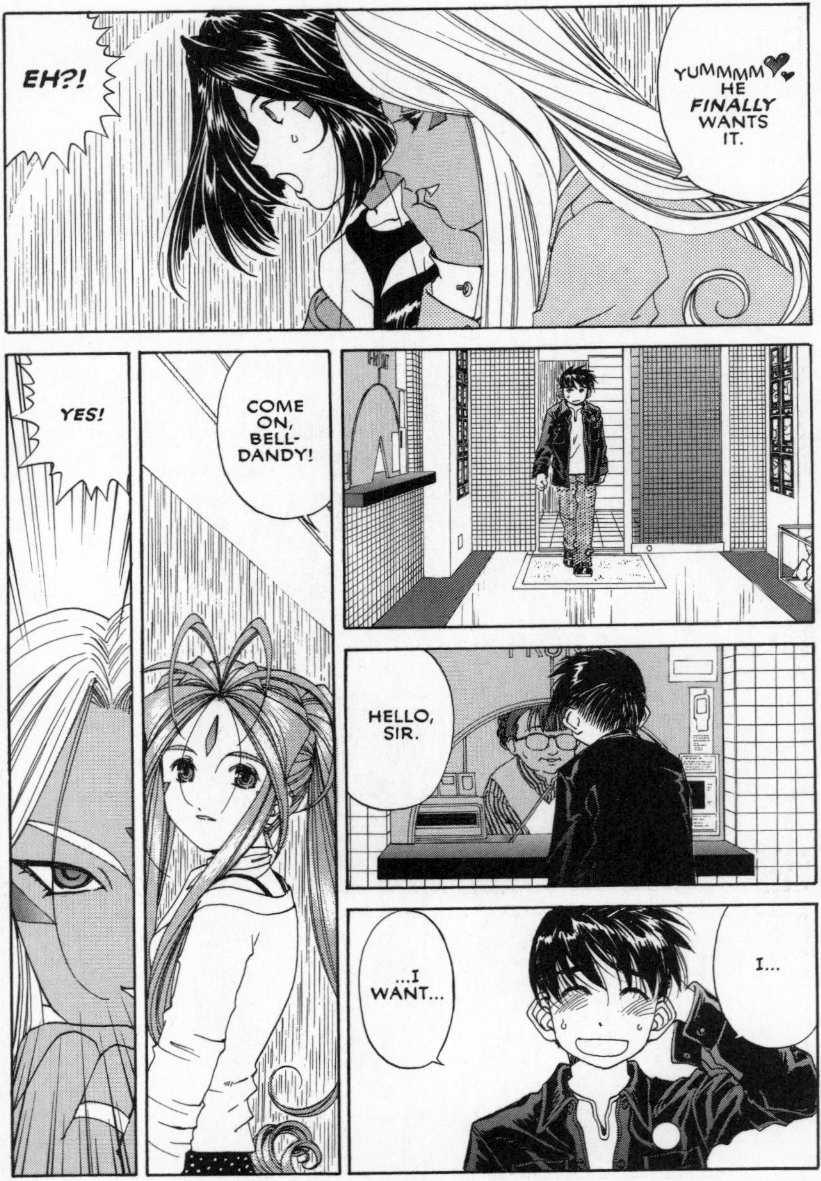
YUMMMM♥ HE FINALLY WANTS IT.
EH?!
HELLO, SIR.
I...
...I WANT...
COME ON, BELL-DANDY!
YES!

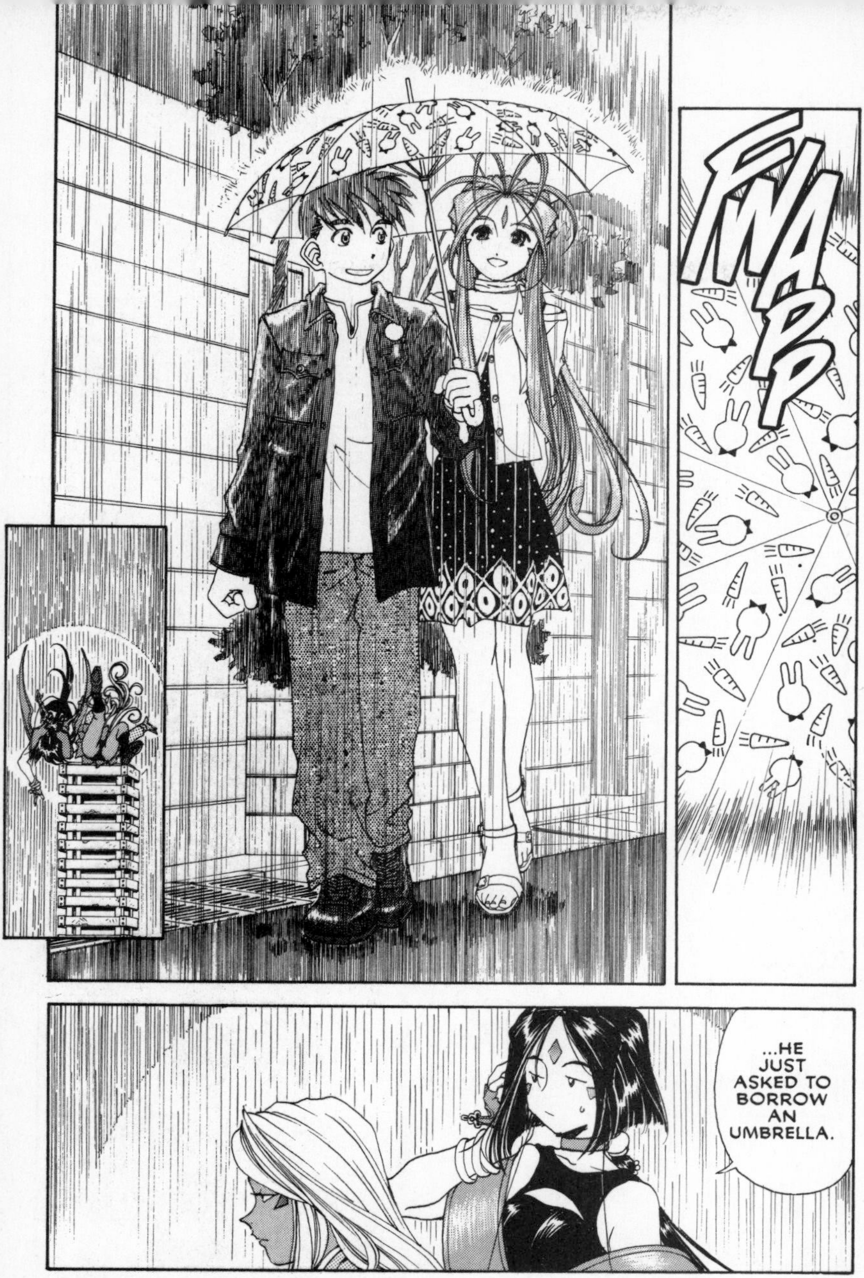
FWAPP
...HE JUST ASKED TO BORROW AN UMBRELLA.

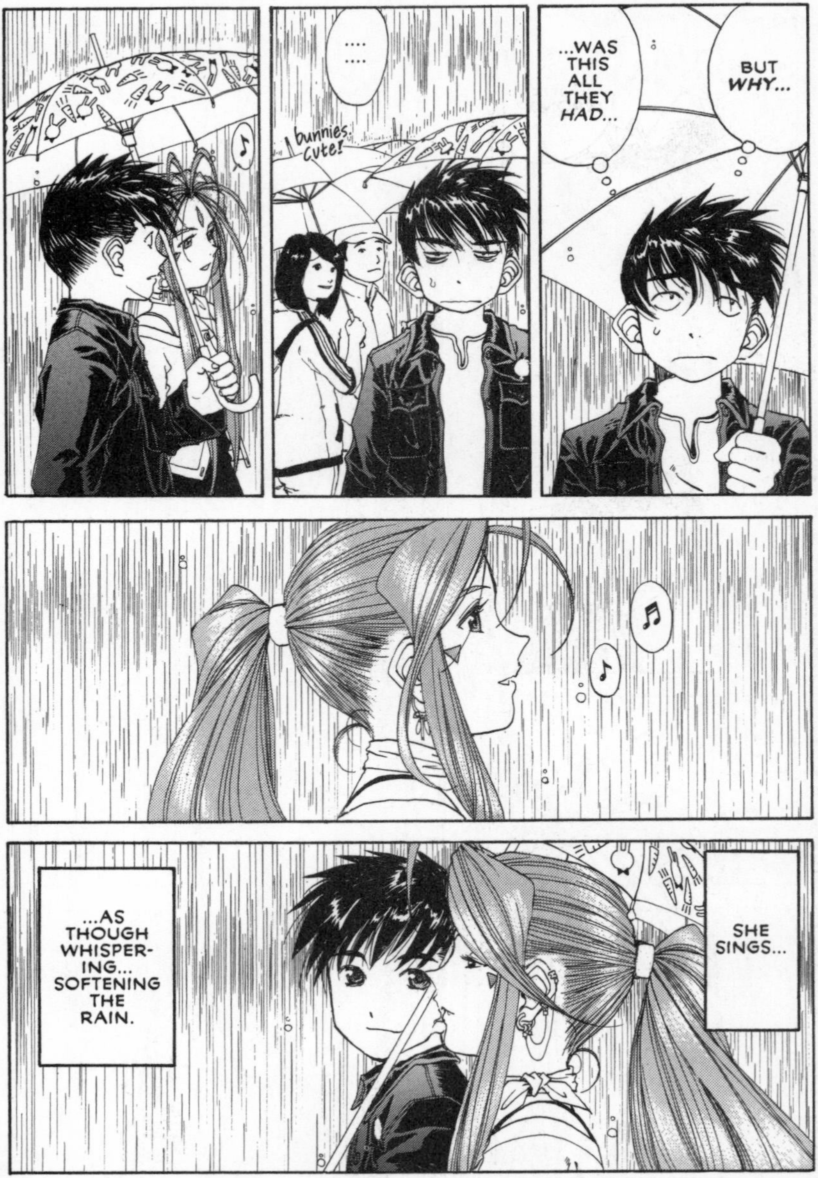
BUT WHY...
...WAS THIS ALL THEY HAD...
....
....
bunnies, cute!
♪
♫
♪
SHE SINGS...
...AS THOUGH WHISPERING... SOFTENING THE RAIN.

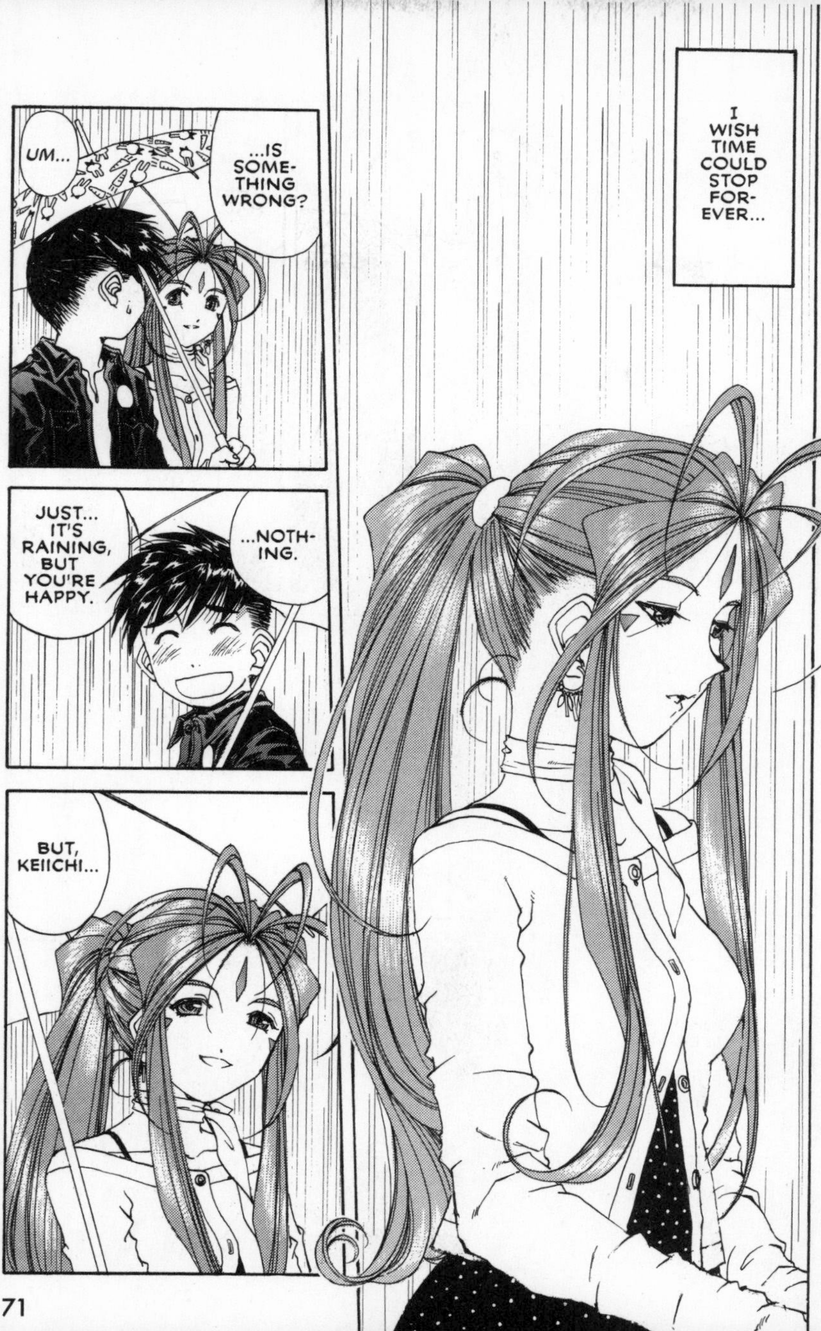
I WISH TIME COULD STOP FOR-EVER...
...IS SOME-THING WRONG?
UM...
...NOTH-ING.
JUST... IT'S RAINING, BUT YOU'RE HAPPY.
BUT, KEIICHI...

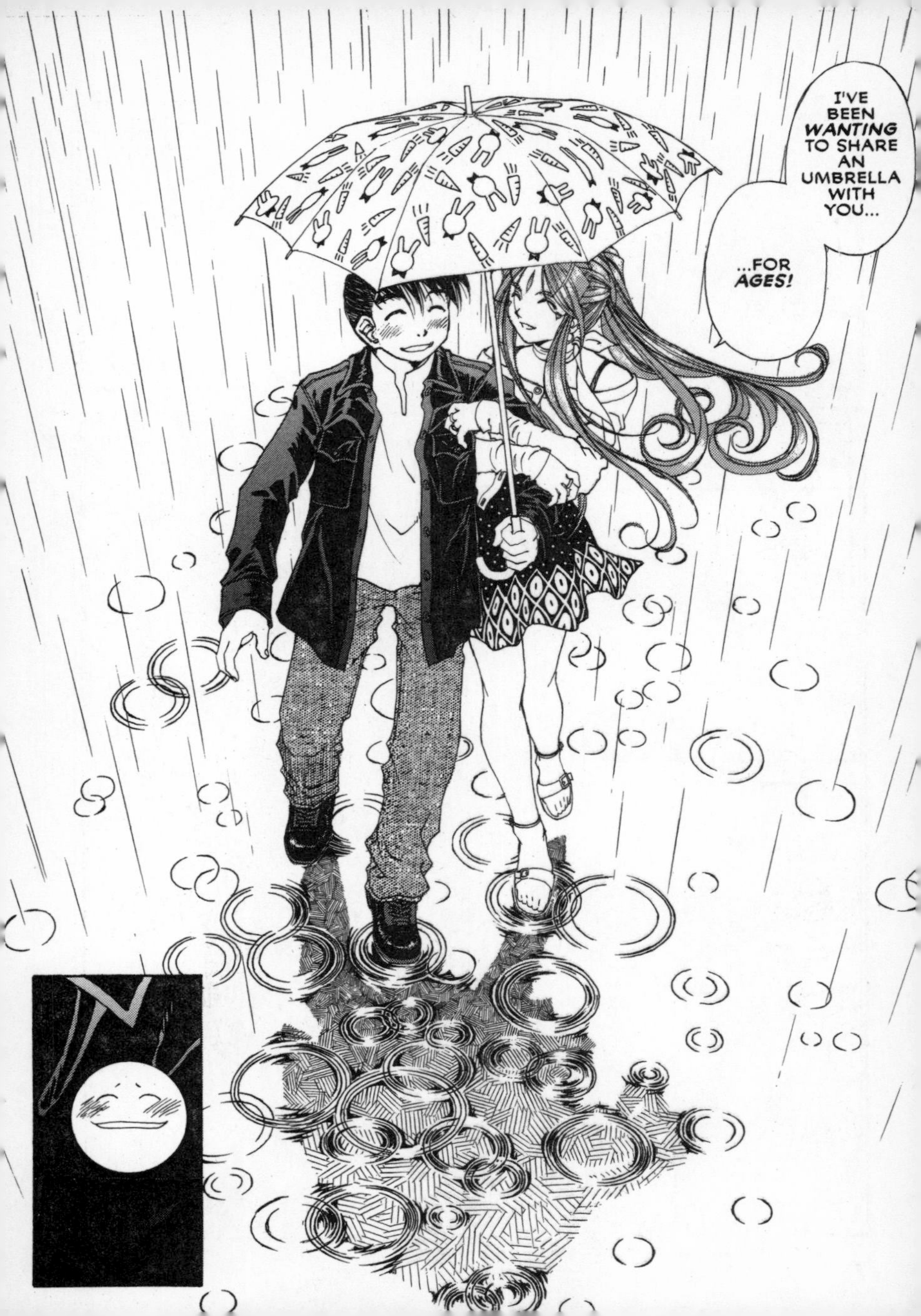
I'VE BEEN WANTING TO SHARE AN UMBRELLA WITH YOU...
...FOR AGES!

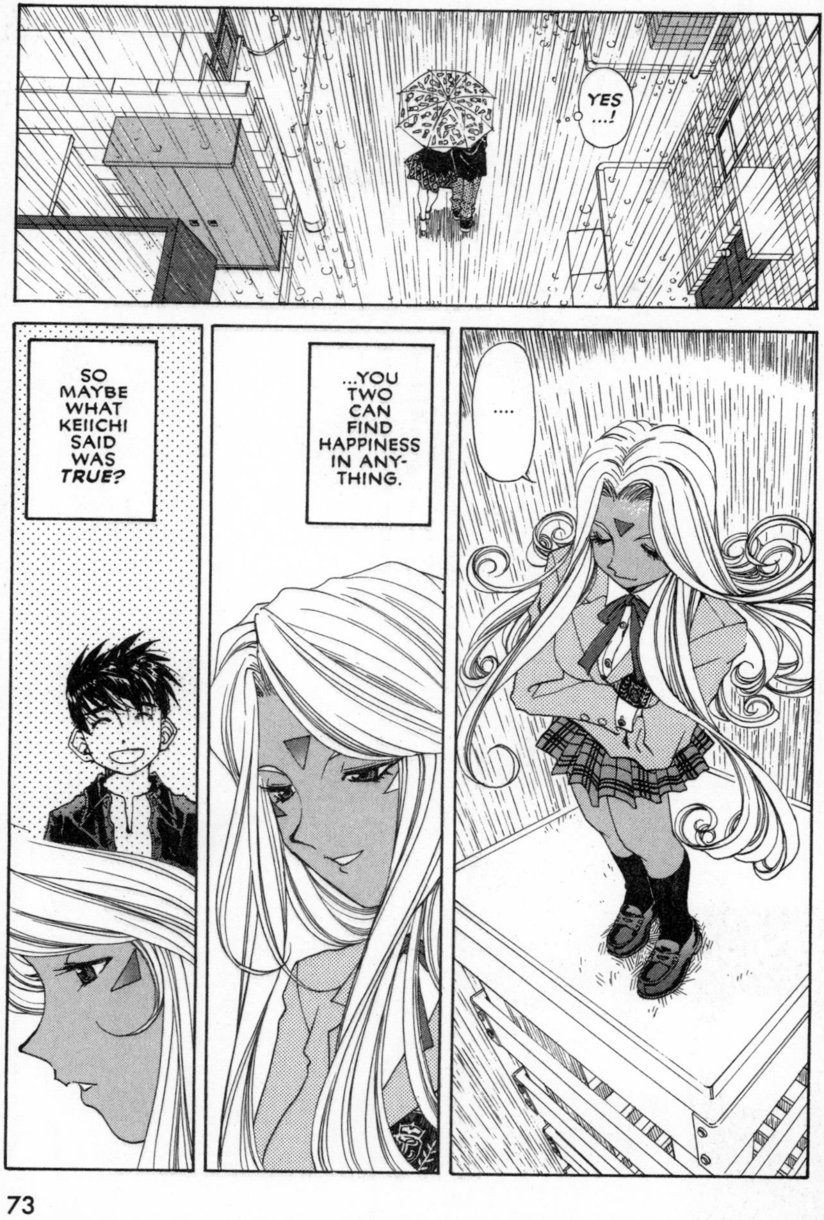
YES ...!
....
...YOU TWO CAN FIND HAPPINESS IN ANY-THING.
SO MAYBE WHAT KEIICHI SAID WAS *TRUE?*

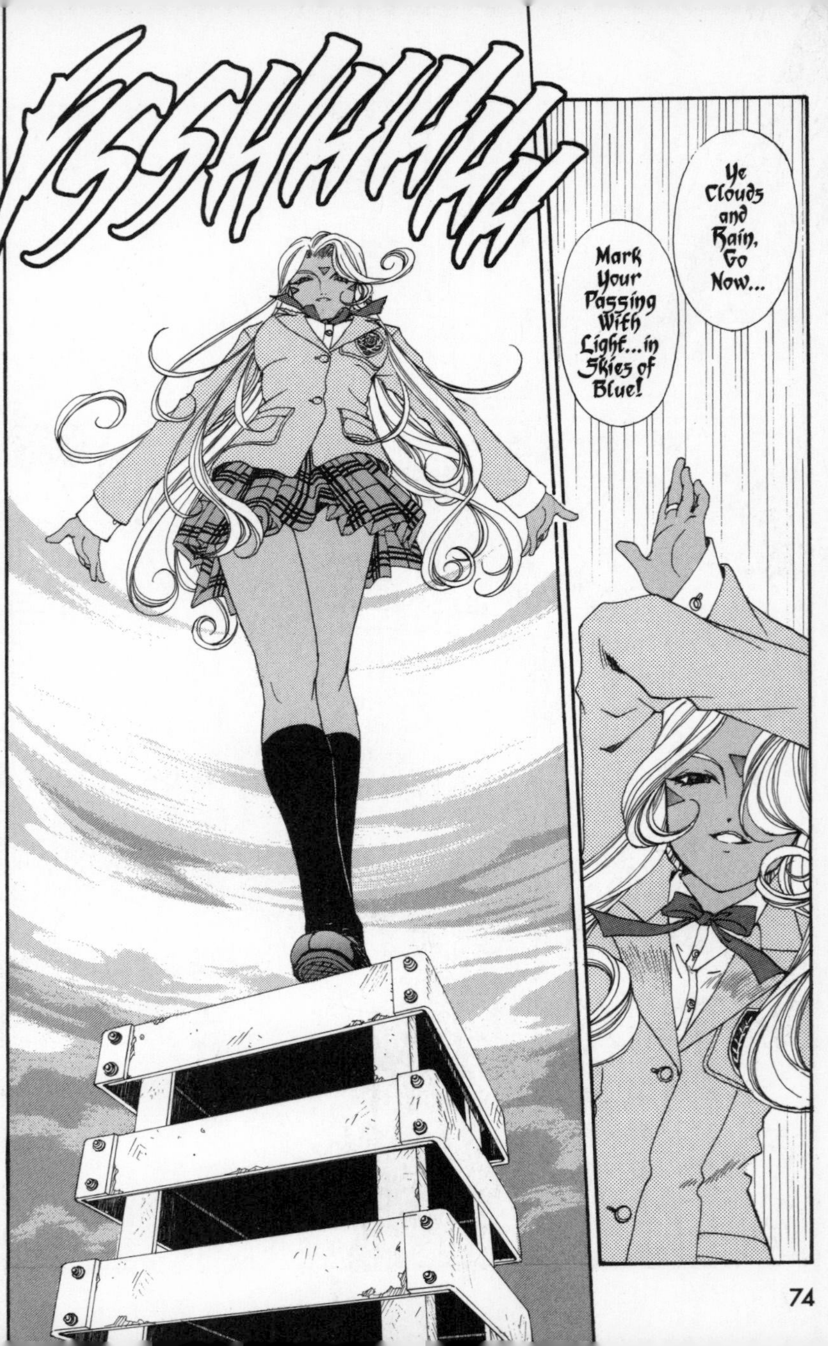
Ye Clouds and Rain, Go Now...
Mark Your Passing With Light...in Skies of Blue!

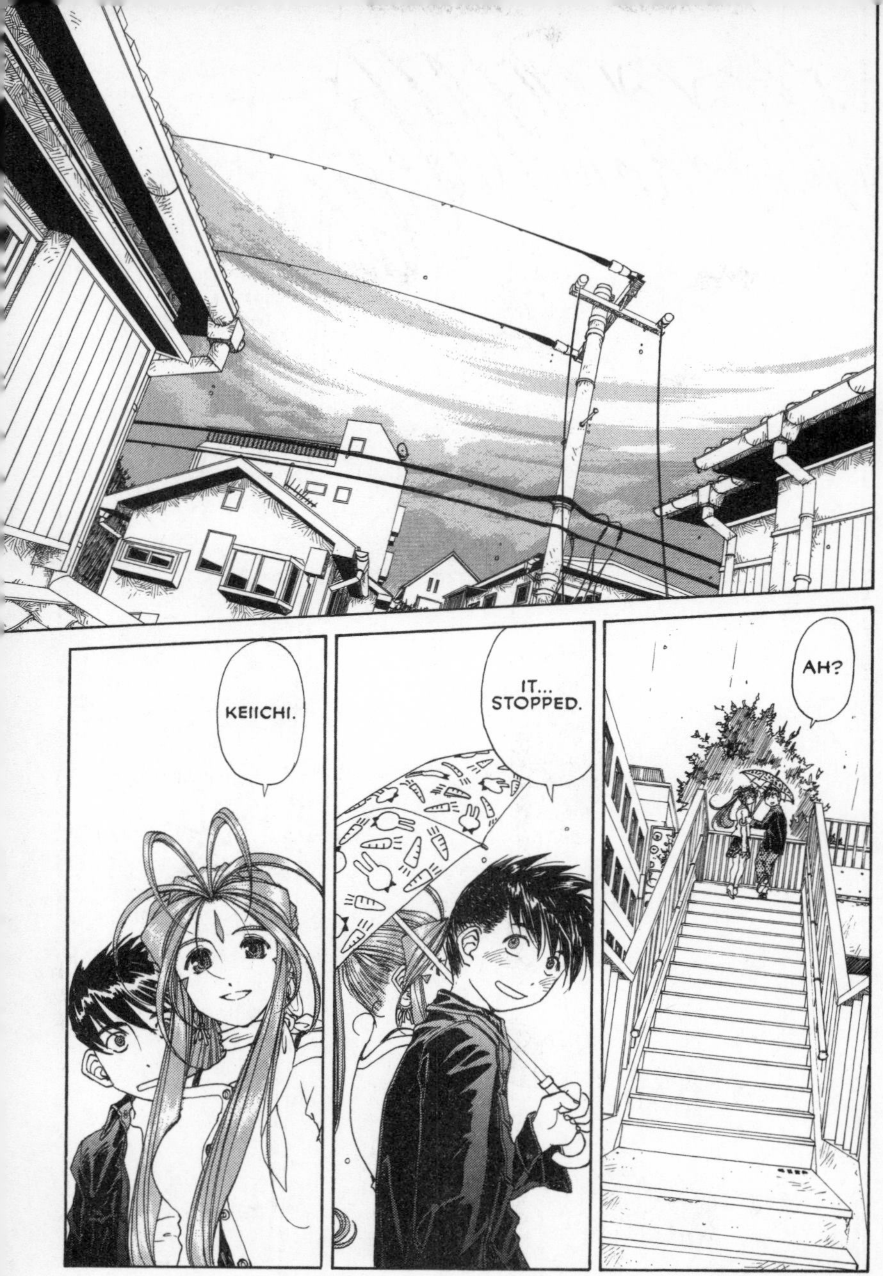
AH?
IT... STOPPED.
KEIICHI.

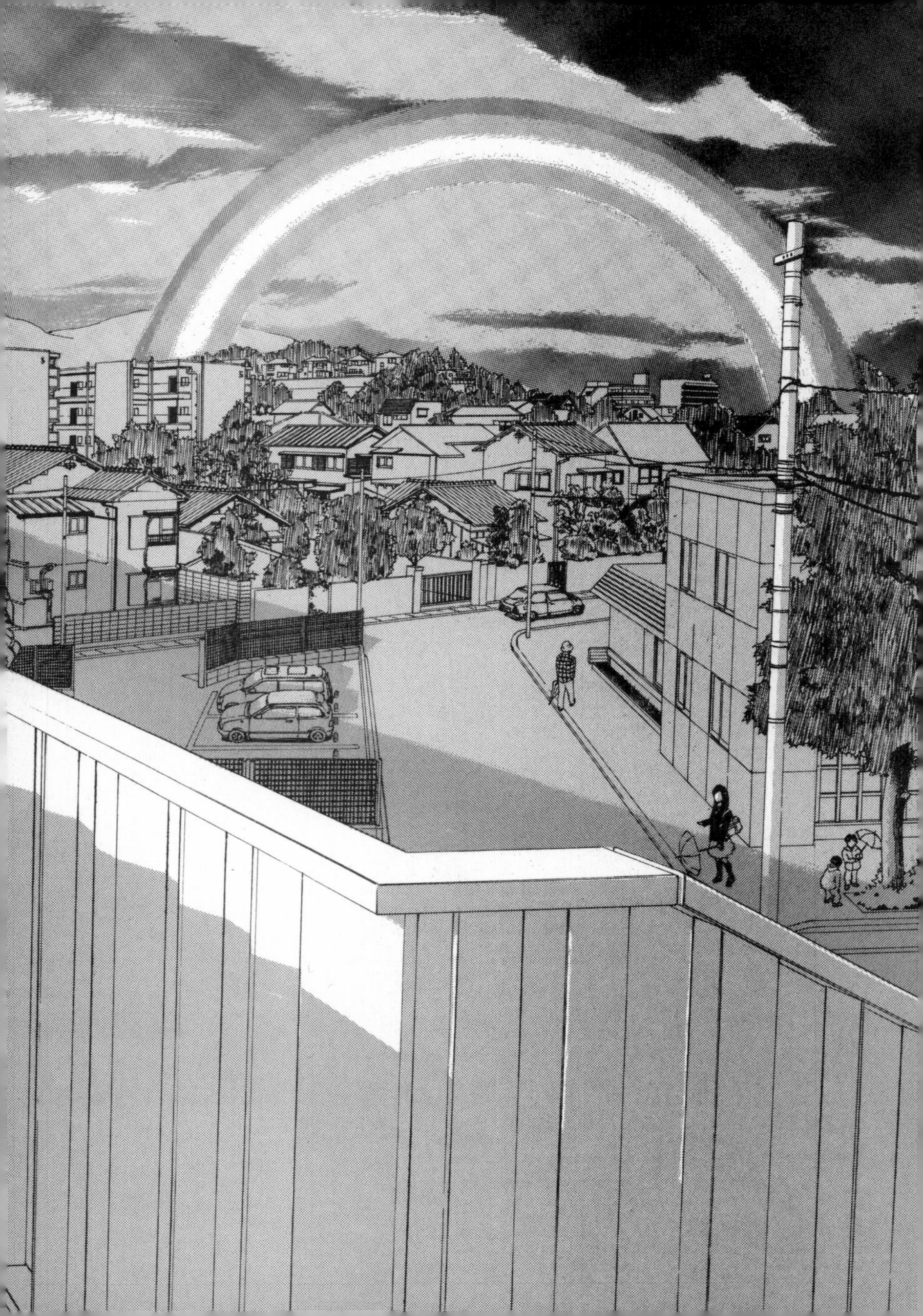

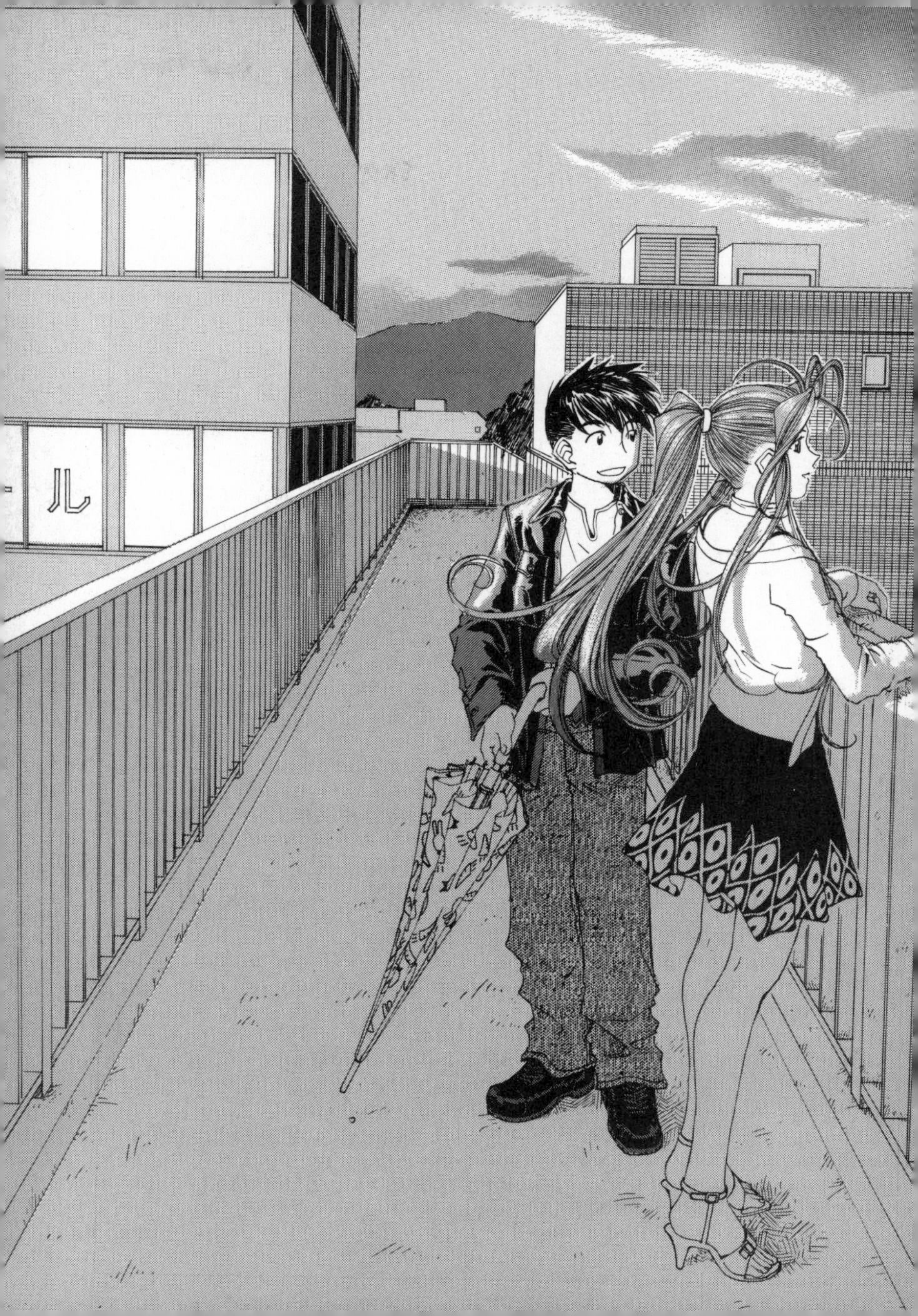

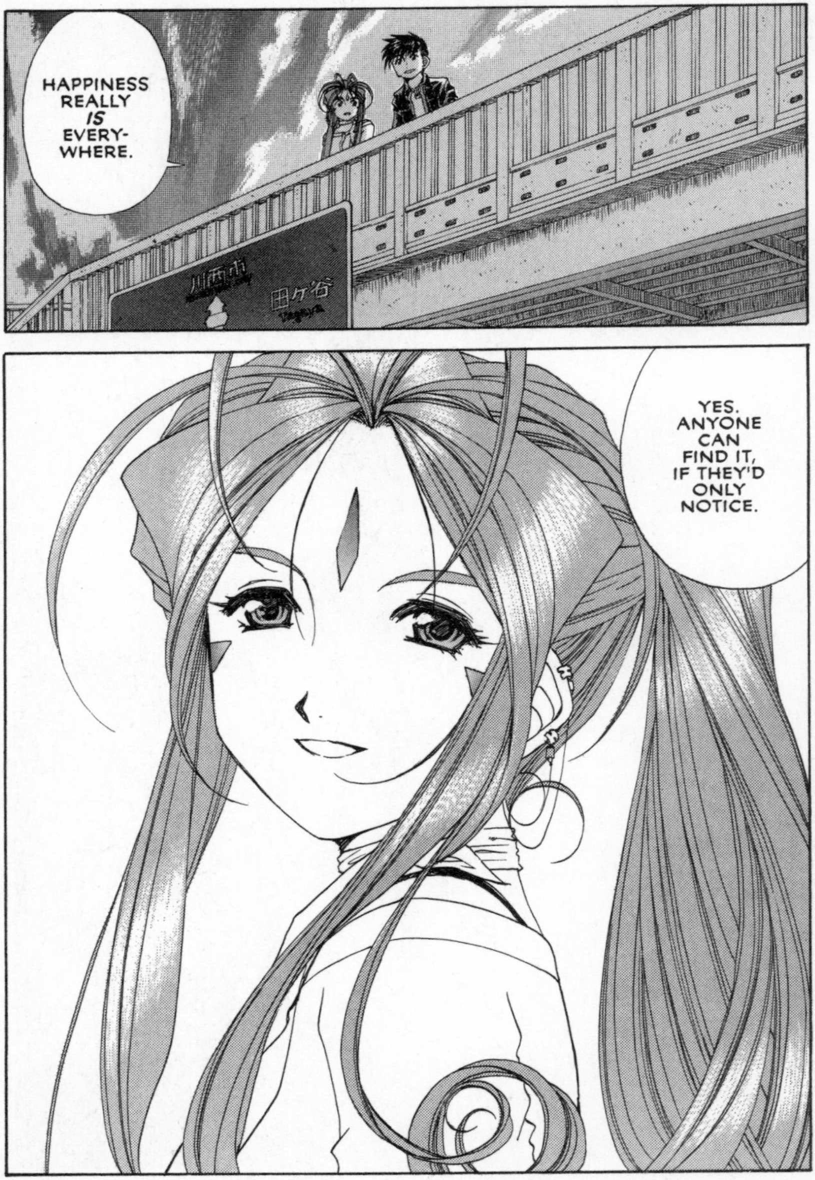
HAPPINESS REALLY *IS* EVERY-WHERE.
川西市
田ヶ谷
YES. ANYONE CAN FIND IT, IF THEY'D ONLY NOTICE.

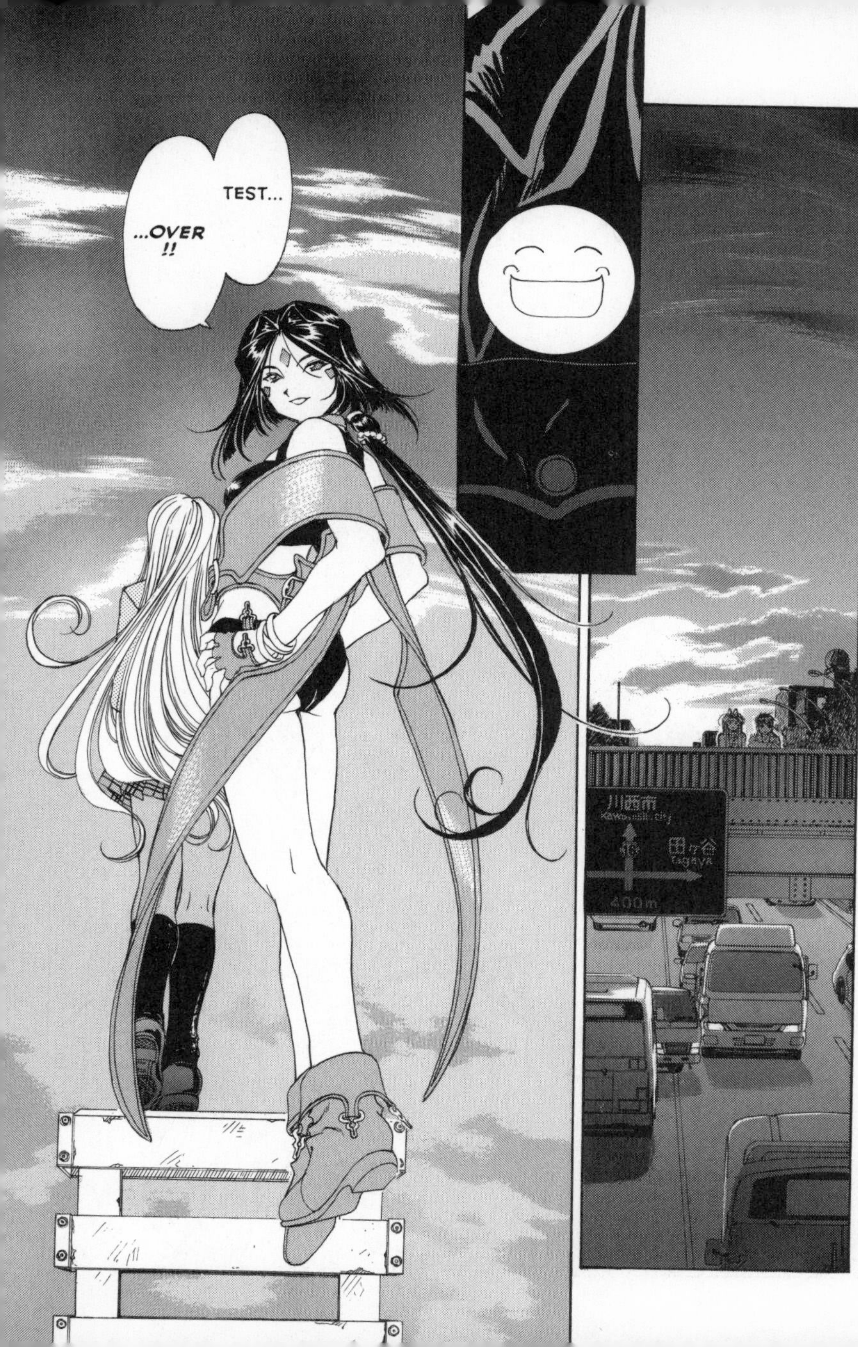
TEST... ...OVER !!
川西市
田ヶ谷
Tagaya
400m

CHAPTER 192

For Whose Sake a First-Class Goddess?

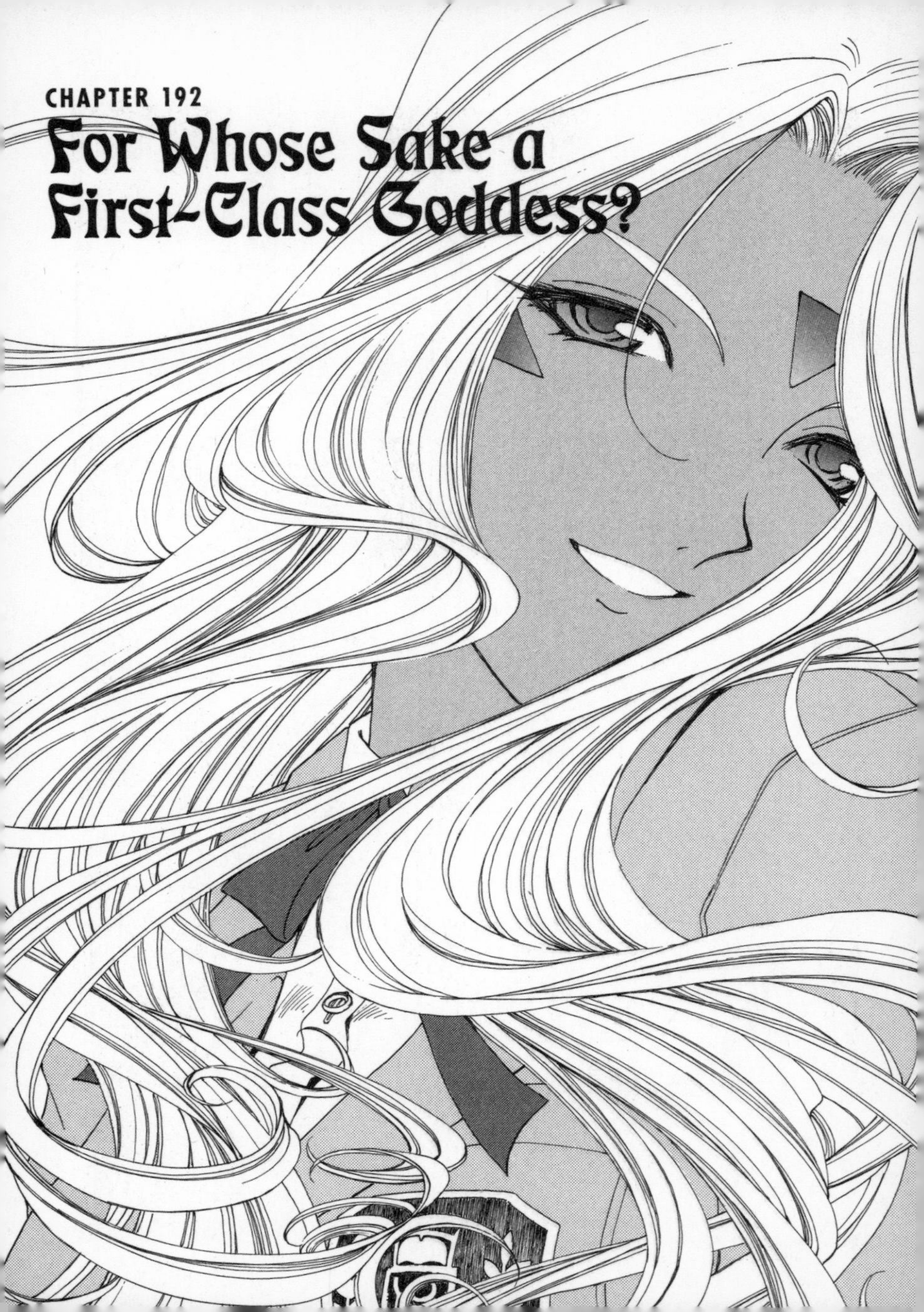

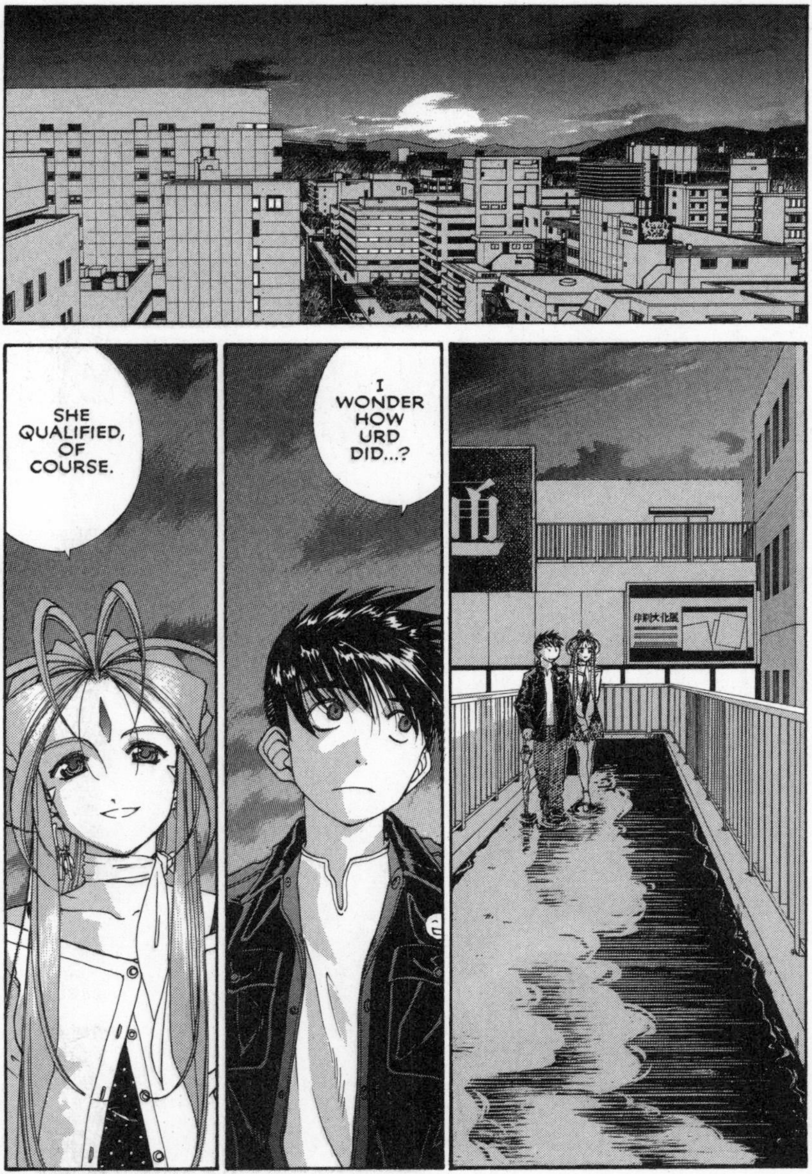
I WONDER HOW URD DID...?
SHE QUALIFIED, OF COURSE.

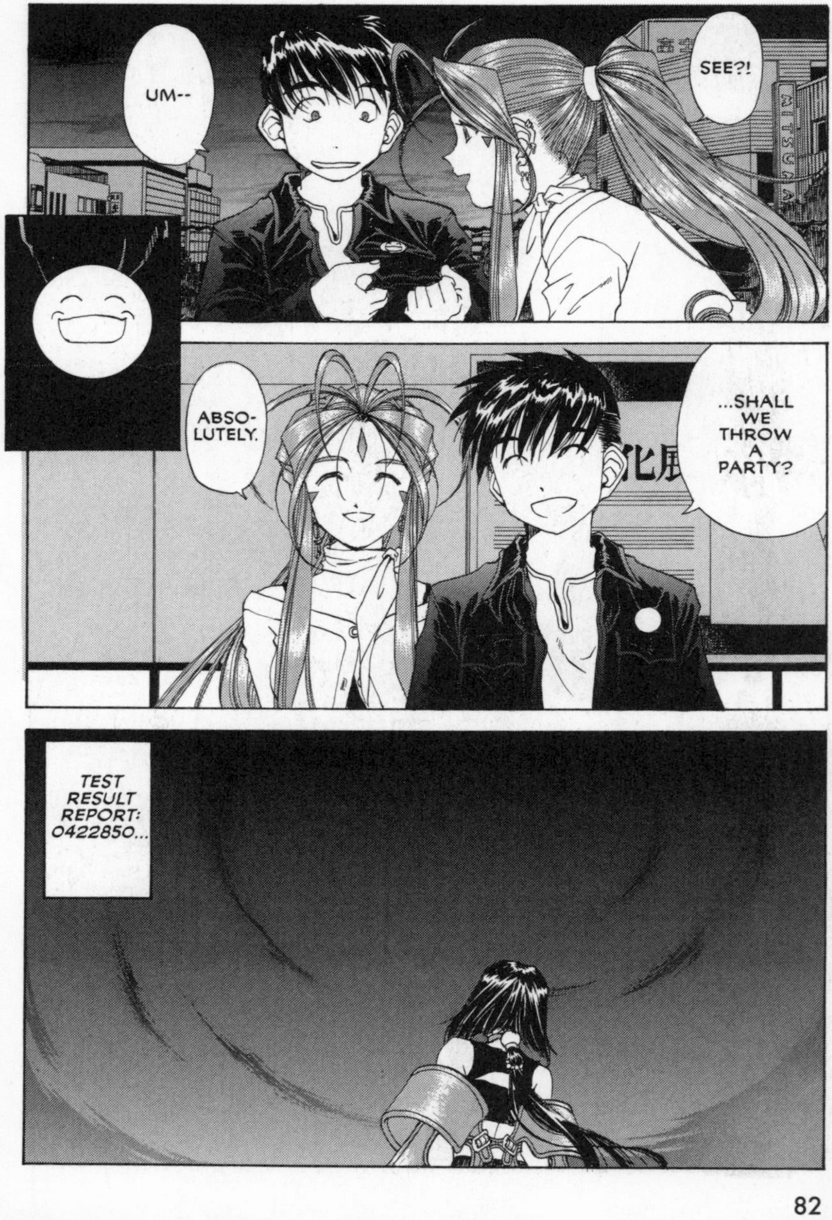
SEE?!
UM--
...SHALL WE THROW A PARTY?
ABSO-LUTELY.
TEST RESULT REPORT: 0422850...

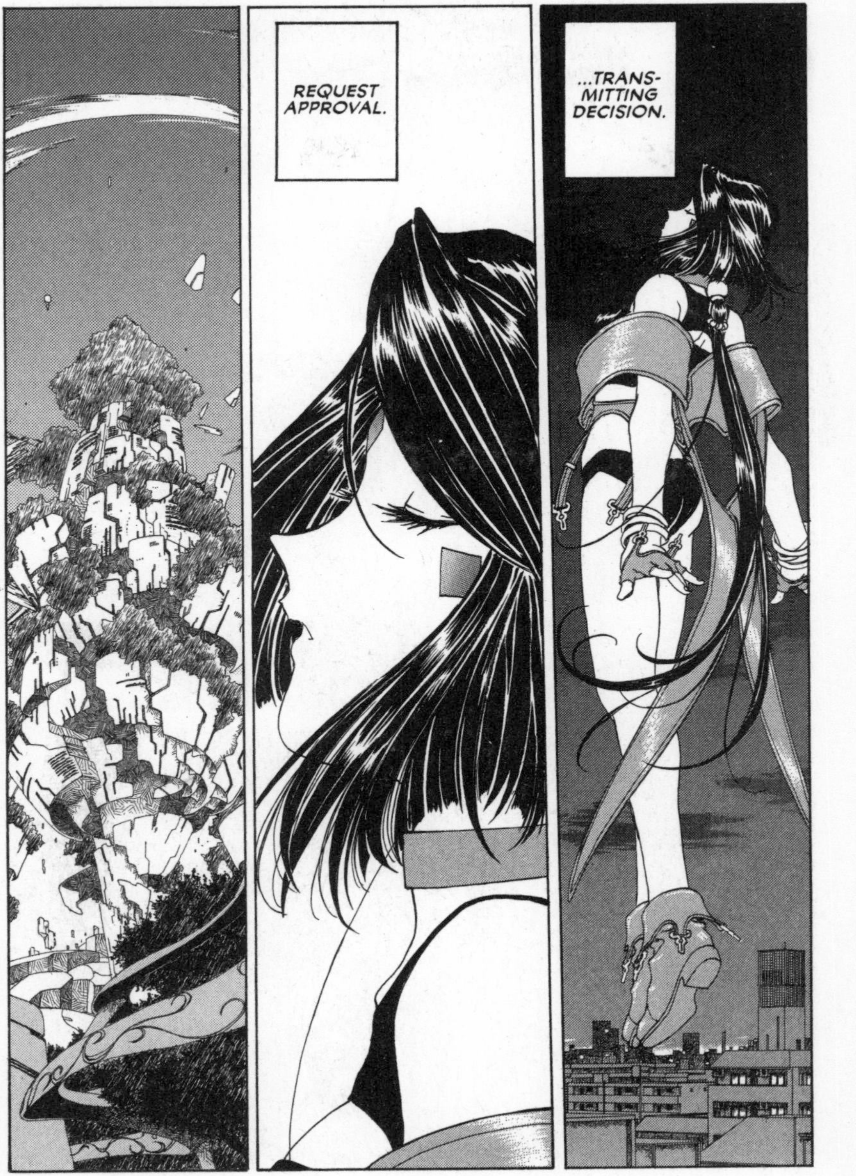
...TRANS-
MITTING
DECISION.
REQUEST
APPROVAL.

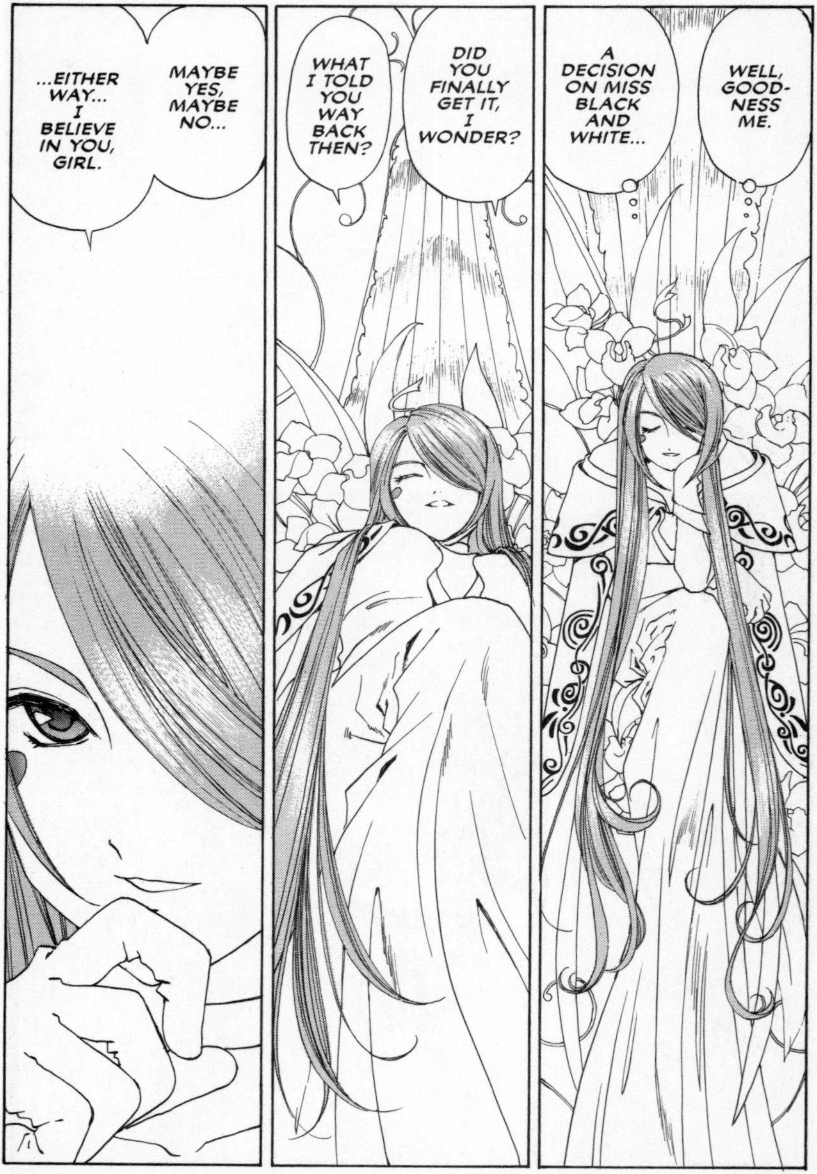
WELL, GOODNESS ME.
A DECISION ON MISS BLACK AND WHITE...
DID YOU FINALLY GET IT, I WONDER?
WHAT I TOLD YOU WAY BACK THEN?
MAYBE YES, MAYBE NO...
...EITHER WAY... I BELIEVE IN YOU, GIRL.

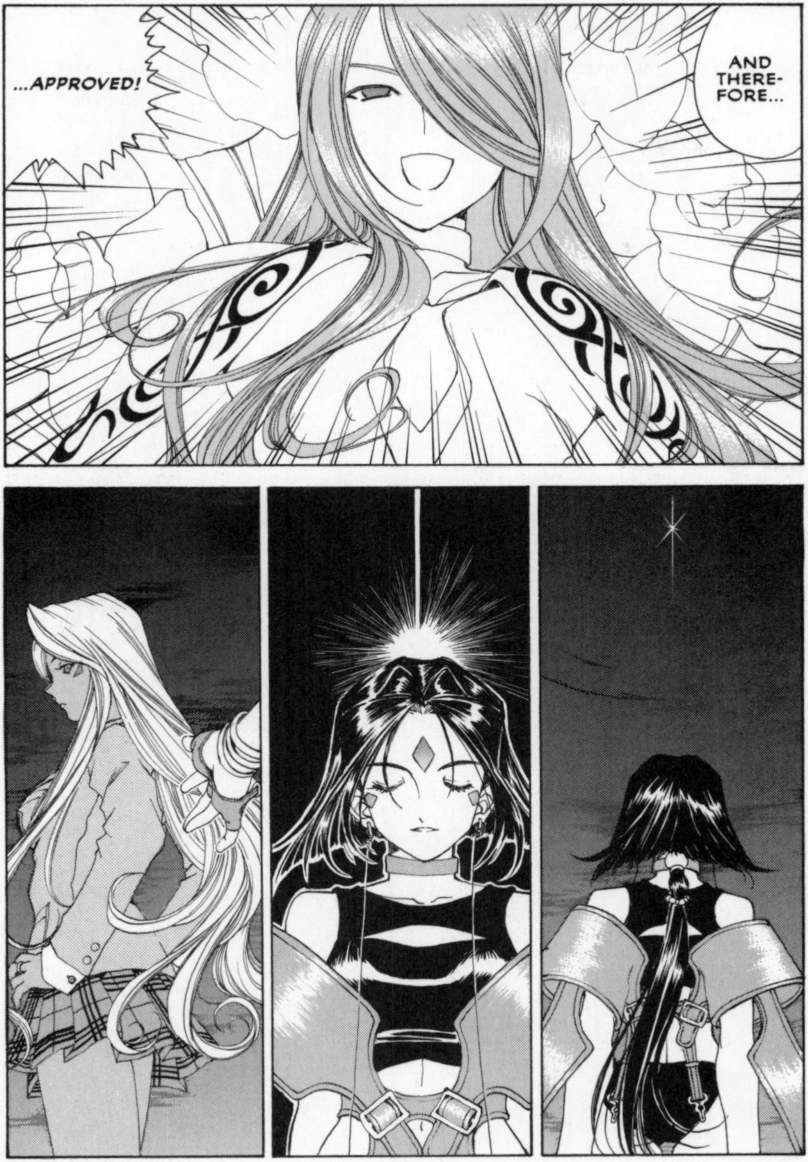
AND THEREFORE...
...APPROVED!

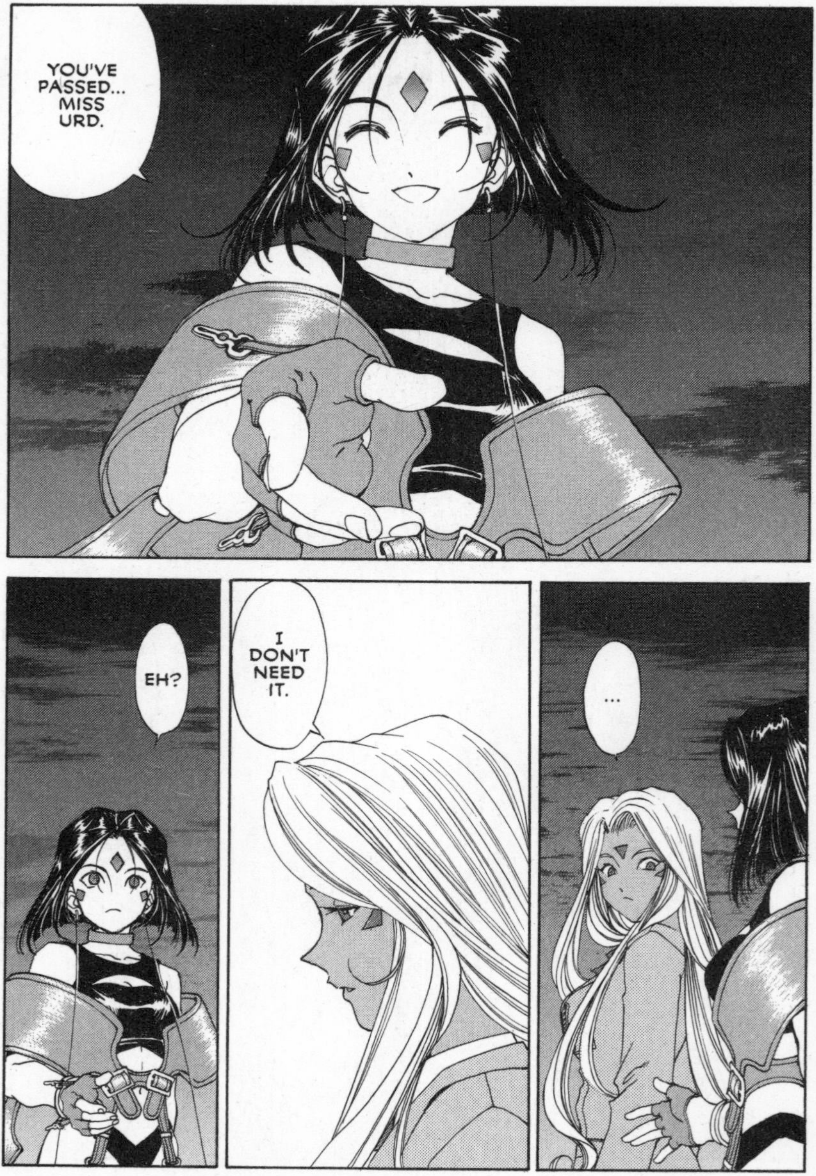
YOU'VE PASSED... MISS URD.
...
I DON'T NEED IT.
EH?

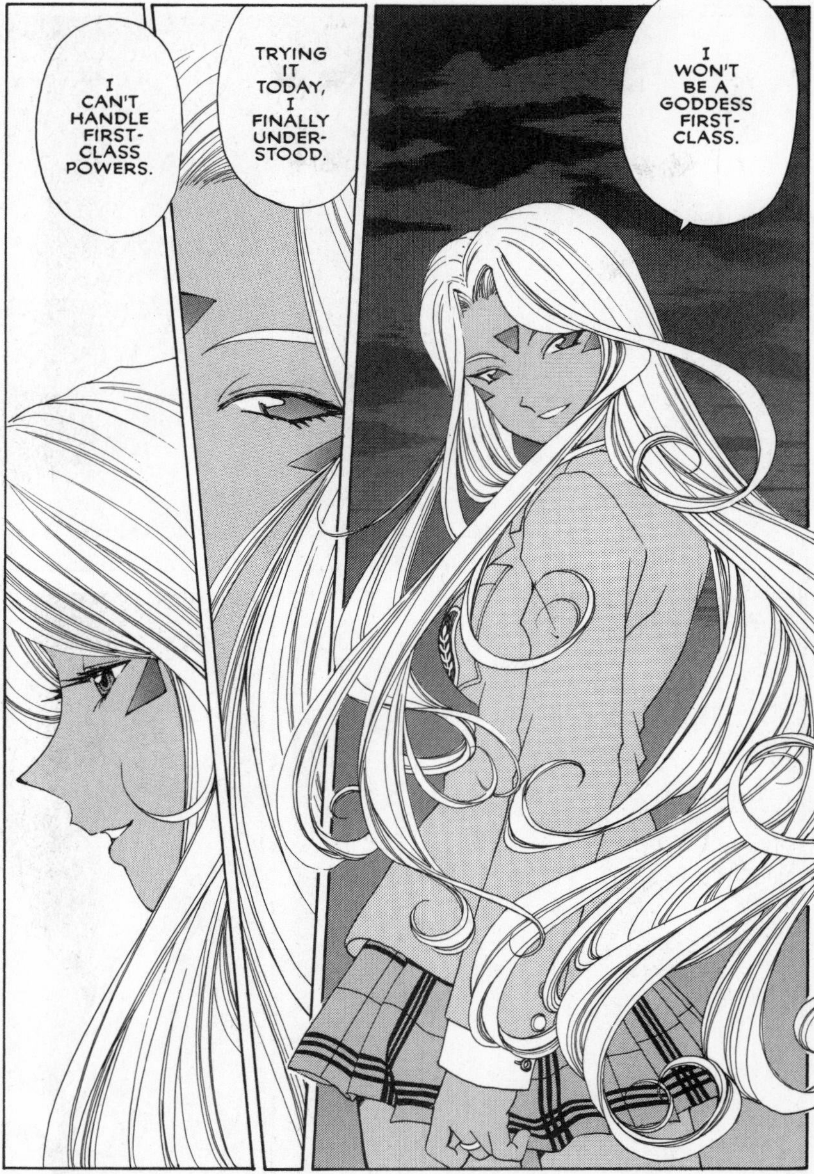
I WON'T BE A GODDESS FIRST-CLASS.
TRYING IT TODAY, I FINALLY UNDERSTOOD.
I CAN'T HANDLE FIRST-CLASS POWERS.

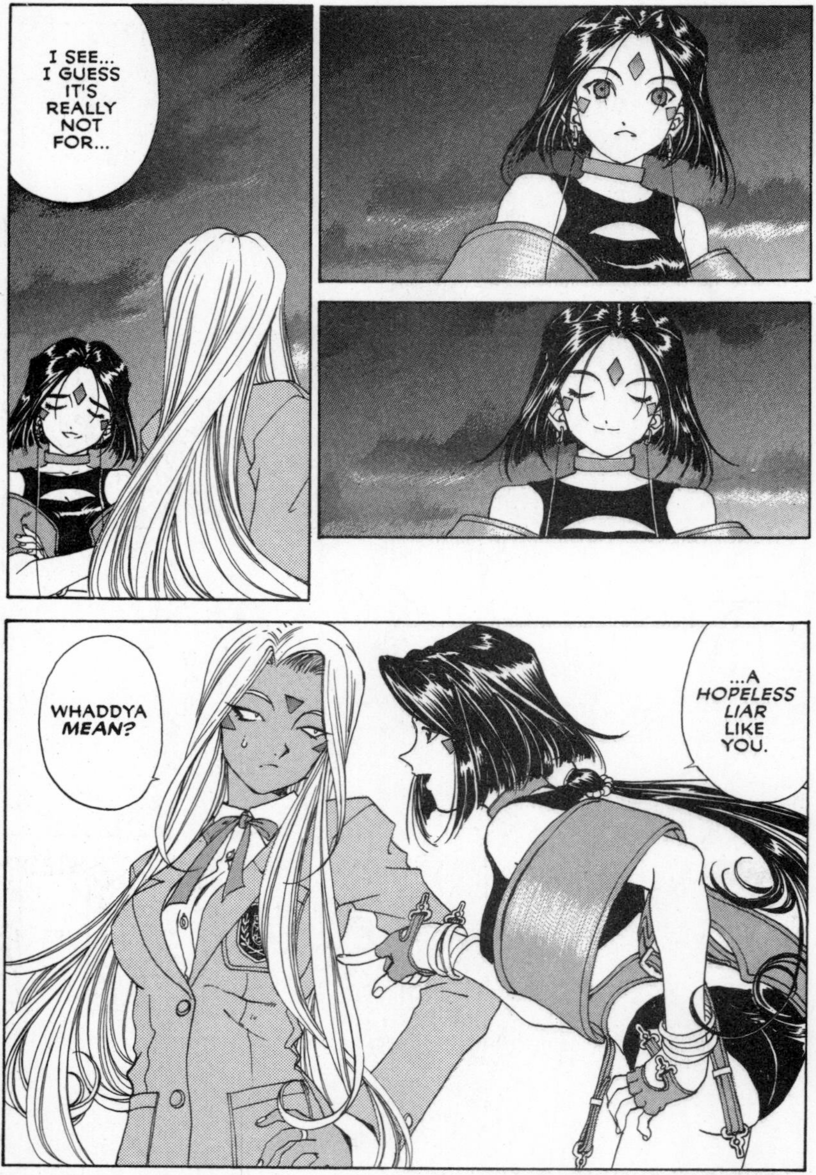
I SEE... I GUESS IT'S REALLY NOT FOR...
...A *HOPELESS* *LIAR* LIKE YOU.
WHADDYA *MEAN?*

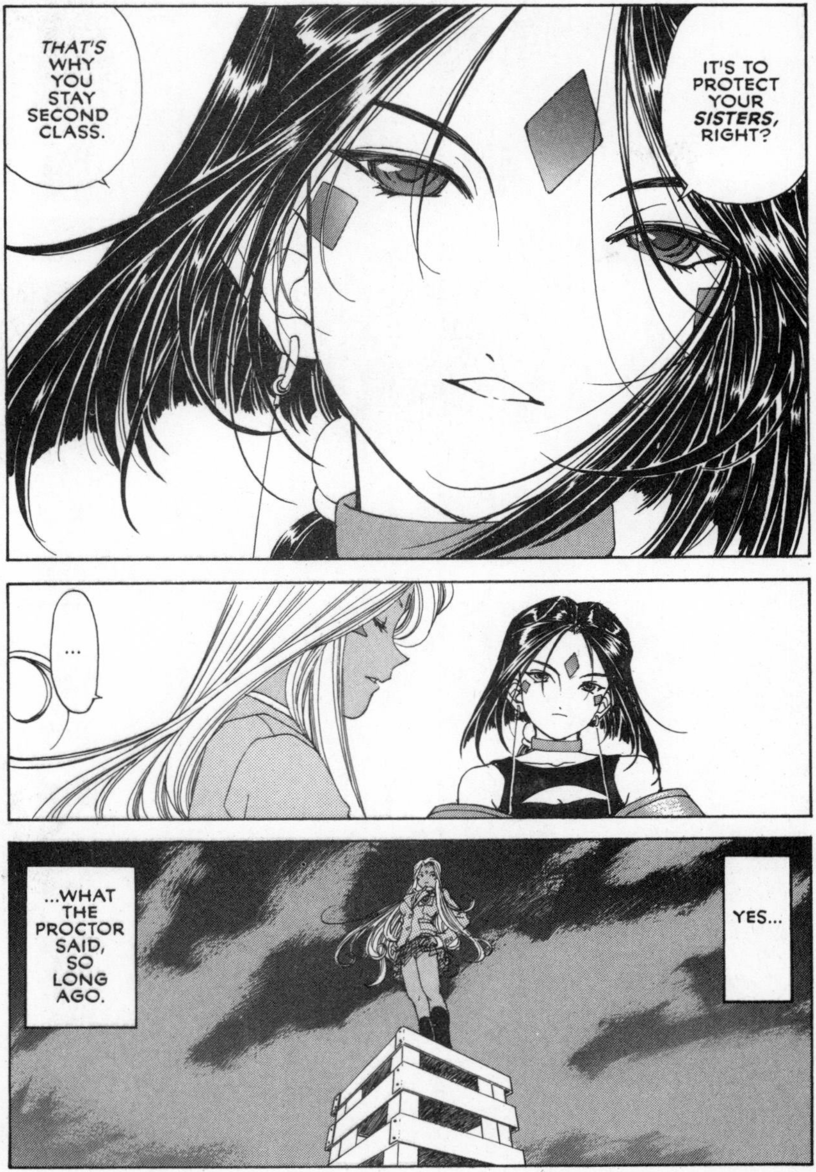
IT'S TO PROTECT YOUR *SISTERS,* RIGHT?
THAT'S WHY YOU STAY SECOND CLASS.
...
YES...
...WHAT THE PROCTOR SAID, SO LONG AGO.

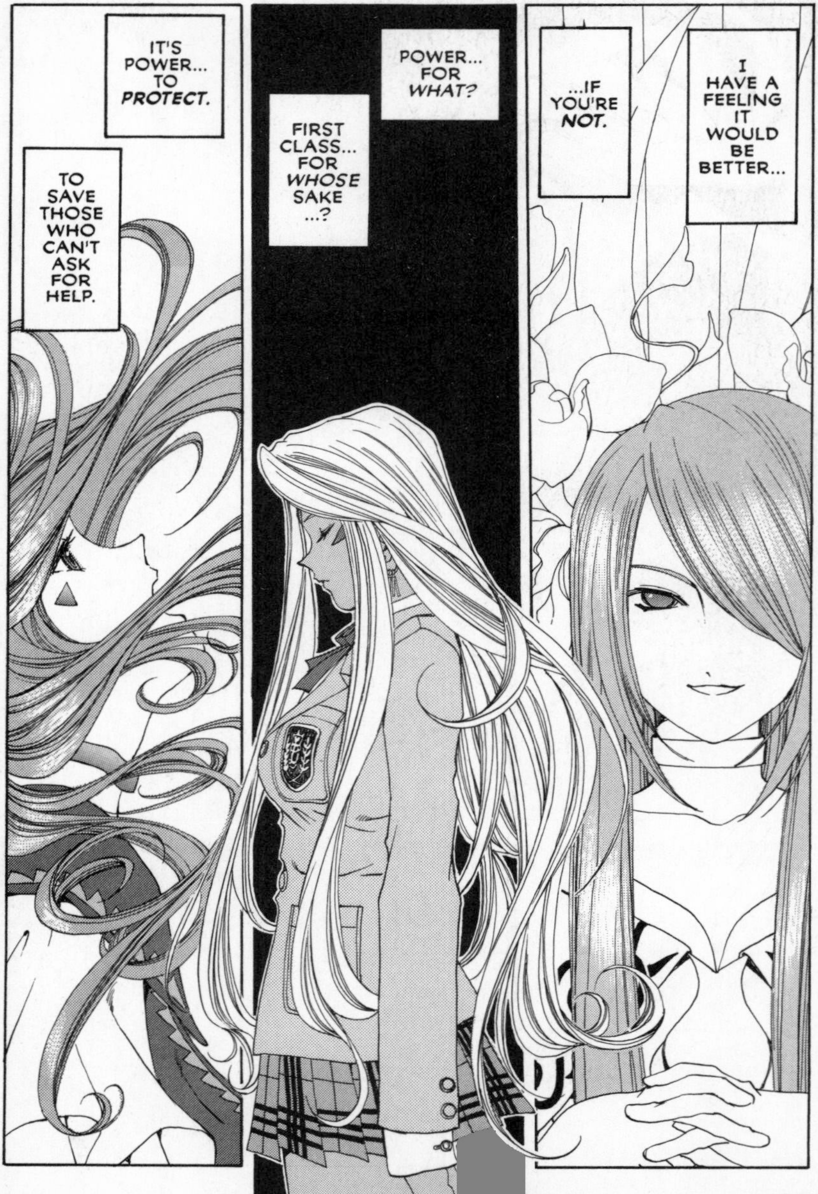
I HAVE A FEELING IT WOULD BE BETTER...
...IF YOU'RE *NOT*.
POWER... FOR *WHAT?*
FIRST CLASS... FOR *WHOSE* SAKE ...?
IT'S POWER... TO *PROTECT*.
TO SAVE THOSE WHO CAN'T ASK FOR HELP.

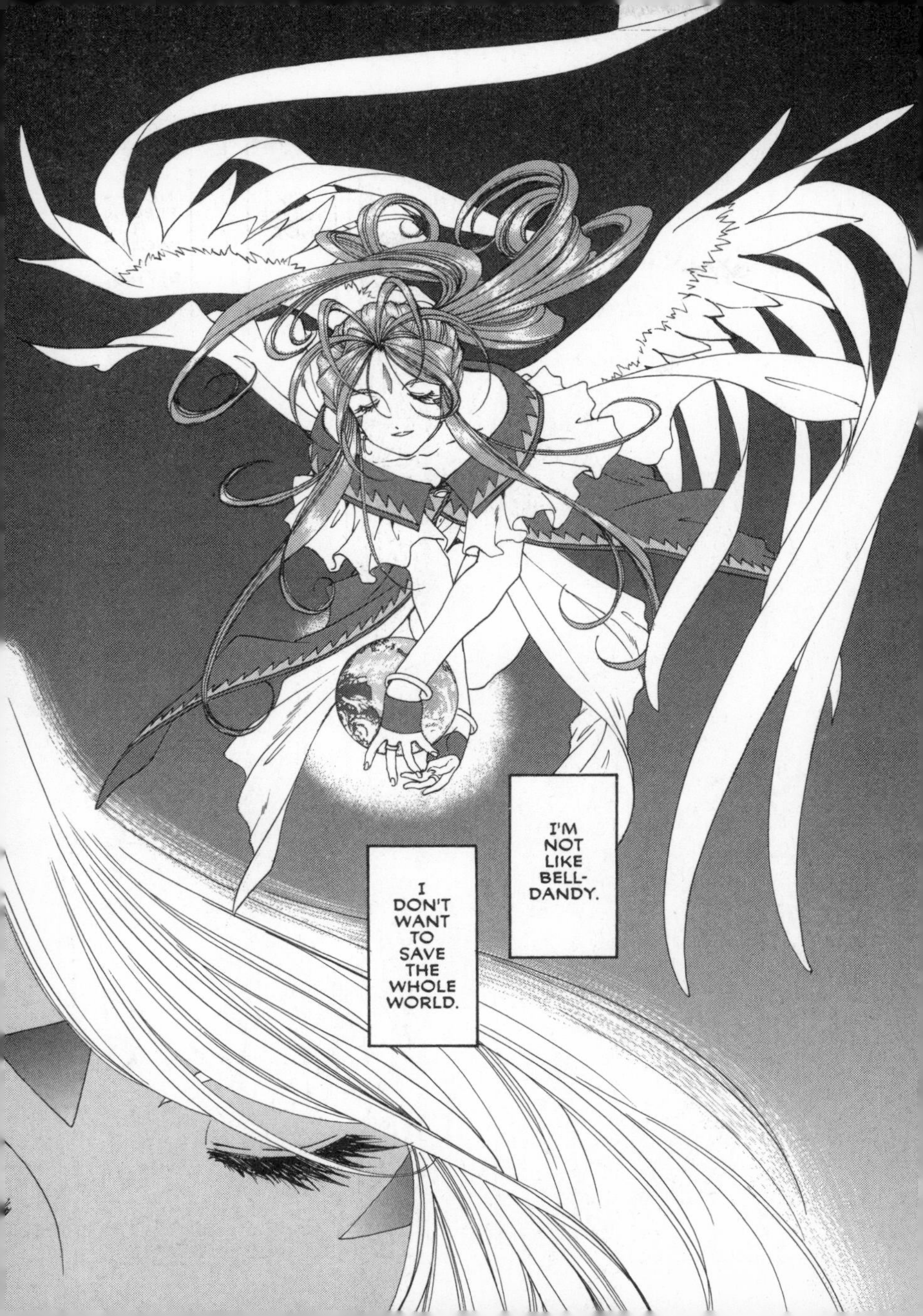
I'M NOT LIKE BELL-DANDY.
I DON'T WANT TO SAVE THE WHOLE WORLD.

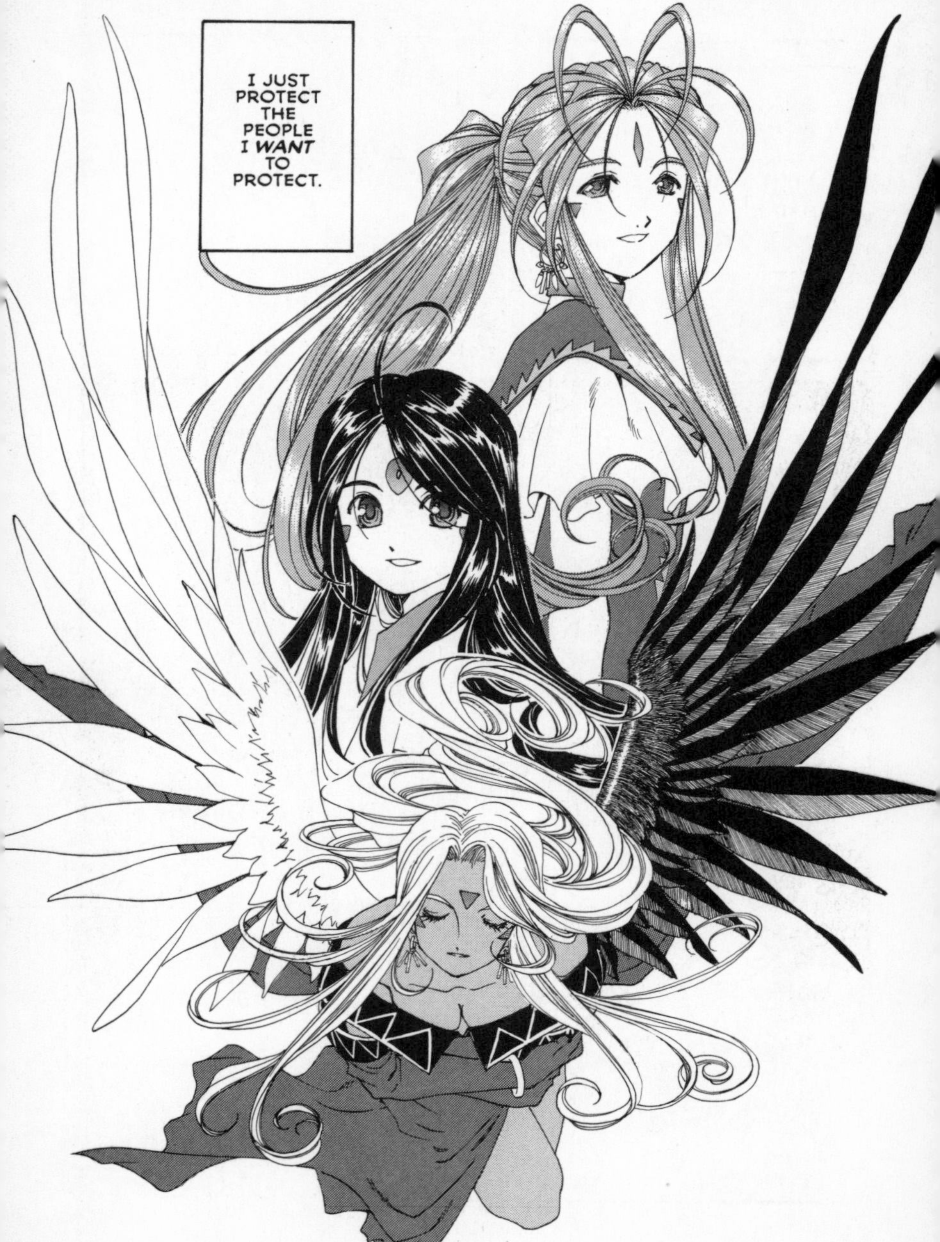
I JUST PROTECT THE PEOPLE I *WANT* TO PROTECT.

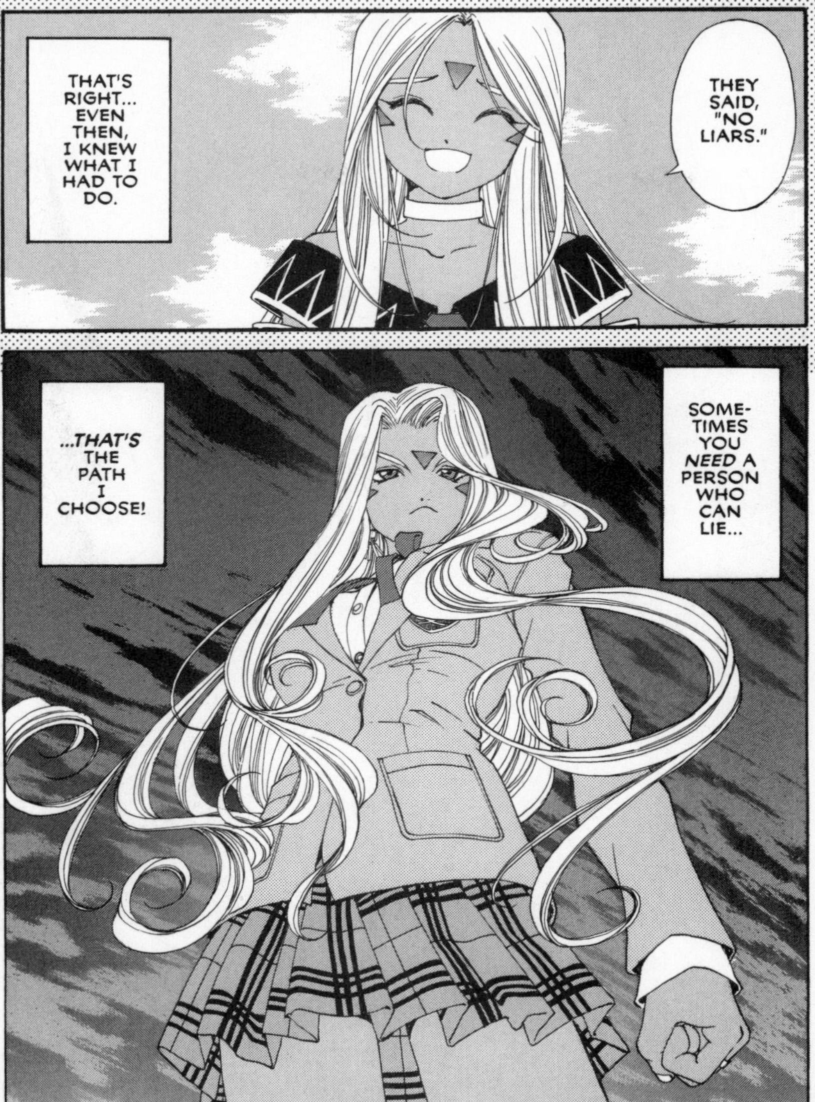
THEY SAID, "NO LIARS."
THAT'S RIGHT... EVEN THEN, I KNEW WHAT I HAD TO DO.
SOME-TIMES YOU *NEED* A PERSON WHO CAN LIE...
...*THAT'S* THE PATH I CHOOSE!

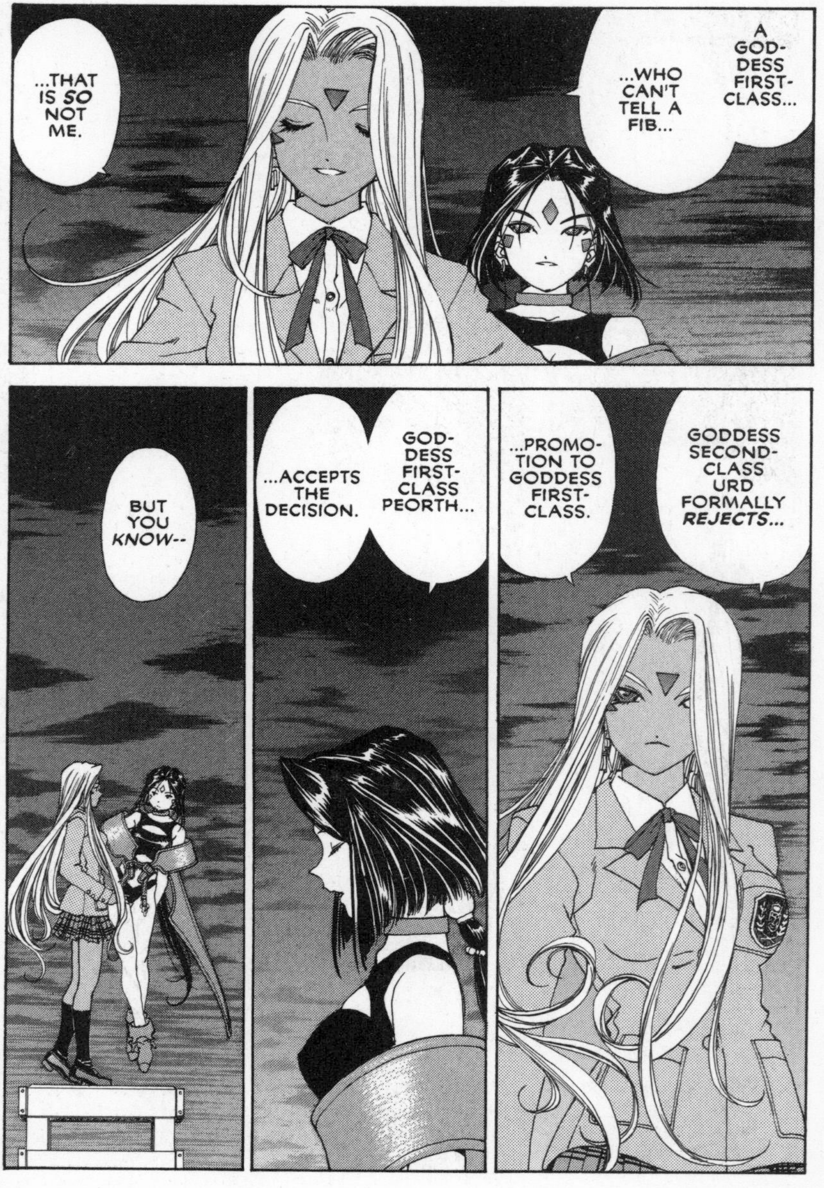
A GODDESS FIRST-CLASS...
...WHO CAN'T TELL A FIB...
...THAT IS *SO* NOT ME.
GODDESS SECOND-CLASS URD FORMALLY *REJECTS...*
...PROMOTION TO GODDESS FIRST-CLASS.
GODDESS FIRST-CLASS PEORTH...
...ACCEPTS THE DECISION.
BUT YOU *KNOW--*

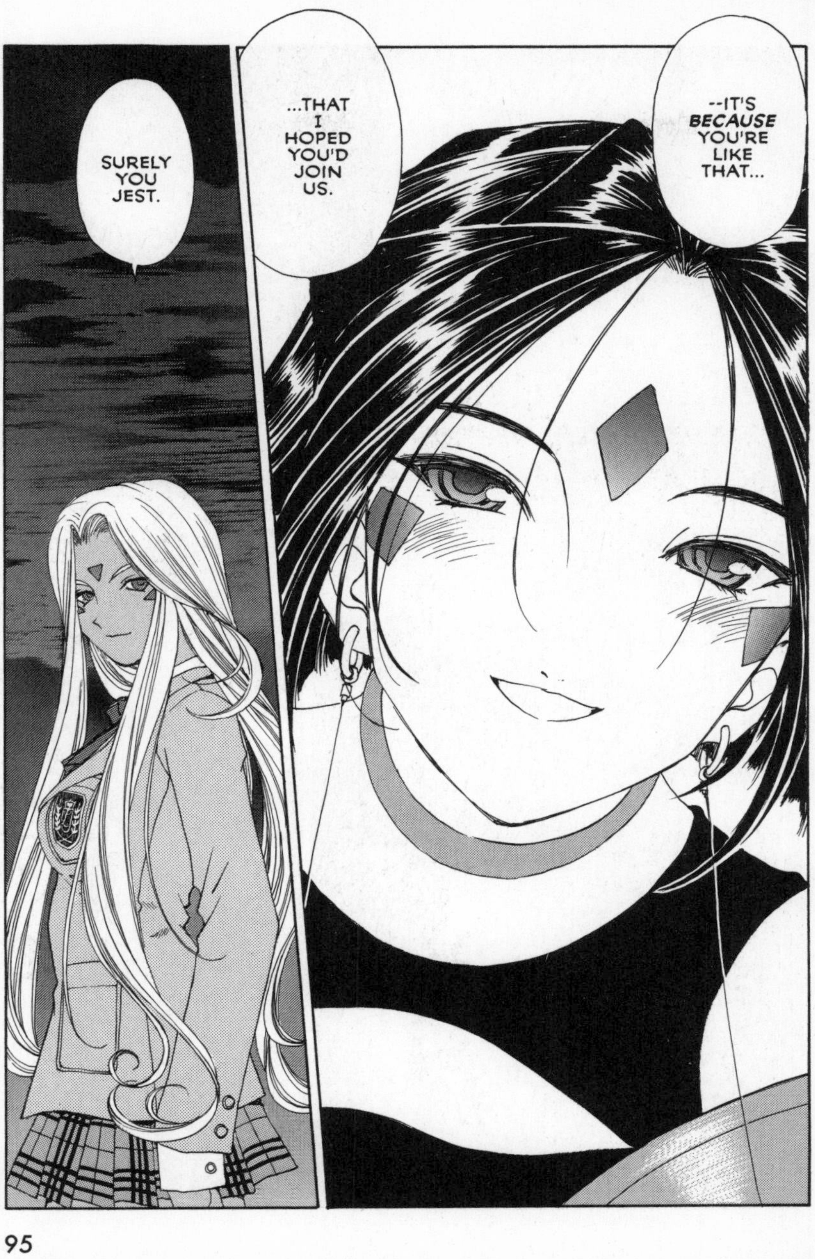
--IT'S *BECAUSE* YOU'RE LIKE THAT...
...THAT I HOPED YOU'D JOIN US.
SURELY YOU JEST.

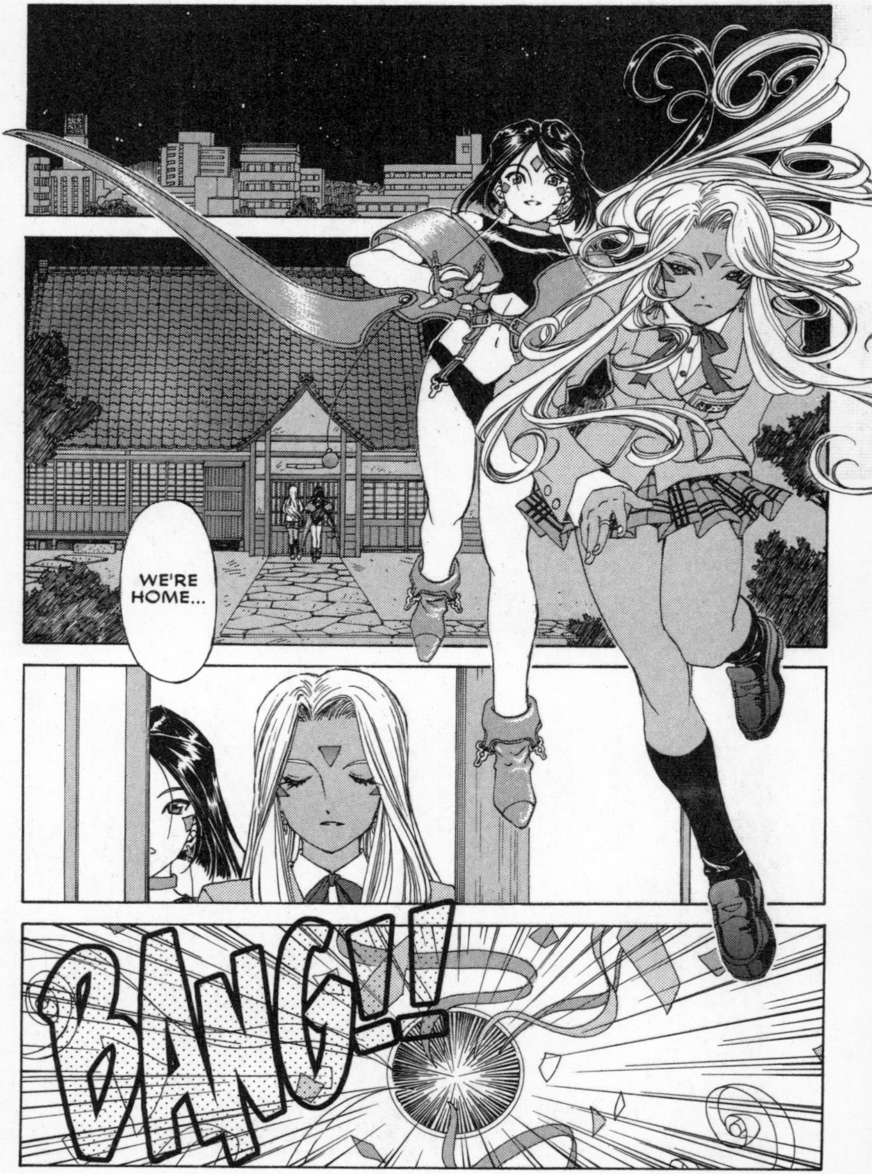
WE'RE HOME...
BANG!!

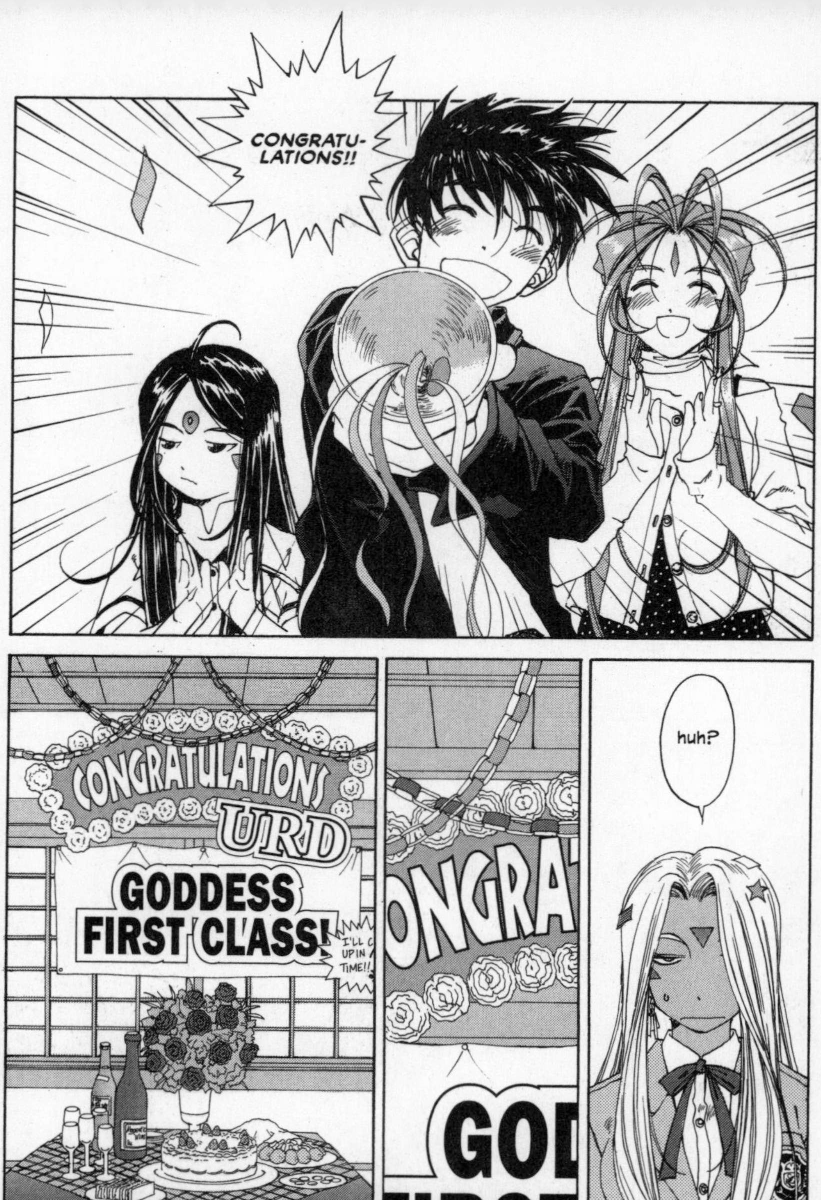
CONGRATU-LATIONS!!
huh?
ONGRAT
GOD
FIRST
CONGRATULATIONS
URD
GODDESS FIRST CLASS!
I'LL C
UP IN TIME!!

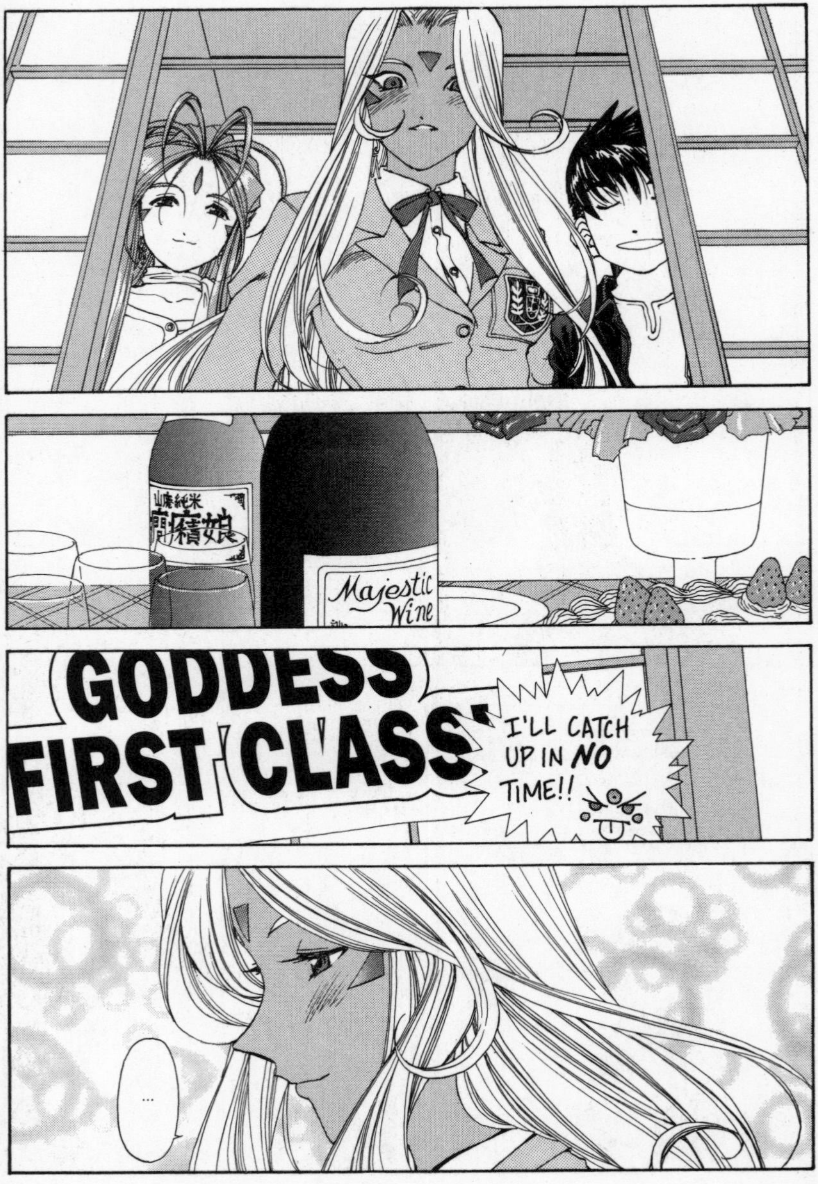
山廃純米
Majestic Wine
GODDESS FIRST CLASS!
I'LL CATCH UP IN NO TIME!!
...

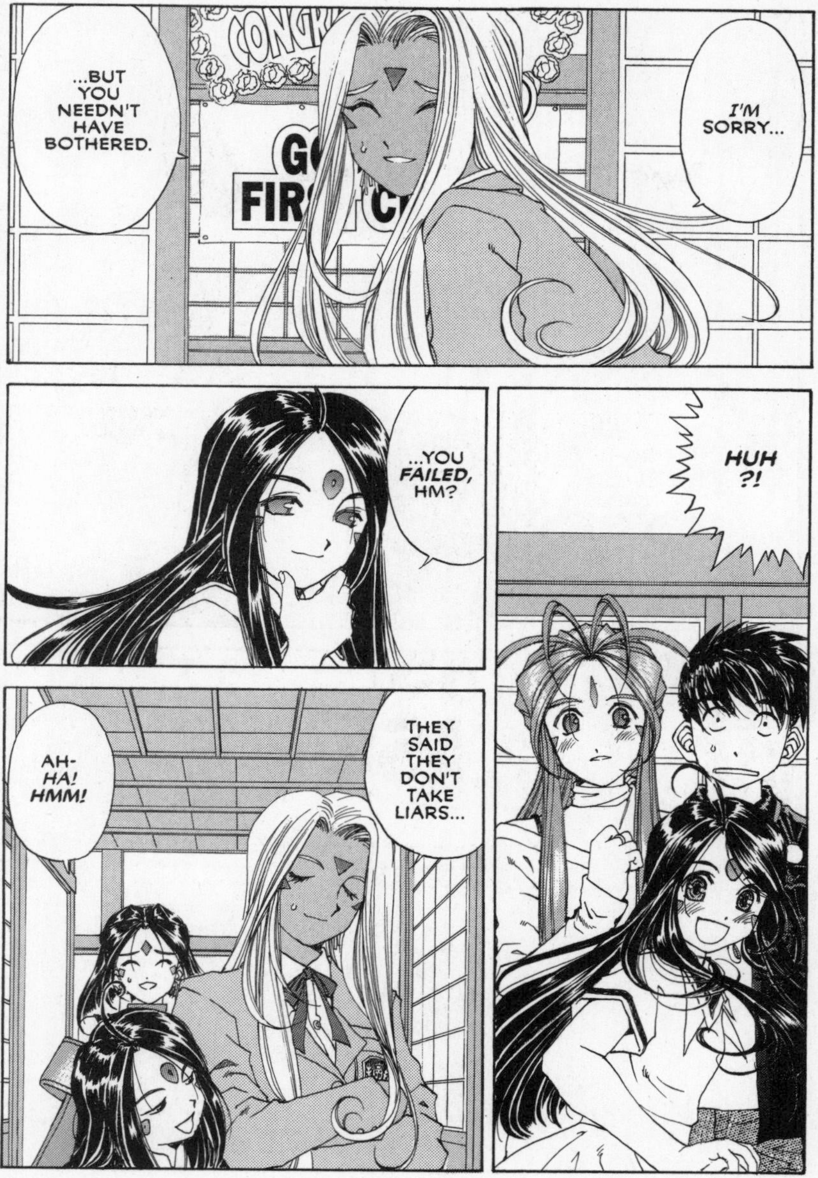
I'M SORRY...
...BUT YOU NEEDN'T HAVE BOTHERED.
HUH ?!
...YOU *FAILED,* HM?
THEY SAID THEY DON'T TAKE LIARS...
AH-*HA! HMM!*

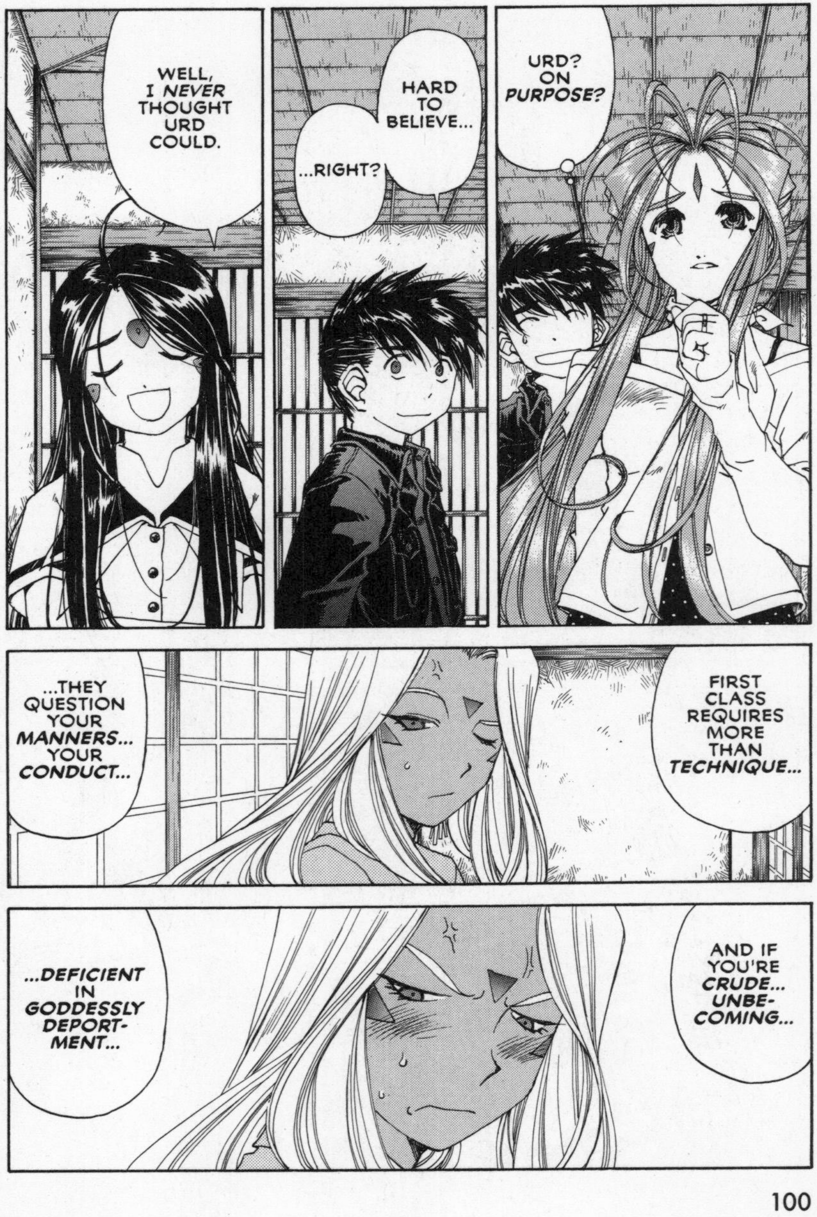
URD? ON *PURPOSE?*
HARD TO BELIEVE...
...RIGHT?
WELL, I *NEVER* THOUGHT URD COULD.
FIRST CLASS REQUIRES MORE THAN *TECHNIQUE...*
...THEY QUESTION YOUR *MANNERS...* YOUR *CONDUCT...*
AND IF YOU'RE *CRUDE... UNBE-COMING...*
...DEFICIENT IN *GODDESSLY DEPORT-MENT...*

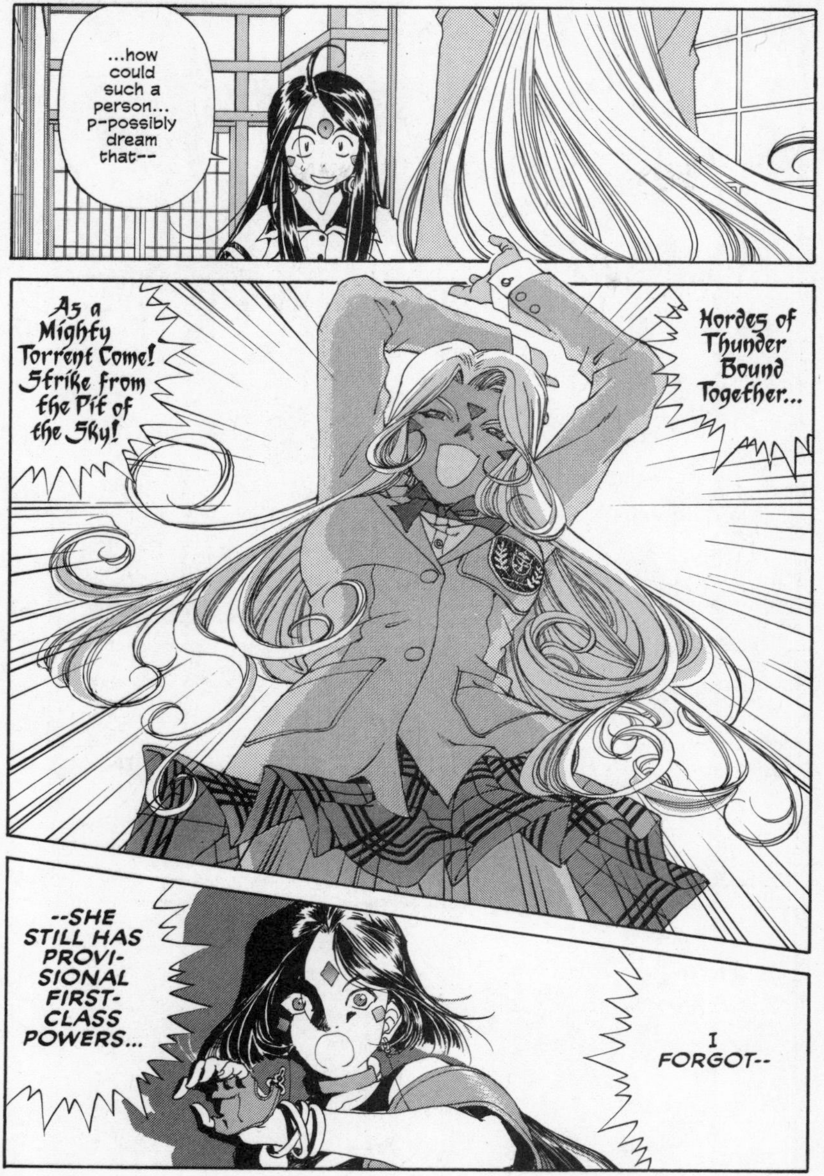
...how could such a person... p-possibly dream that--
Hordes of Thunder Bound Together...
As a Mighty Torrent Come! Strike from the Pit of the Sky!
I FORGOT--
--SHE STILL HAS PROVISIONAL FIRST-CLASS POWERS...

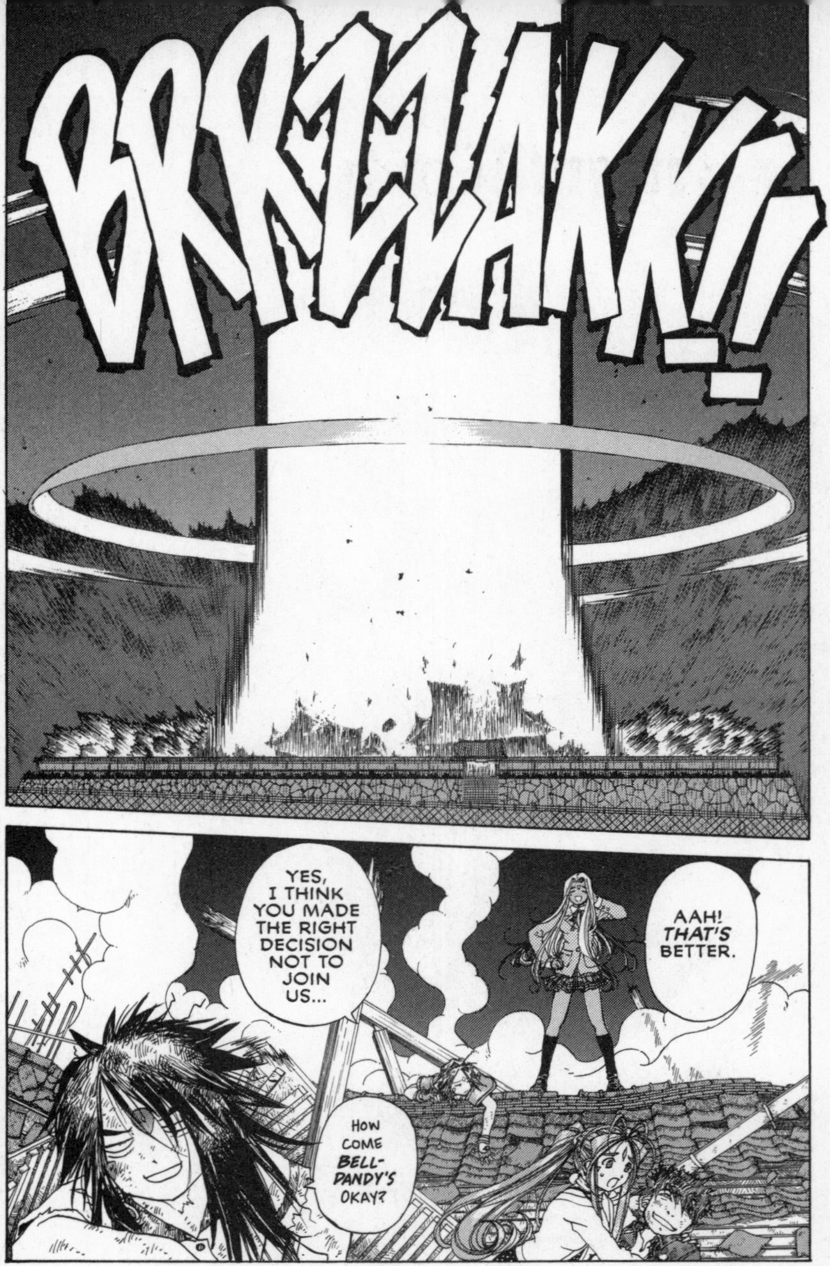
BRRZZAKK!!
AAH! *THAT'S* BETTER.
YES, I THINK YOU MADE THE RIGHT DECISION NOT TO JOIN US...
HOW COME *BELL-DANDY'S* OKAY?

CHAPTER 193

Important Words

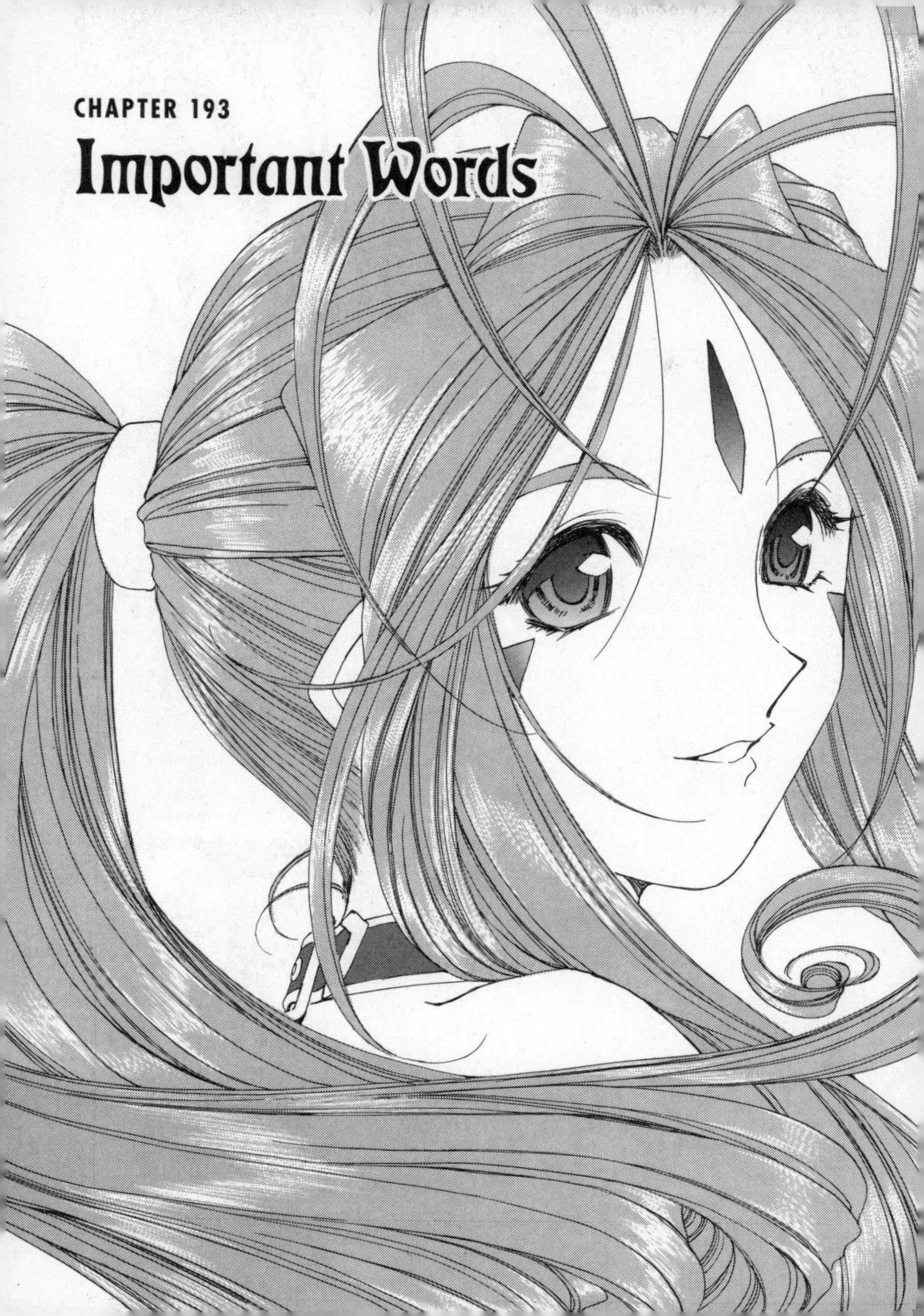

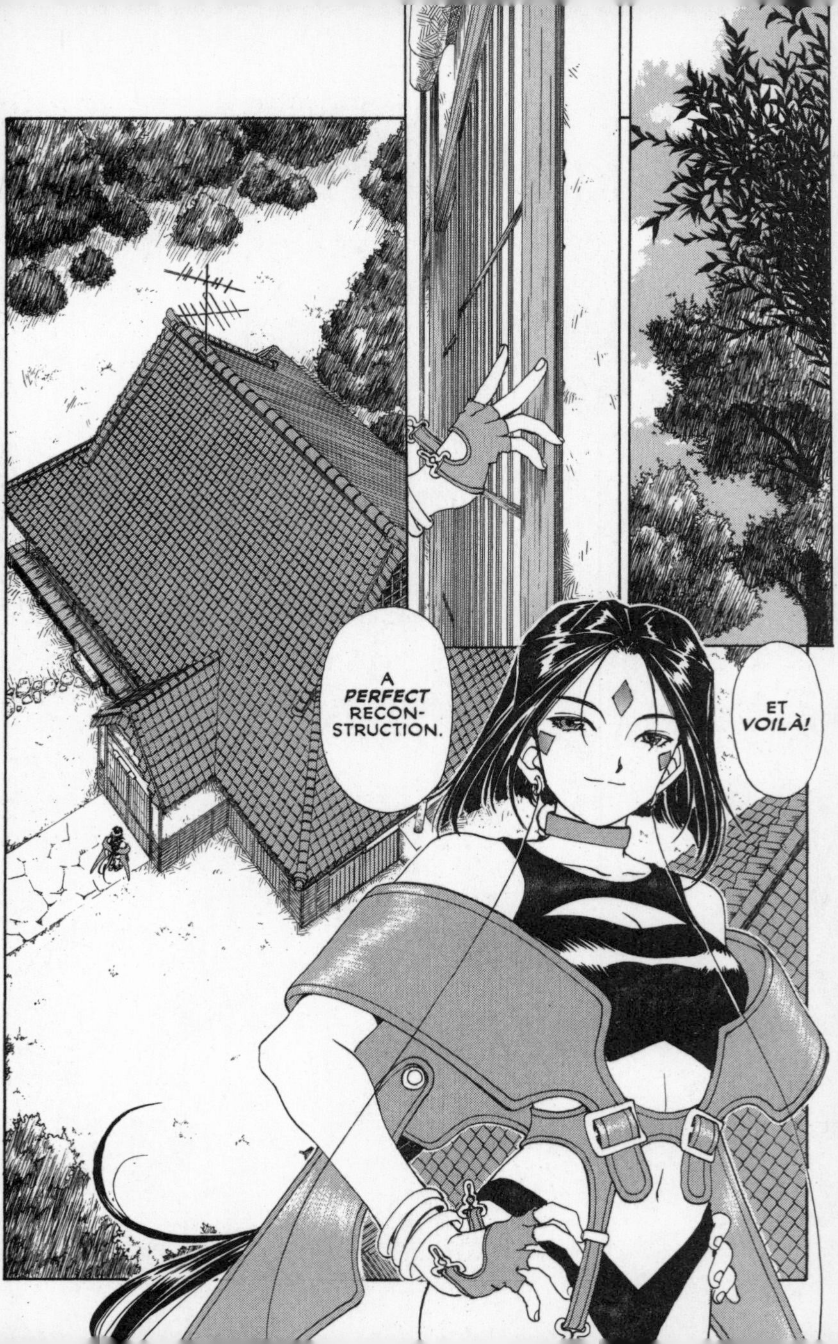
ET *VOILÀ!*
A *PERFECT* RECON-STRUCTION.

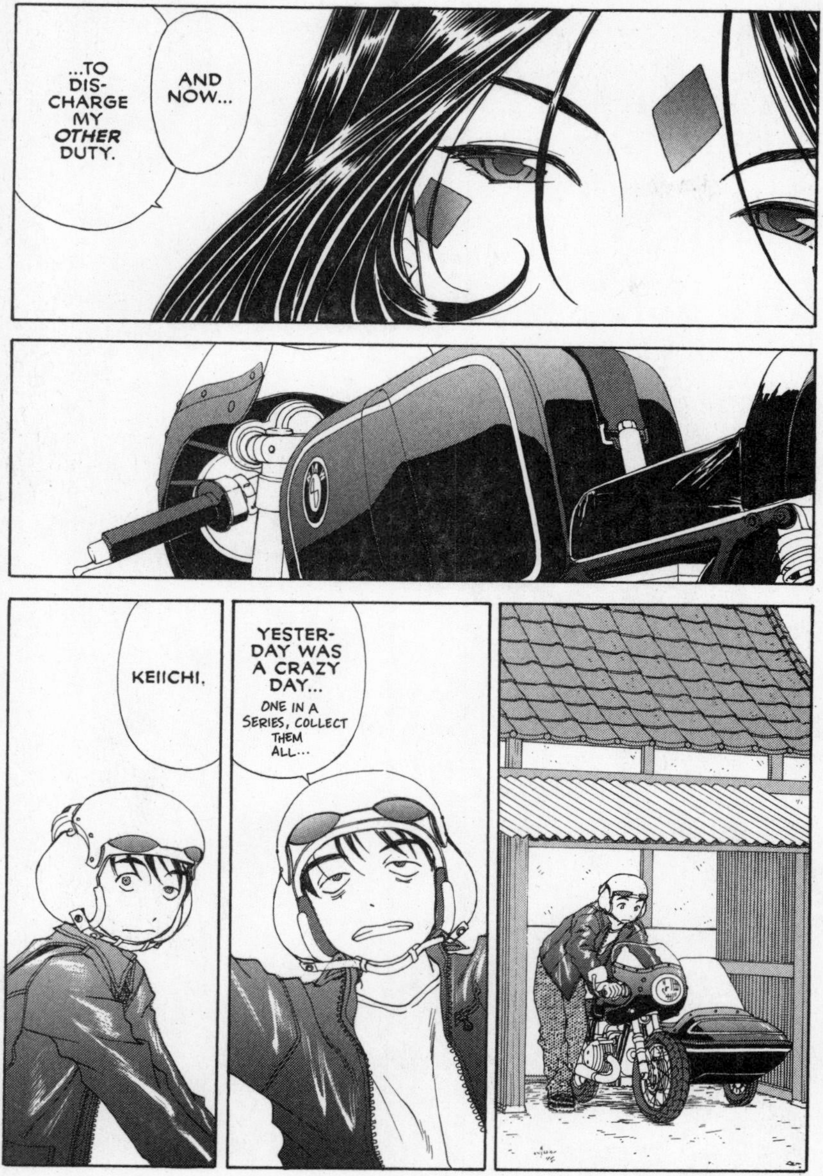
AND NOW...
...TO DIS-CHARGE MY *OTHER* DUTY.
YESTER-DAY WAS A CRAZY DAY...
ONE IN A SERIES, COLLECT THEM ALL...
KEIICHI.

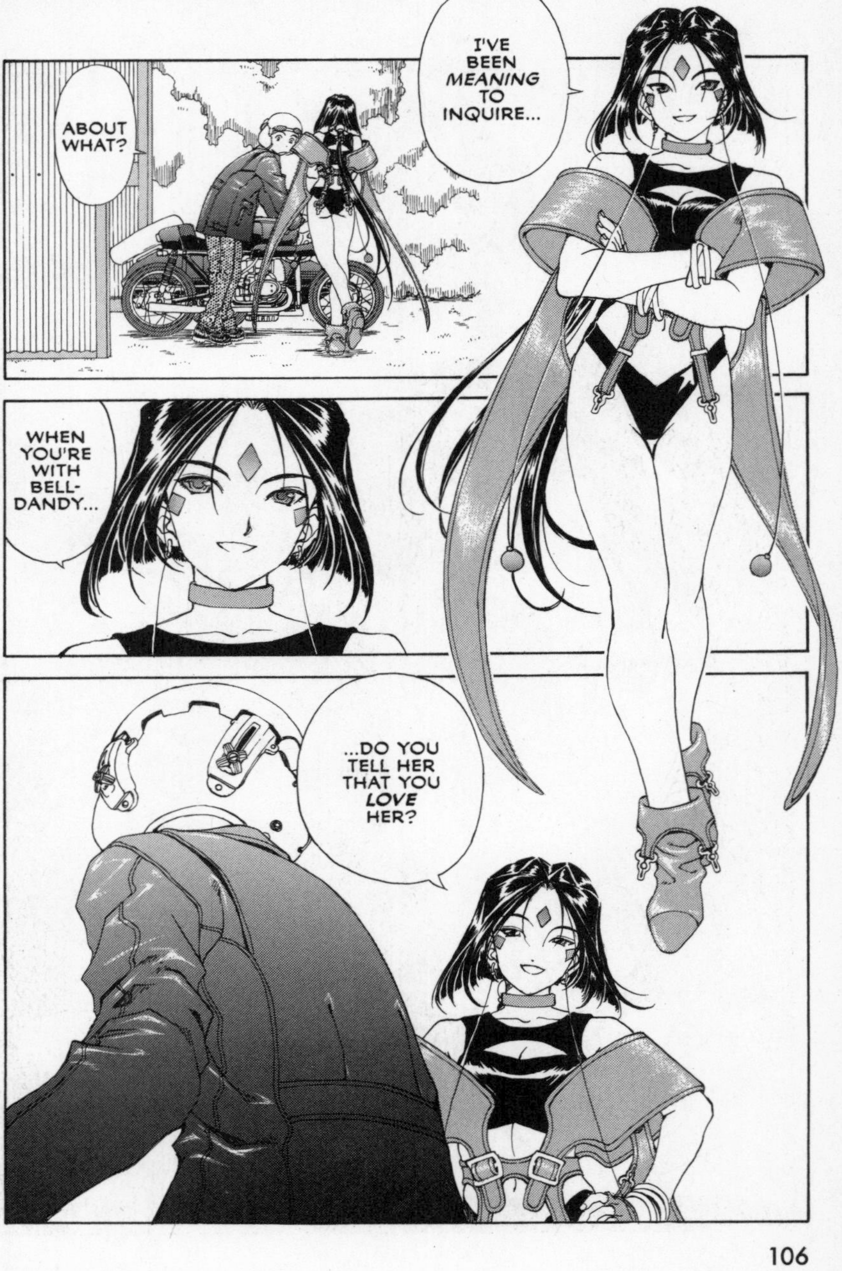
I'VE BEEN *MEANING* TO INQUIRE...
ABOUT WHAT?
WHEN YOU'RE WITH BELL-DANDY...
...DO YOU TELL HER THAT YOU *LOVE* HER?

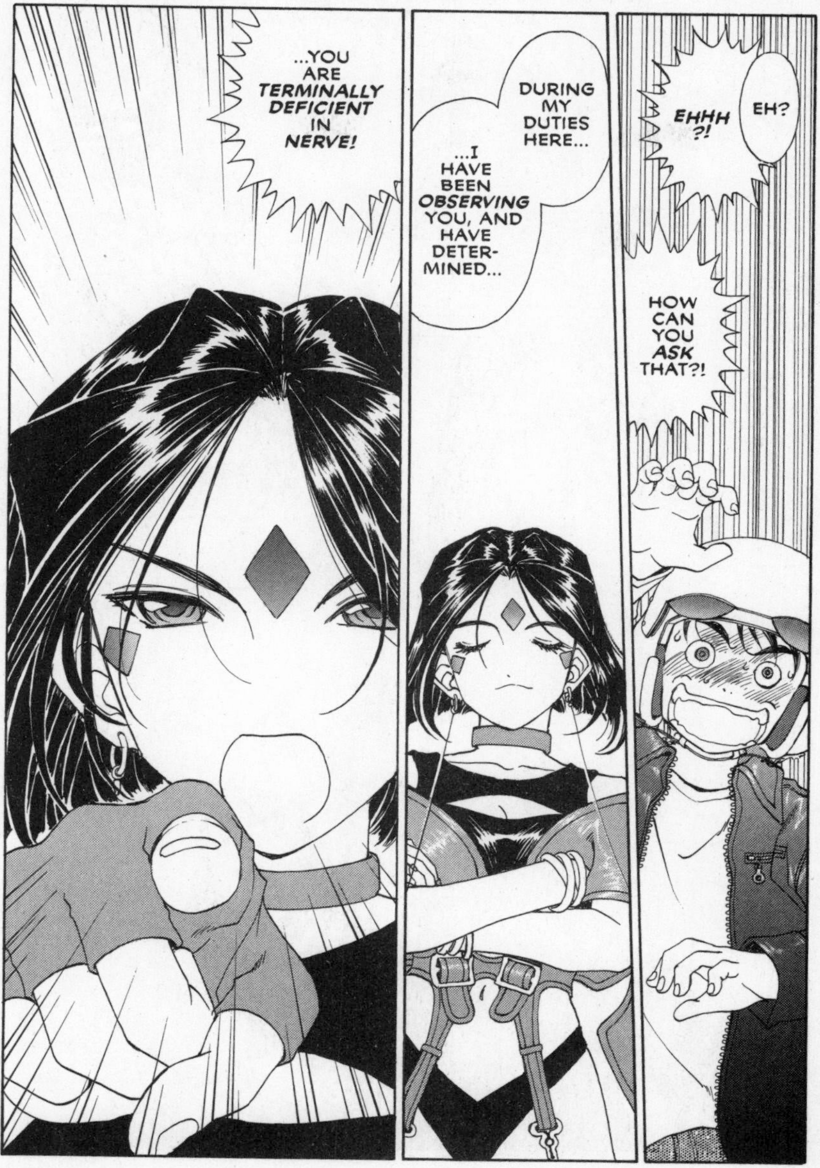
EH?
EHHH ?!
HOW CAN YOU ASK THAT?!
DURING MY DUTIES HERE...
...I HAVE BEEN OBSERVING YOU, AND HAVE DETERMINED...
...YOU ARE TERMINALLY DEFICIENT IN NERVE!

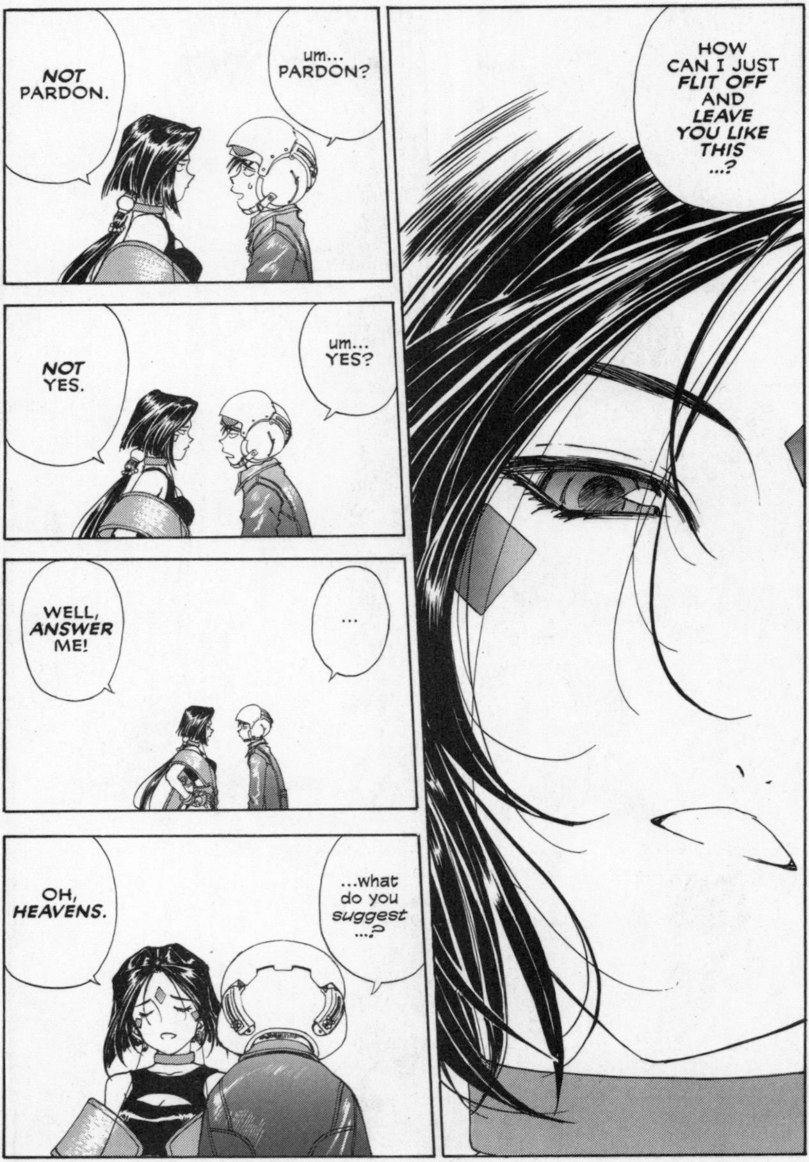
HOW CAN I JUST *FLIT OFF* AND *LEAVE* YOU LIKE *THIS* ...?
um... PARDON?
NOT PARDON.
um... YES?
NOT YES.
...
WELL, *ANSWER* ME!
...what do you *suggest* ...?
OH, *HEAVENS.*

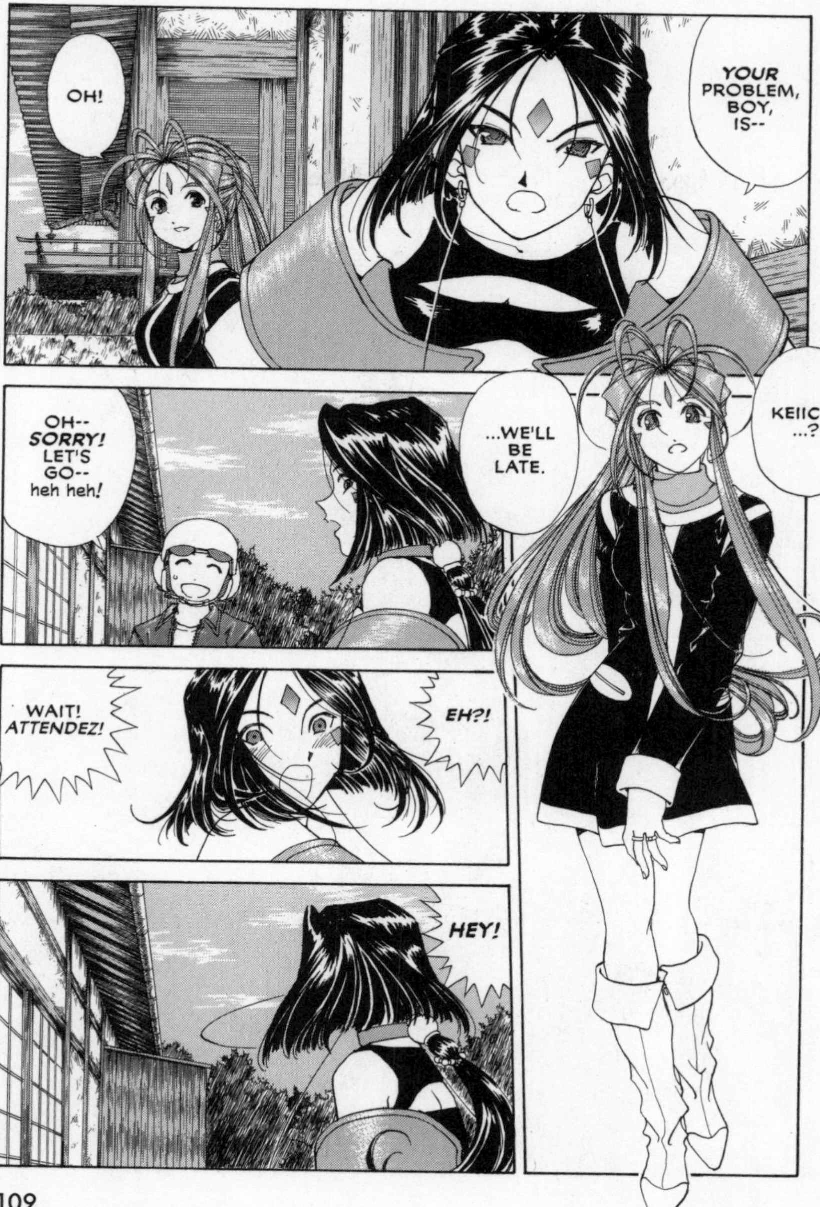
YOUR PROBLEM, BOY, IS--
OH!
KEIICHI ...?
...WE'LL BE LATE.
OH-- SORRY! LET'S GO-- heh heh!
EH?!
WAIT! ATTENDEZ!
HEY!

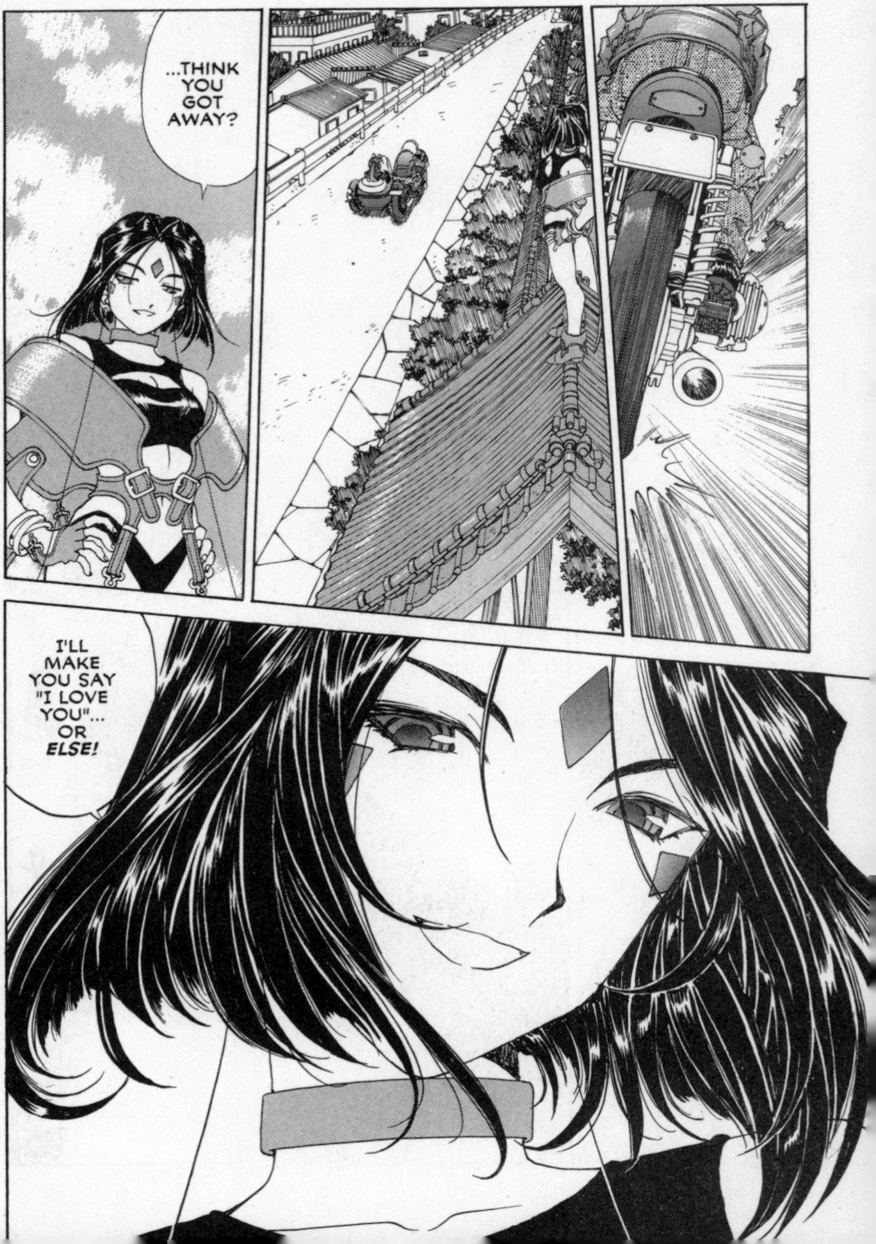
...THINK YOU GOT AWAY?
I'LL MAKE YOU SAY "I LOVE YOU"... OR *ELSE!*

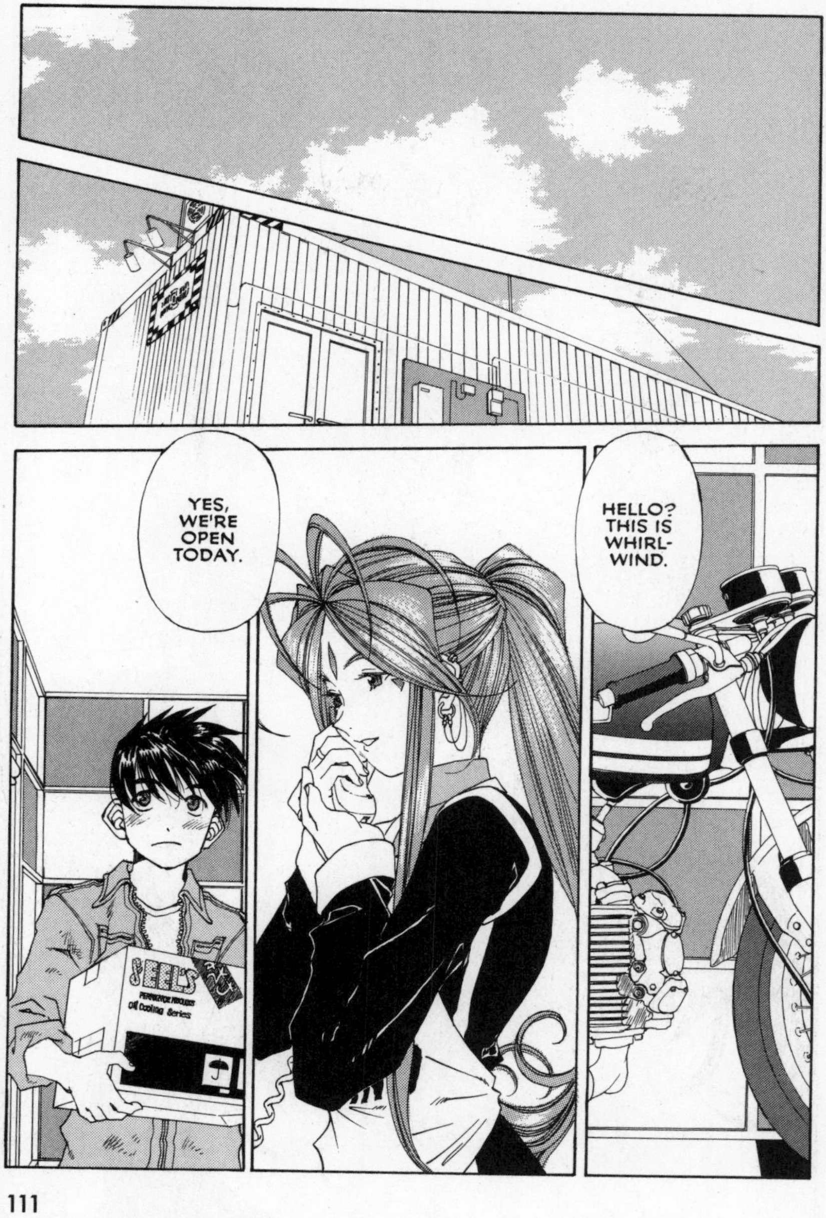
HELLO? THIS IS WHIRL-WIND.
YES, WE'RE OPEN TODAY.

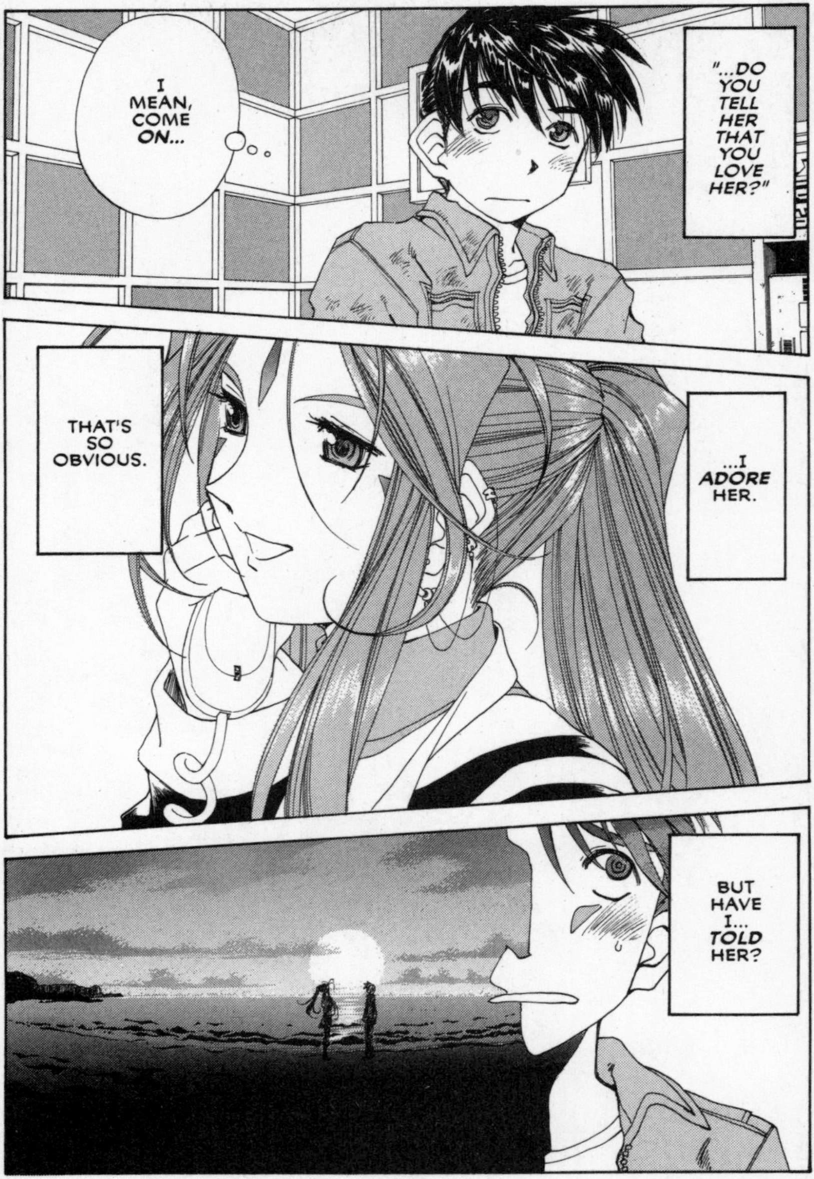
"...DO YOU TELL HER THAT YOU LOVE HER?"
I MEAN, COME *ON*...
...I *ADORE* HER.
THAT'S SO OBVIOUS.
BUT HAVE I... *TOLD* HER?

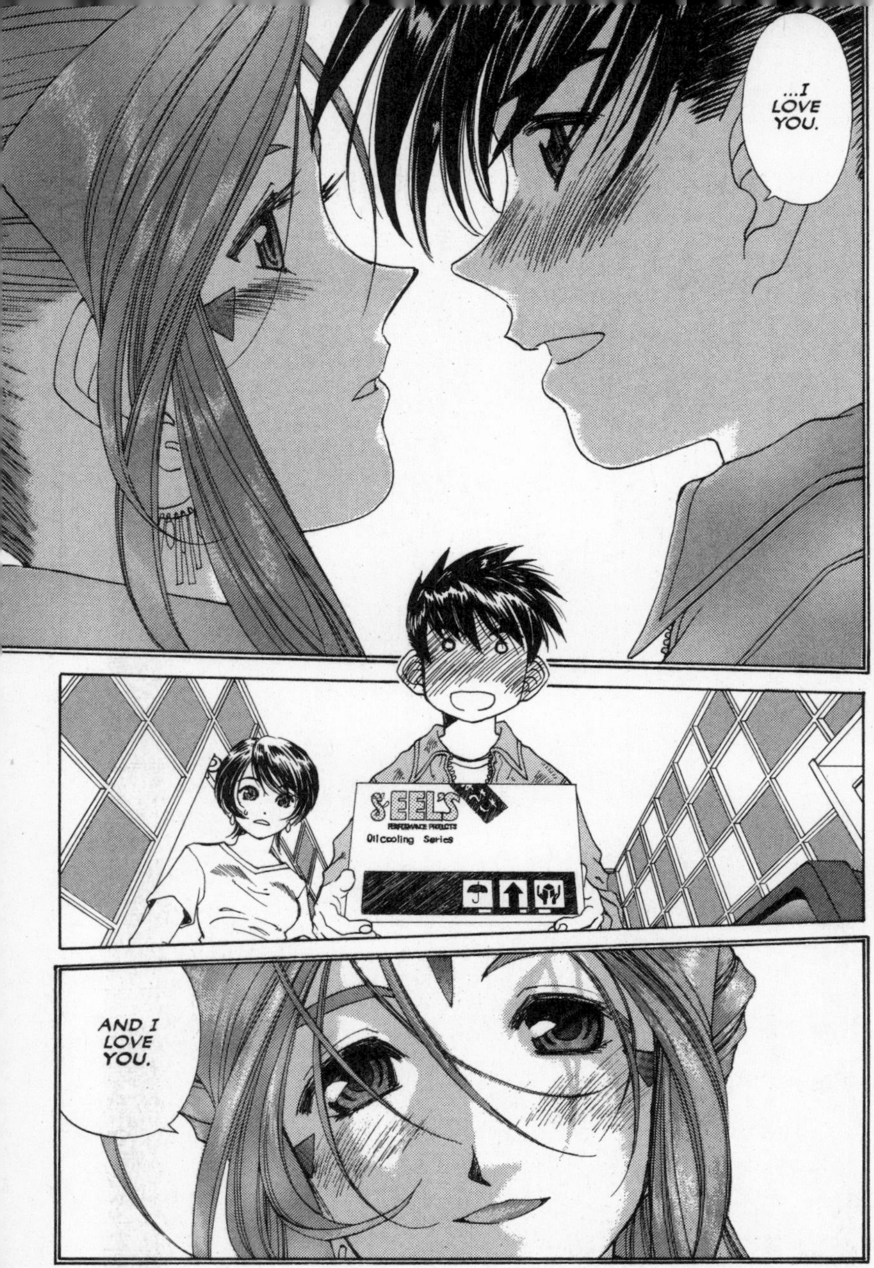
...I LOVE YOU.
S'EEL'S
Oilcooling Series
AND I LOVE YOU.

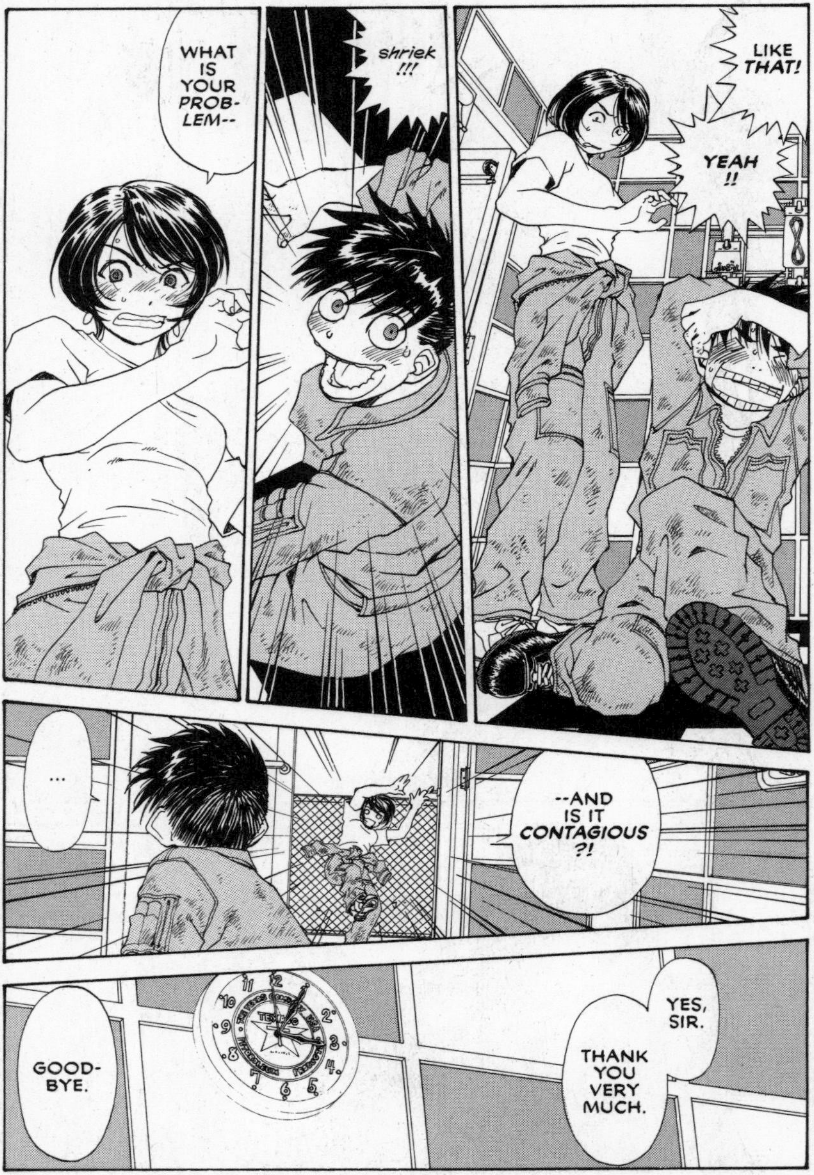
LIKE THAT!
YEAH !!
shriek !!!
WHAT IS YOUR PROB-LEM--
--AND IS IT CONTAGIOUS ?!
...
YES, SIR.
THANK YOU VERY MUCH.
GOOD-BYE.

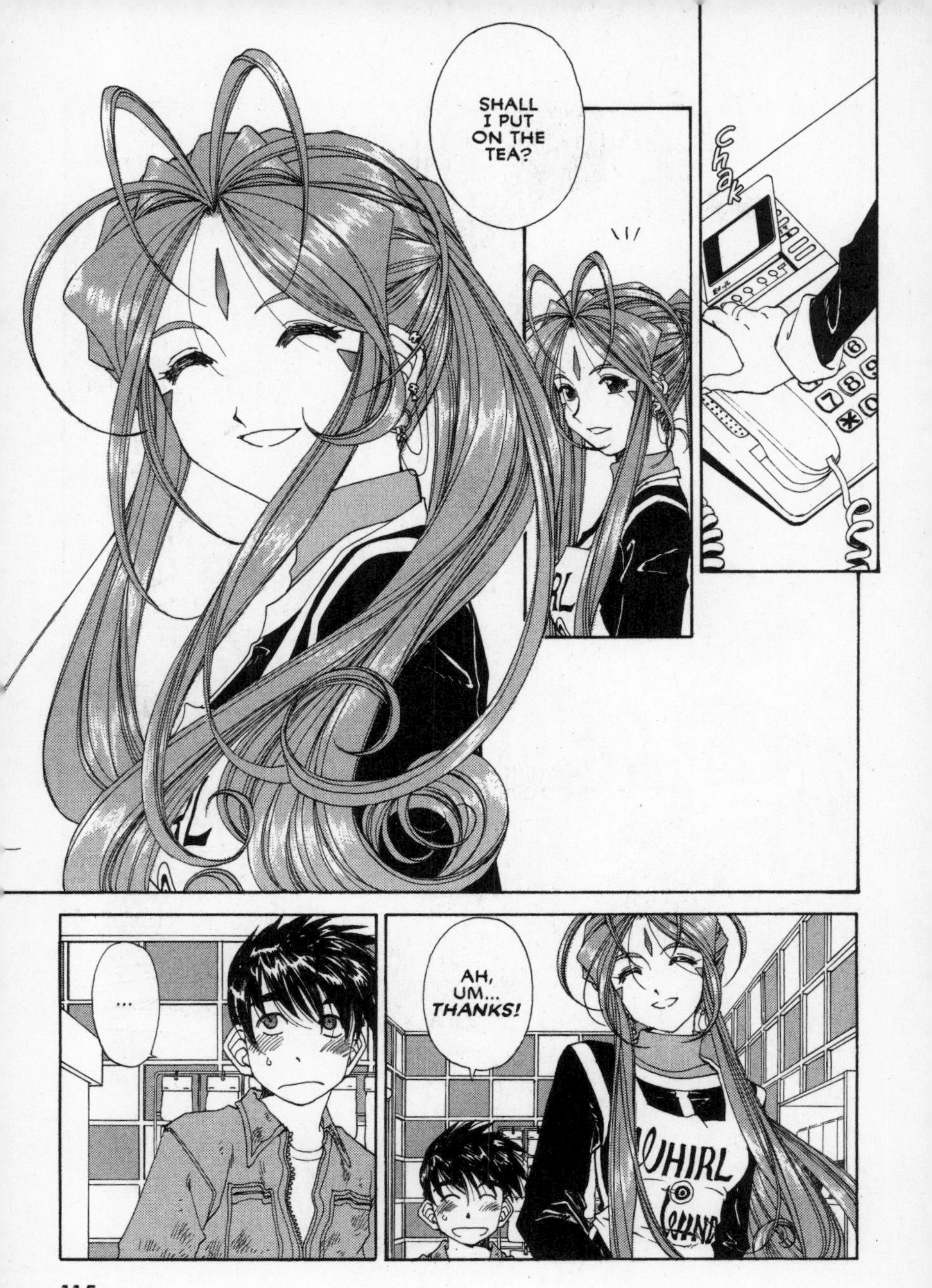
chak
SHALL I PUT ON THE TEA?
AH, UM... THANKS!
...

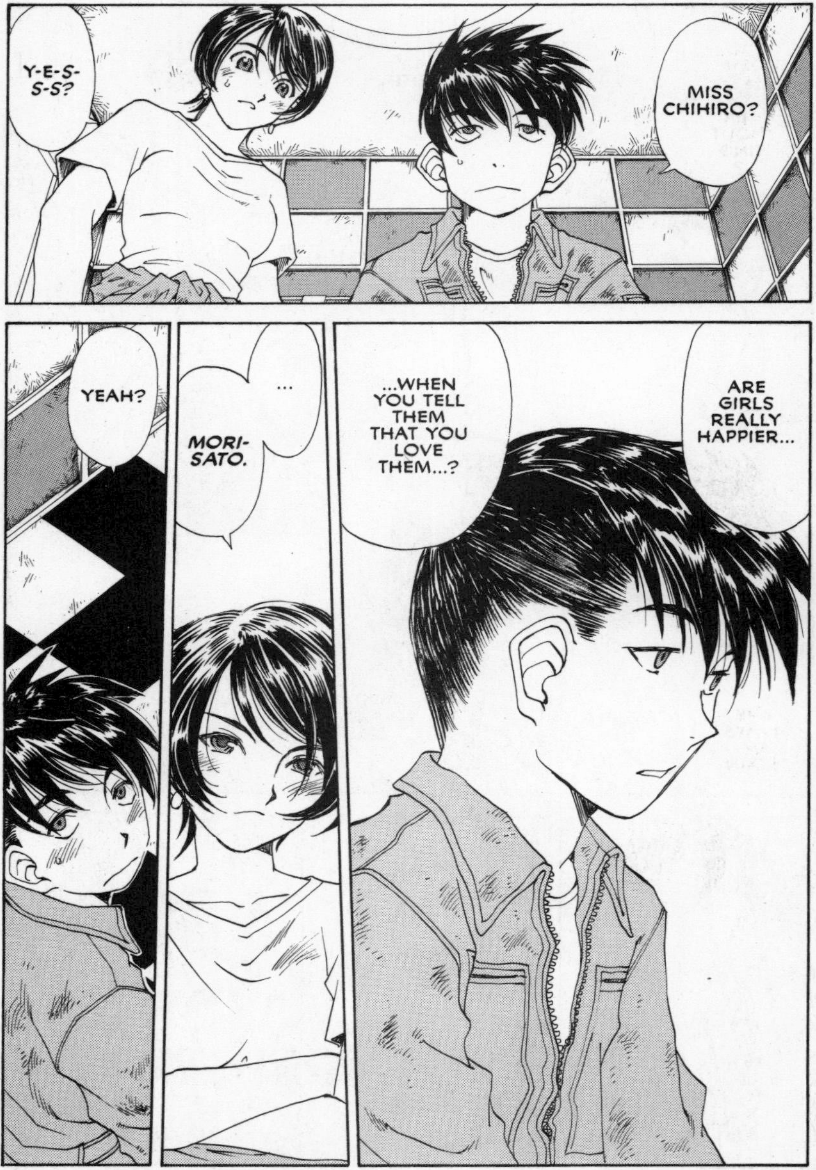
MISS CHIHIRO?
Y-E-S-S-S?
ARE GIRLS REALLY HAPPIER...
...WHEN YOU TELL THEM THAT YOU LOVE THEM...?
...
MORI-SATO.
YEAH?

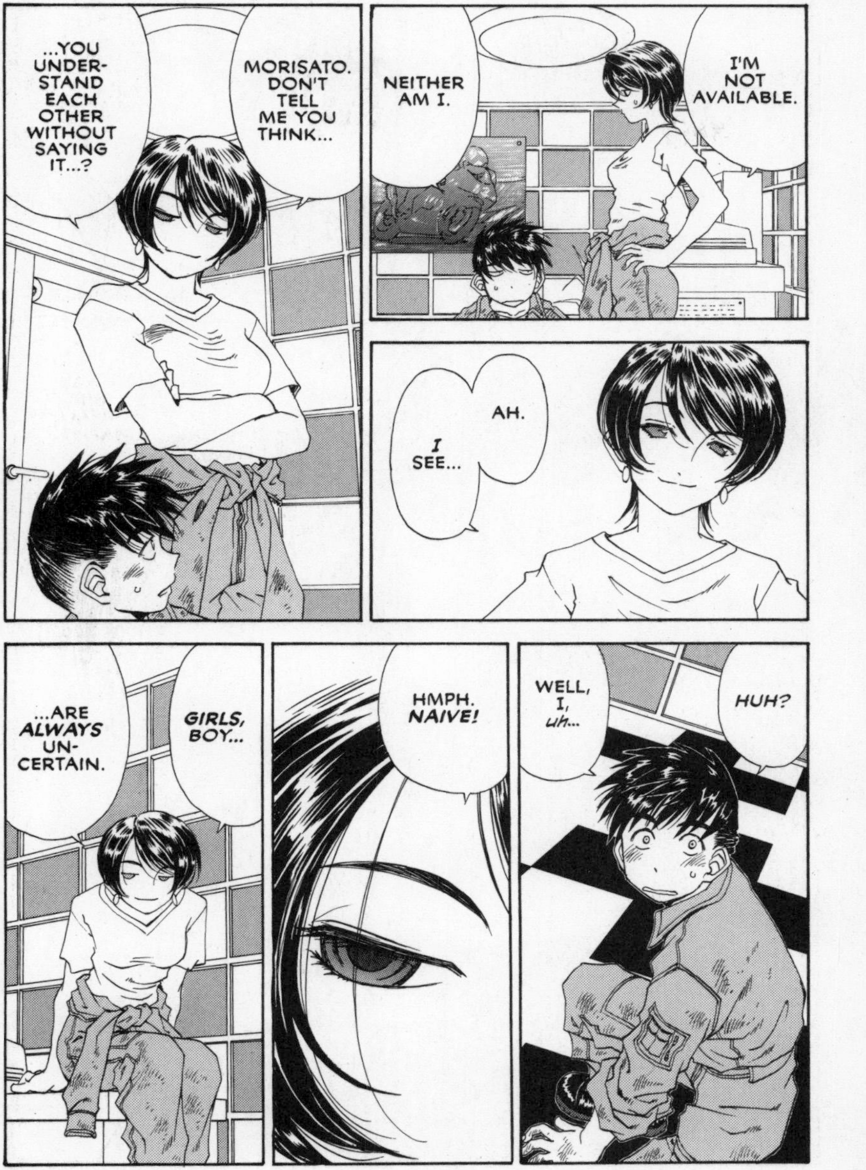
I'M NOT AVAILABLE.
NEITHER AM I.
AH.
I SEE...
MORISATO. DON'T TELL ME YOU THINK...
...YOU UNDER-STAND EACH OTHER WITHOUT SAYING IT...?
HUH?
WELL, I, *uh...*
HMPH. *NAIVE!*
GIRLS, BOY...
...ARE *ALWAYS* UN-CERTAIN.

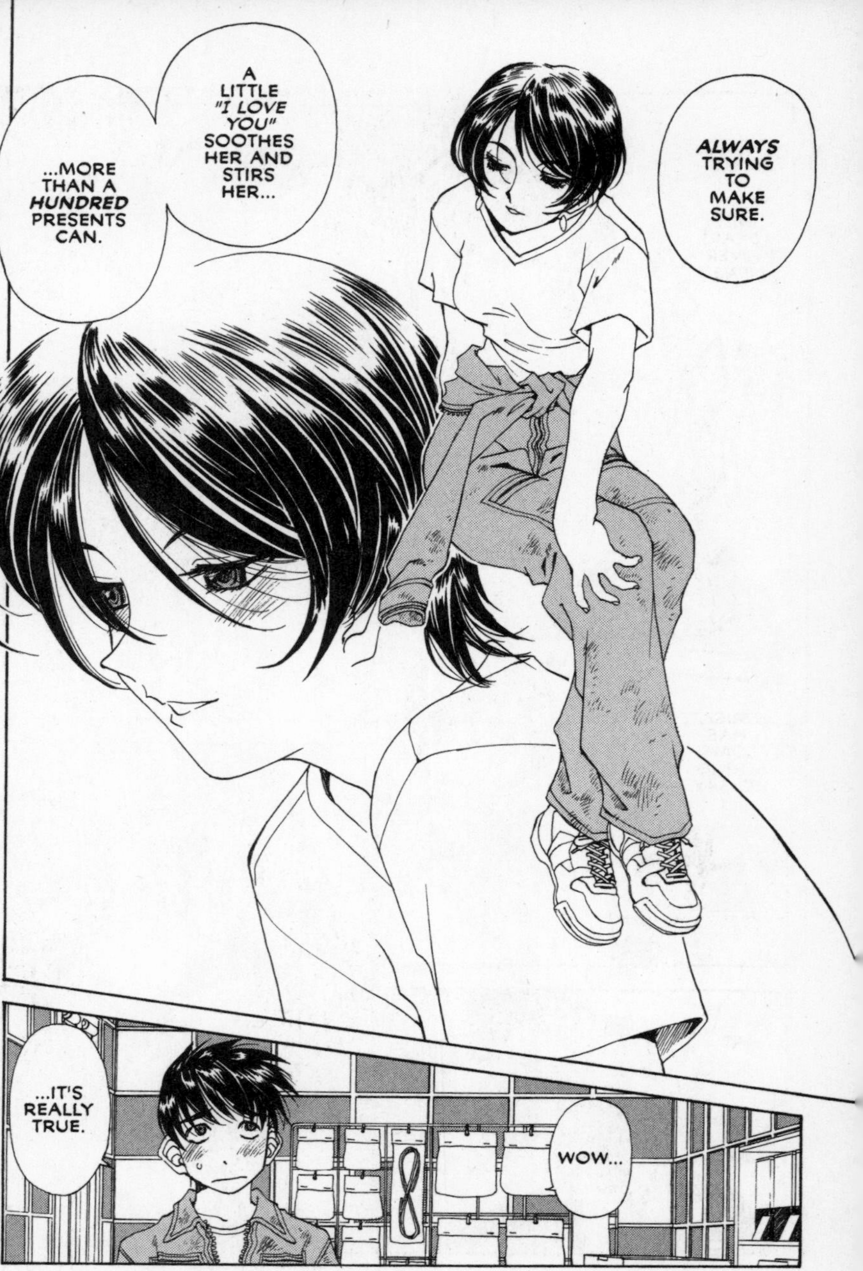
ALWAYS TRYING TO MAKE SURE.
A LITTLE "I LOVE YOU" SOOTHES HER AND STIRS HER...
...MORE THAN A HUNDRED PRESENTS CAN.
WOW...
...IT'S REALLY TRUE.

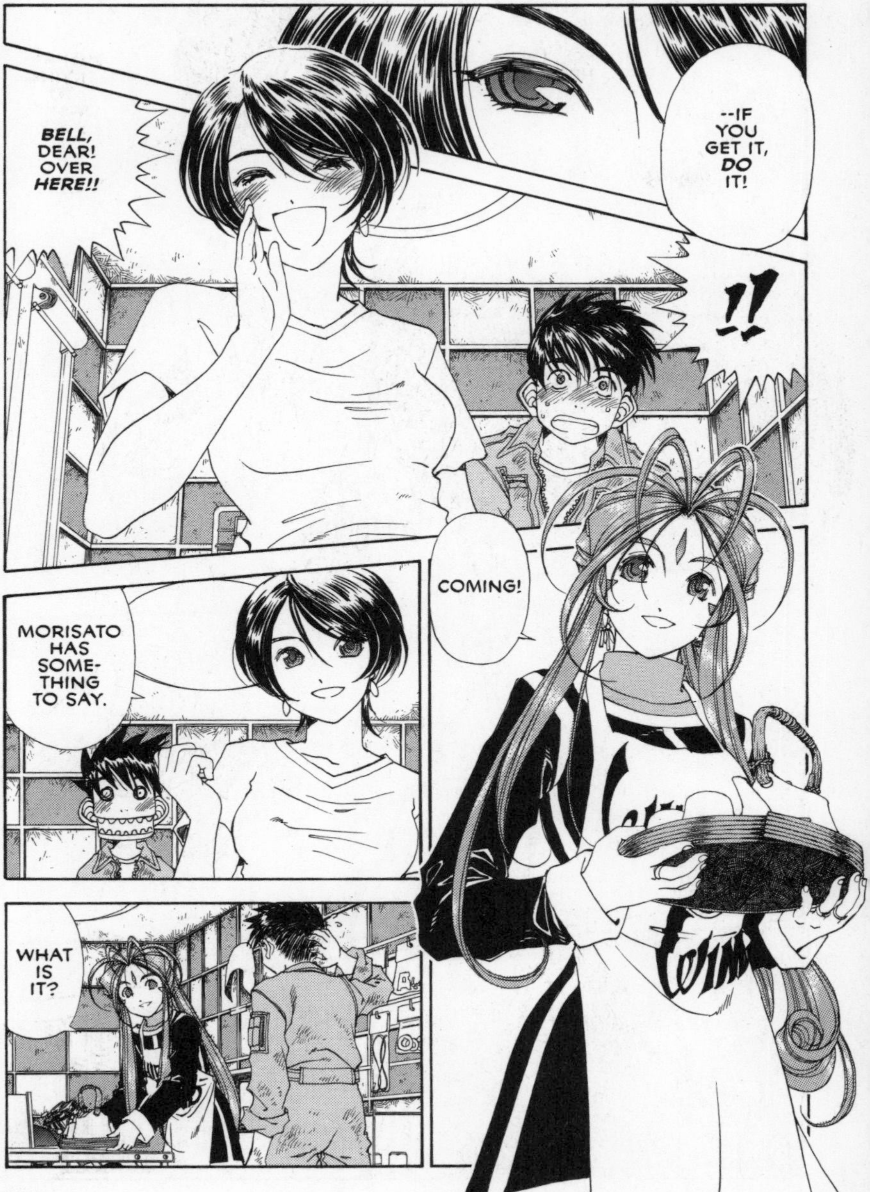
--IF YOU GET IT, *DO* IT!
BELL, DEAR! OVER HERE!!
!!
COMING!
MORISATO HAS SOME-THING TO SAY.
WHAT IS IT?

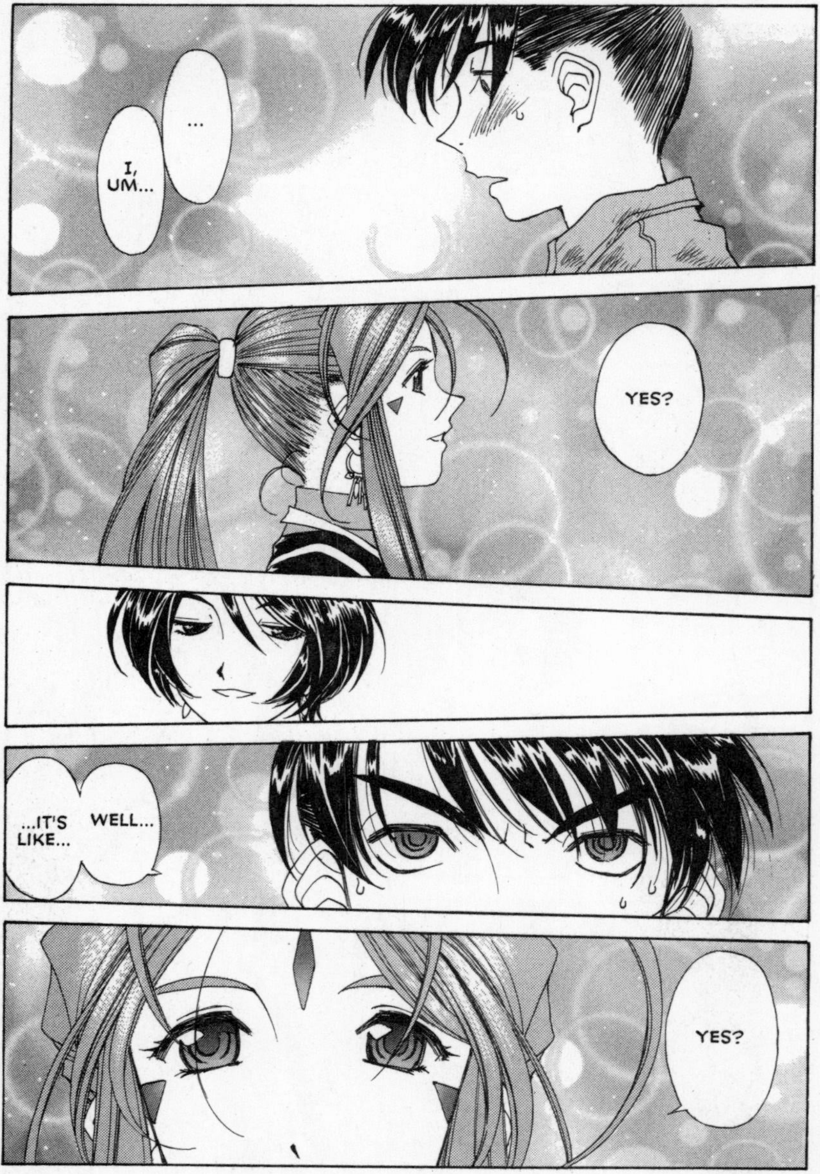
...
I, UM...
YES?
WELL...
...IT'S LIKE...
YES?

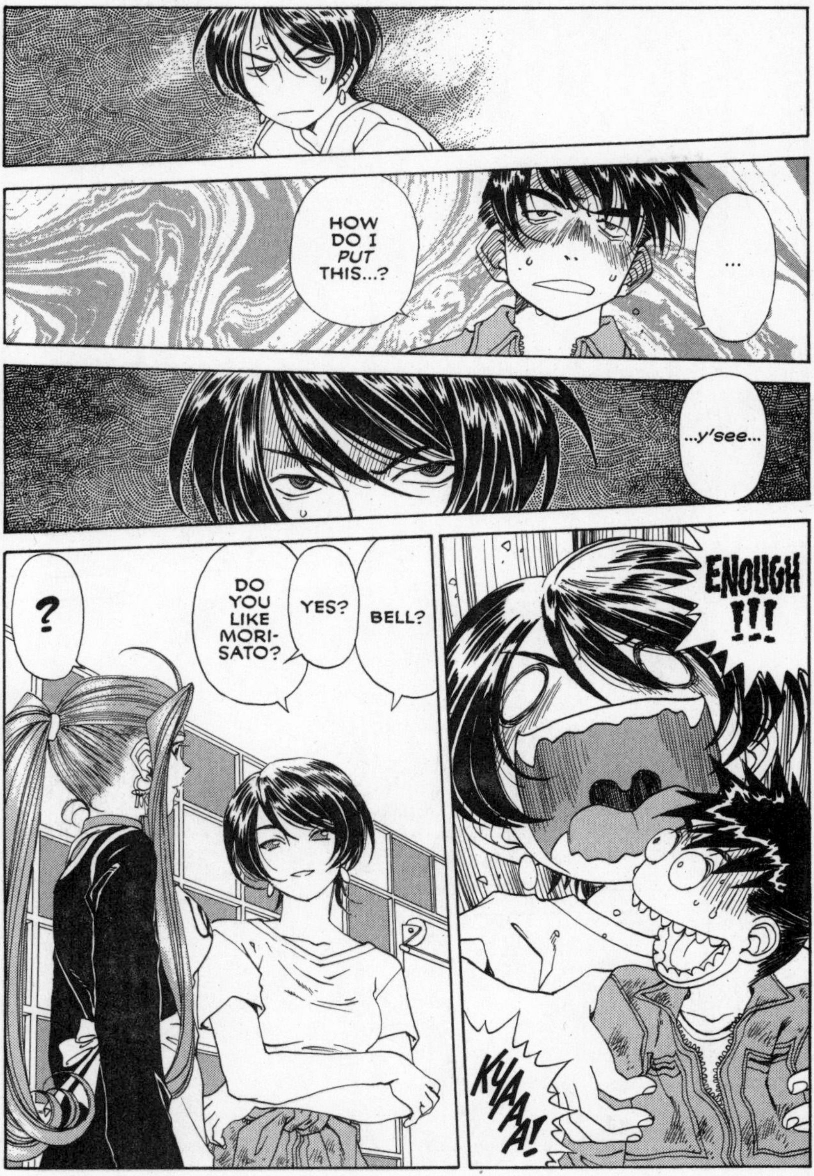
...
HOW DO I PUT THIS...?
...y'see...
ENOUGH !!!
KYAAAA!
BELL?
YES?
DO YOU LIKE MORI-SATO?
?

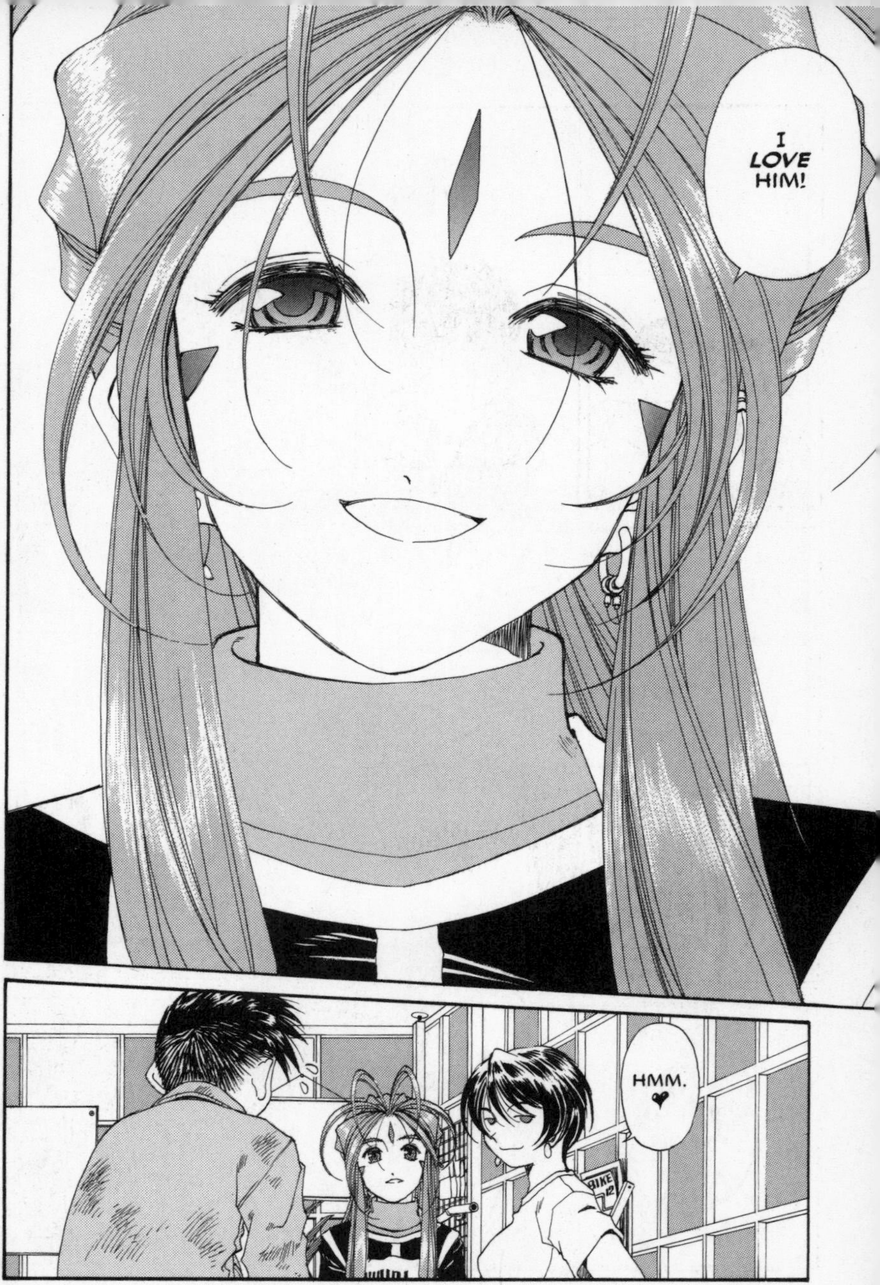
I *LOVE* HIM!
HMM. ♥

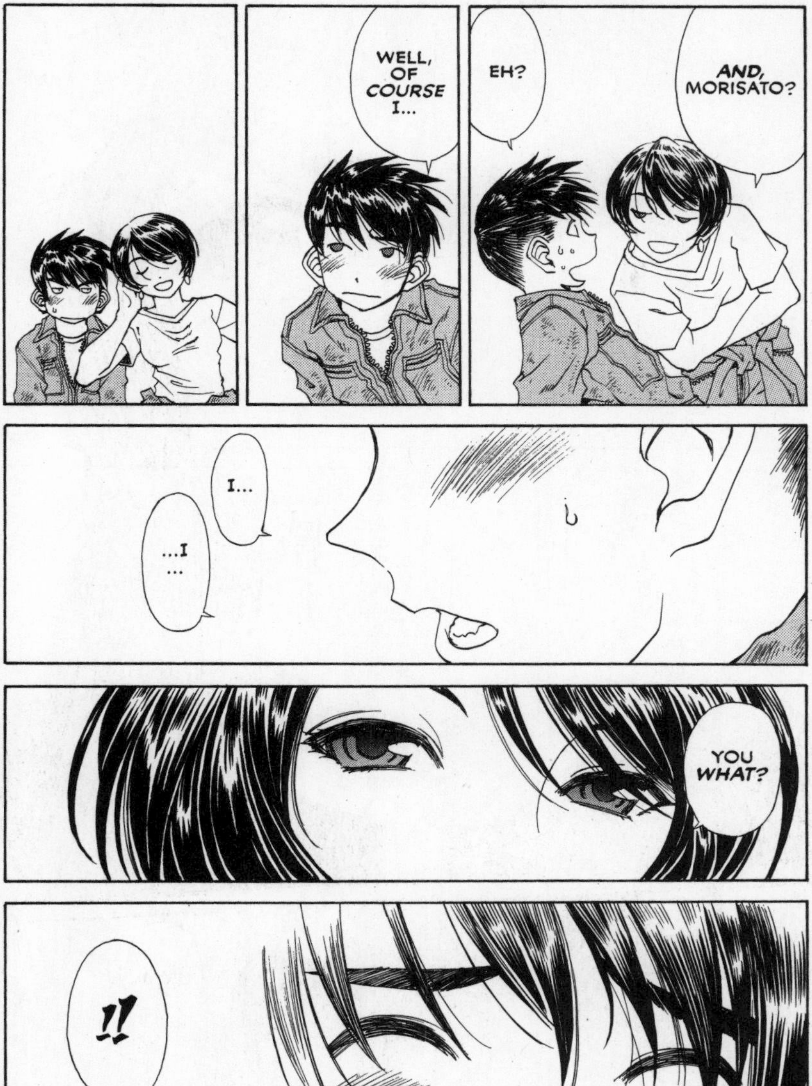
AND, MORISATO?
EH?
WELL, OF COURSE I...
I...
...I ...
YOU WHAT?
!!

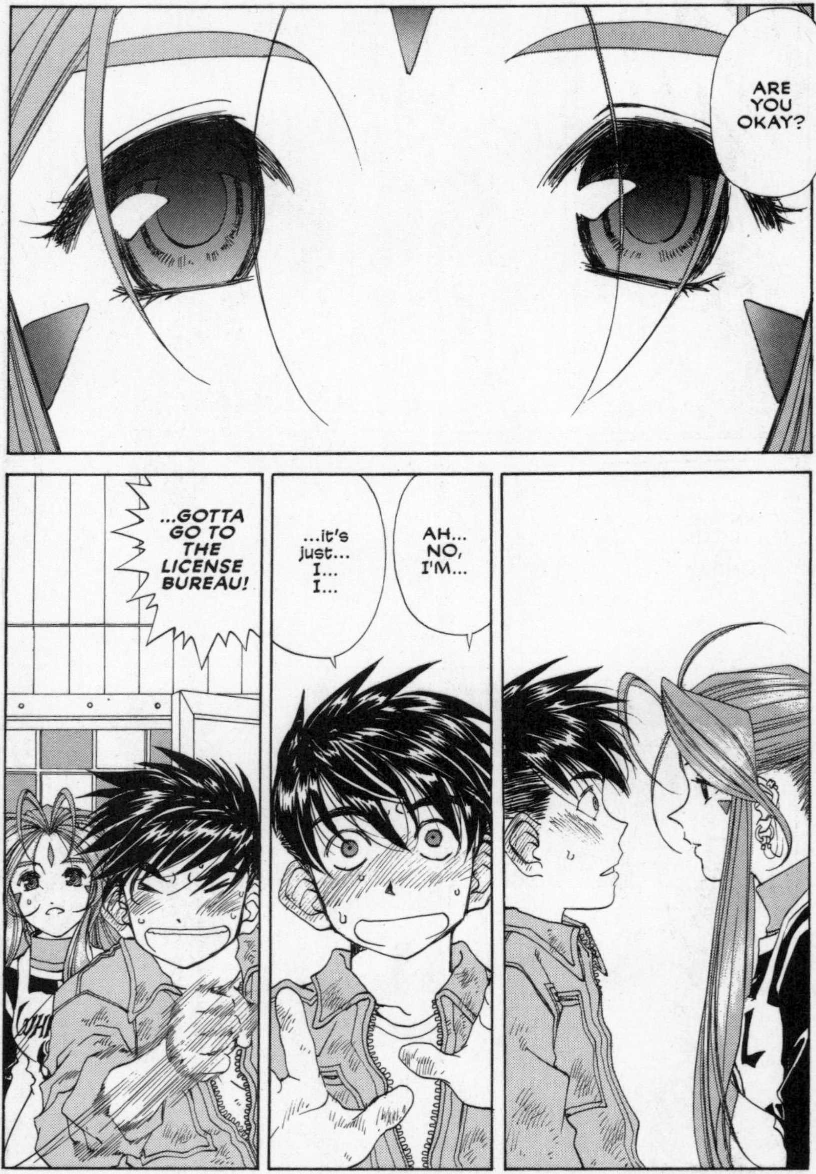
ARE YOU OKAY?
AH... NO, I'M...
...it's just... I... I...
...GOTTA GO TO THE LICENSE BUREAU!

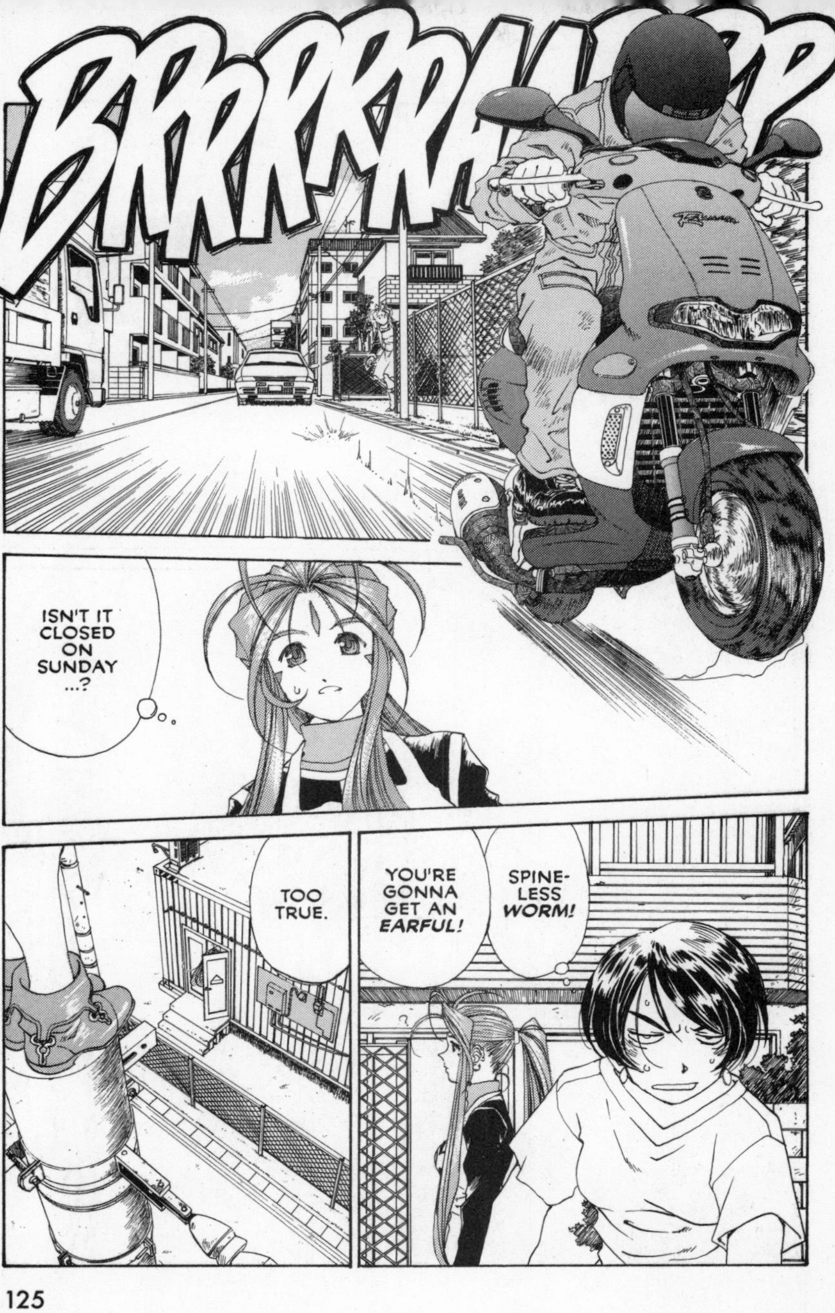
ISN'T IT CLOSED ON SUNDAY ...?
SPINE-LESS *WORM!*
YOU'RE GONNA GET AN *EARFUL!*
TOO TRUE.

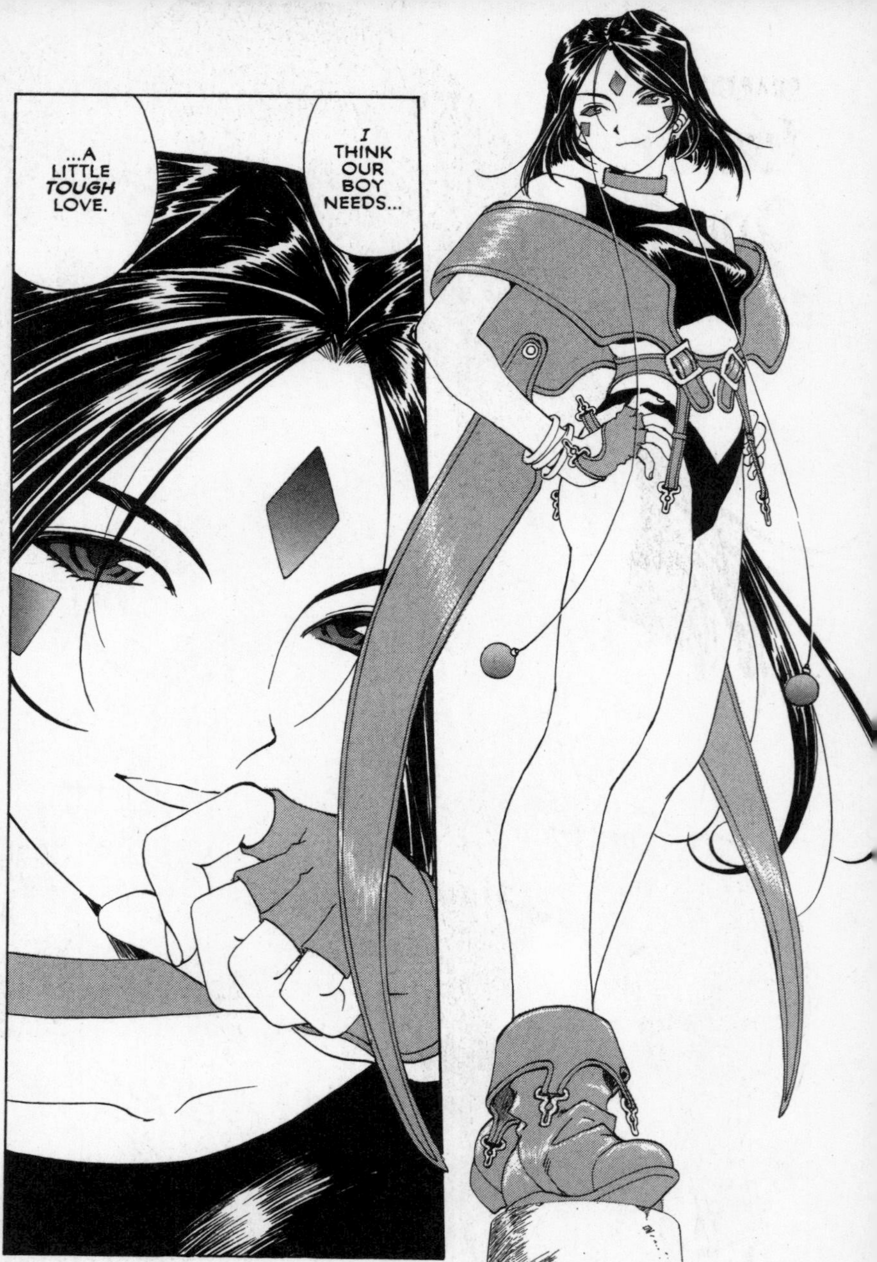
I THINK OUR BOY NEEDS...
...A LITTLE *TOUGH* LOVE.

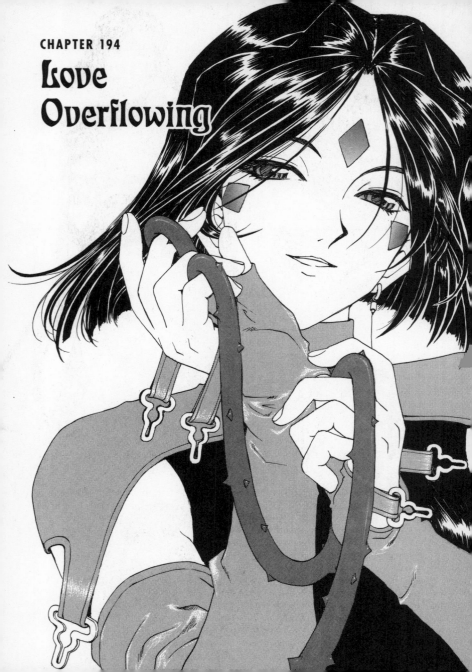

CHAPTER 194
Love Overflowing

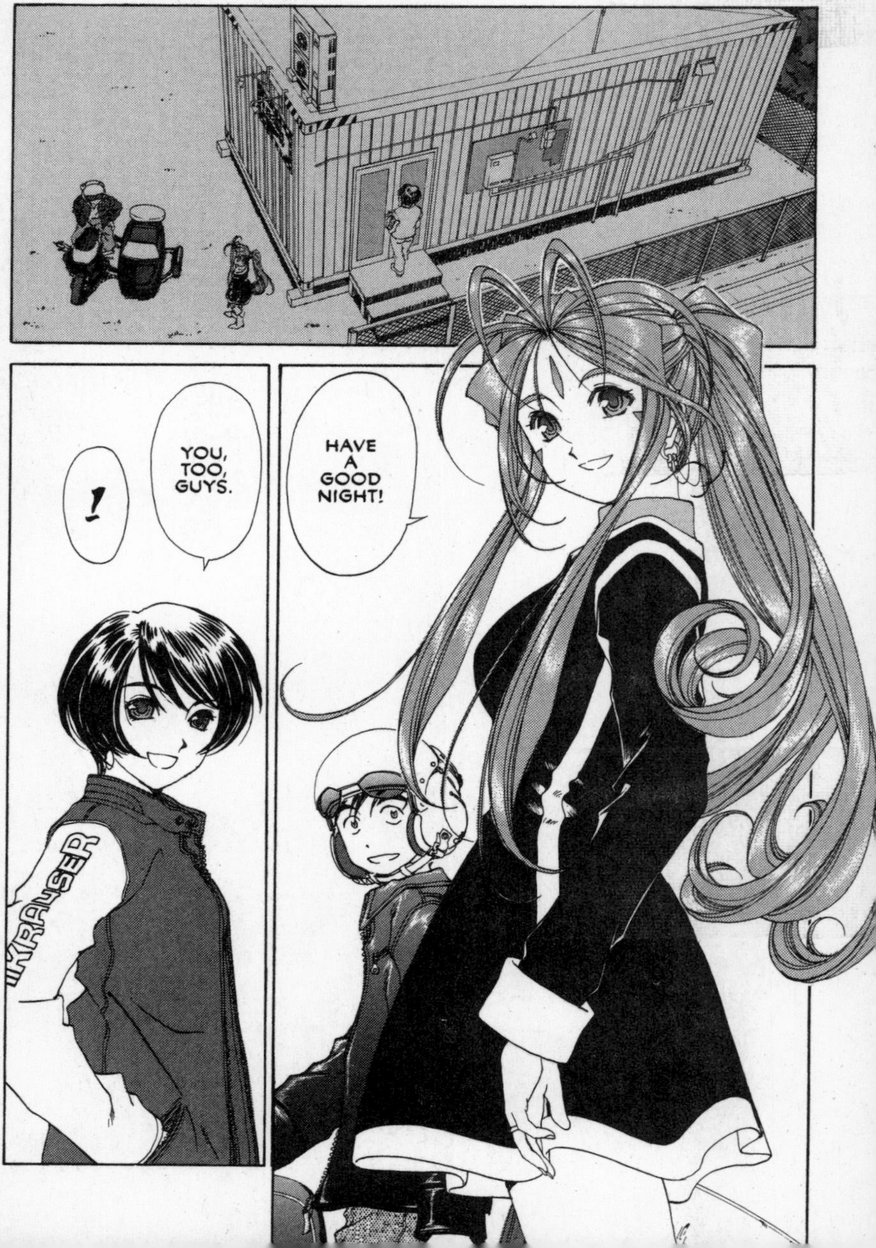
HAVE A GOOD NIGHT!
YOU, TOO, GUYS.
!
KRAUSER

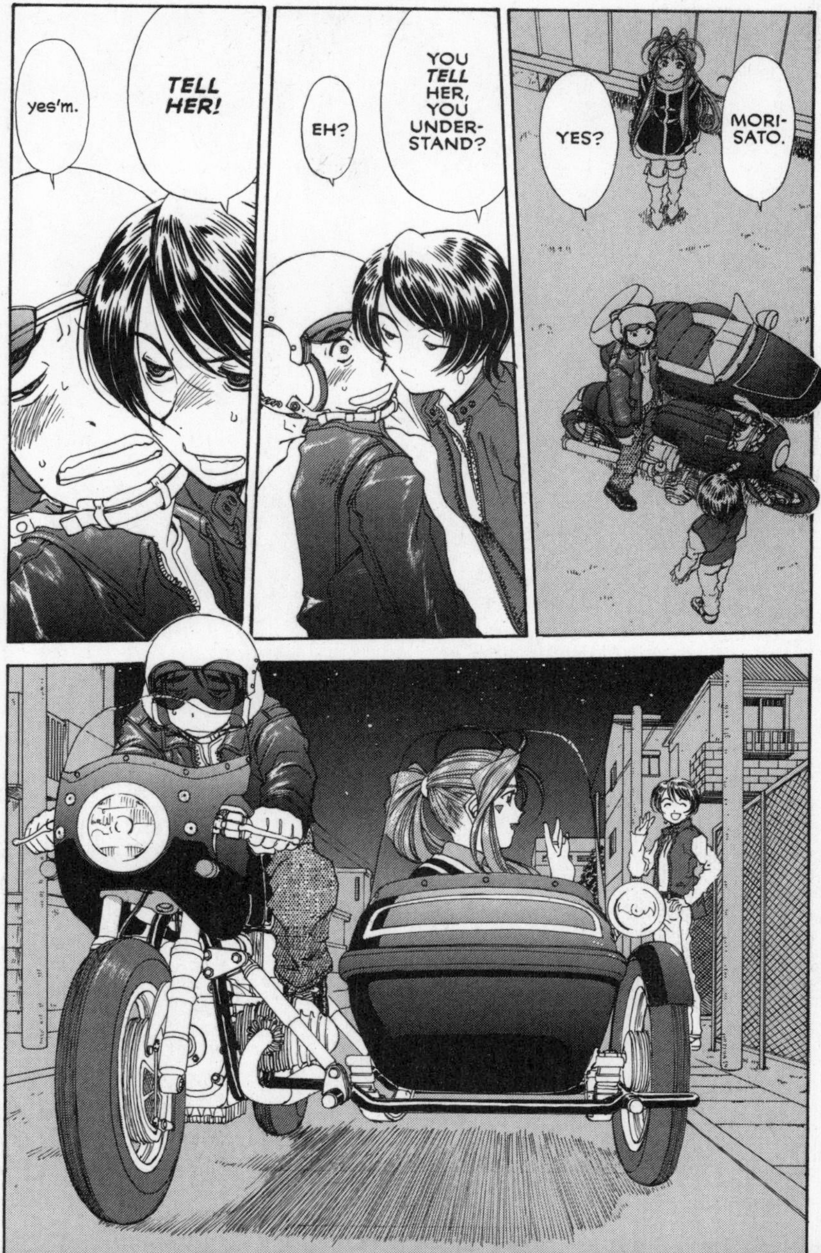
MORI-SATO.
YES?
YOU TELL HER, YOU UNDERSTAND?
EH?
TELL HER!
yes'm.

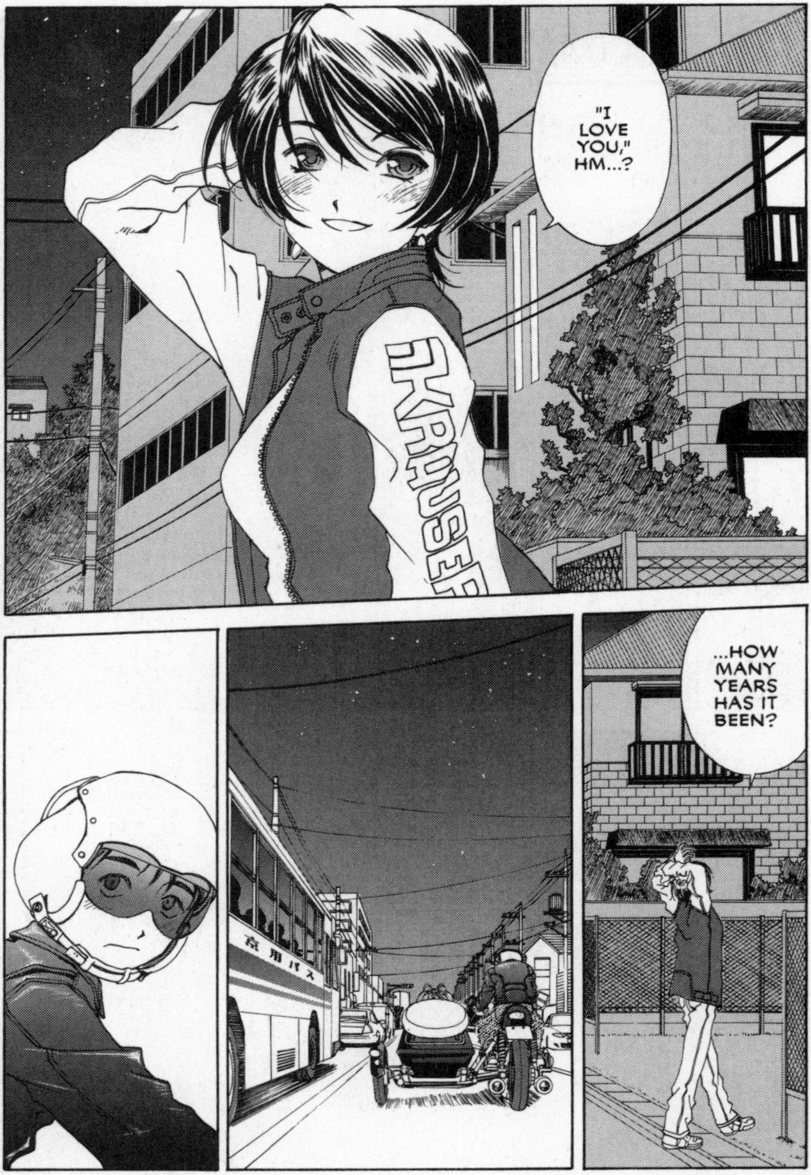
KRAUSER
"I LOVE YOU," HM...?
...HOW MANY YEARS HAS IT BEEN?
京用バス

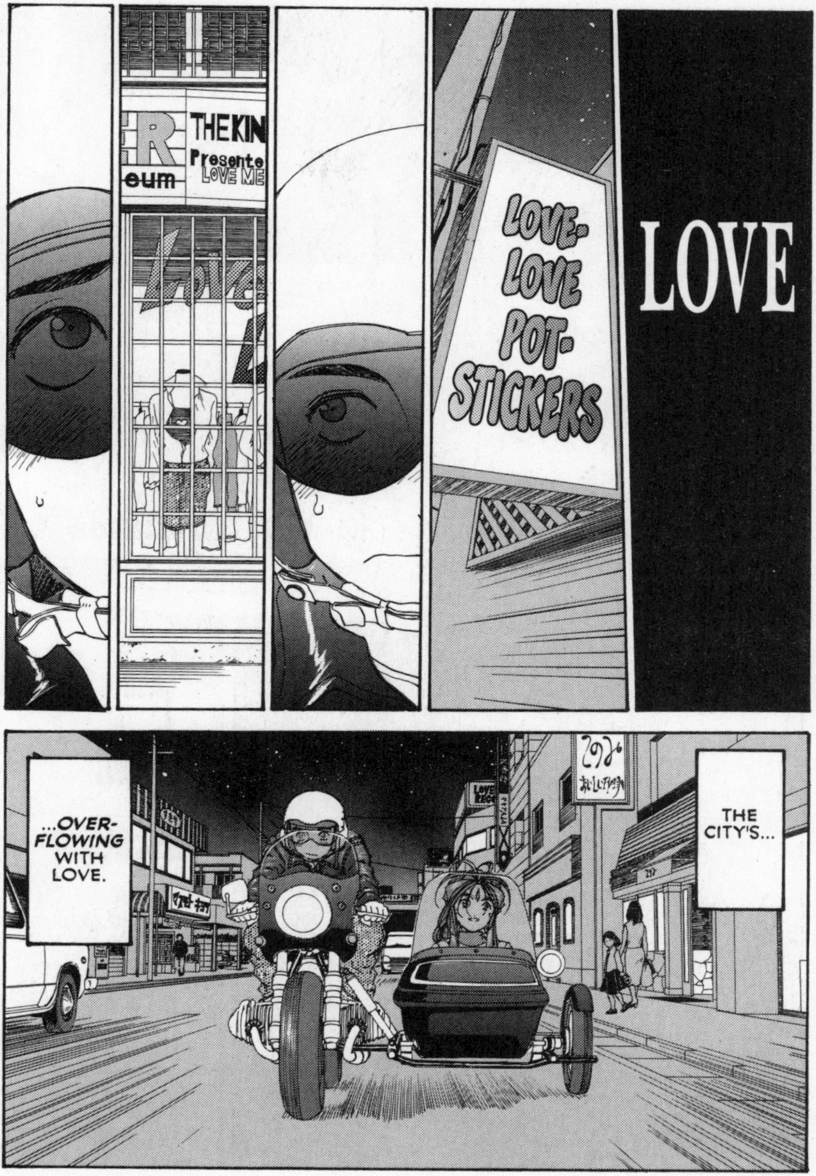
LOVE
LOVE-LOVE POT-STICKERS
THEKIN
Presente
LOVE ME
eum
THE CITY'S...
...OVER-FLOWING WITH LOVE.

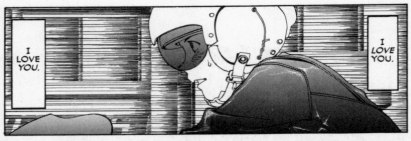

I LOVE YOU.

I LOVE YOU.

THIS GIRL I *ADORE?*

BUT TO *HER?*

...TO *SAY* IT...?

WHY IS IT SO *HARD...*

IT FEELS LIKE... I COULD SAY IT *NOW.*

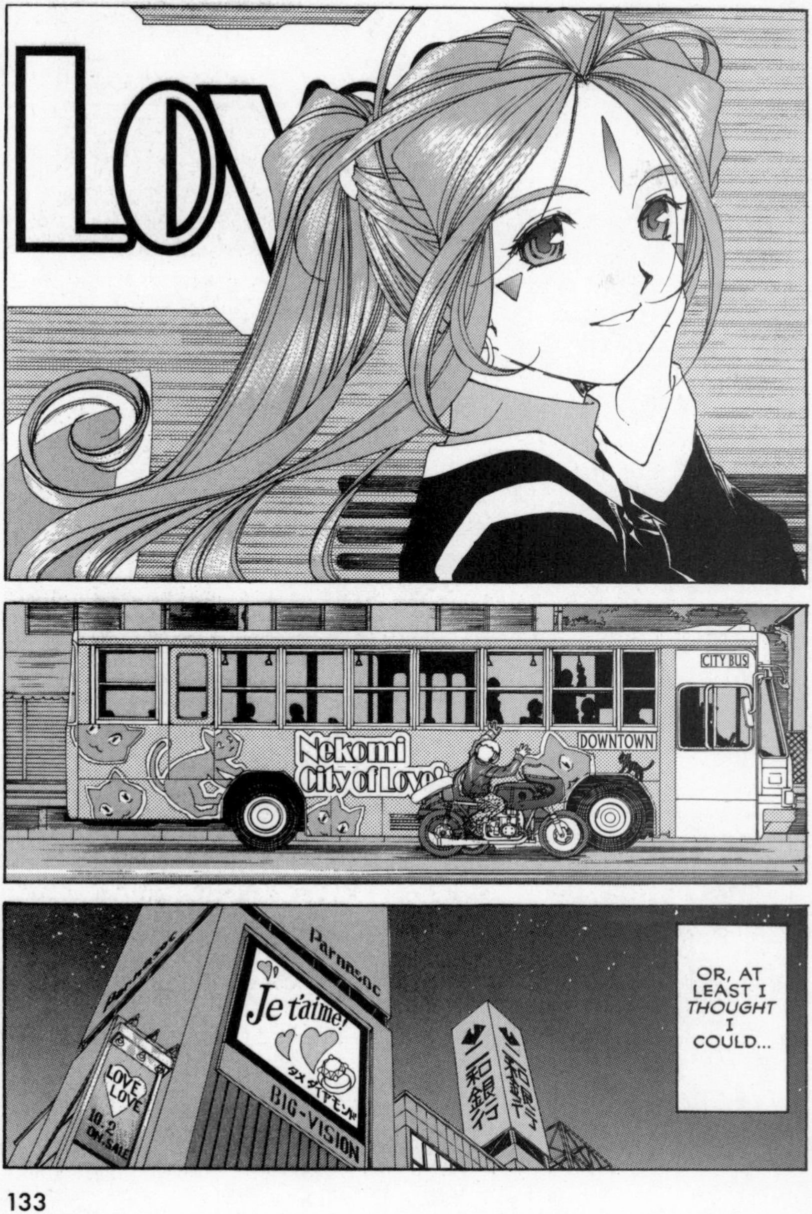
LOV
CITY BUS
DOWNTOWN
Nekomi City of Love!
OR, AT LEAST I *THOUGHT* I COULD...
Parnasoc
Je t'aime!
BIG-VISION
LOVE LOVE
10.2 ON.SALE

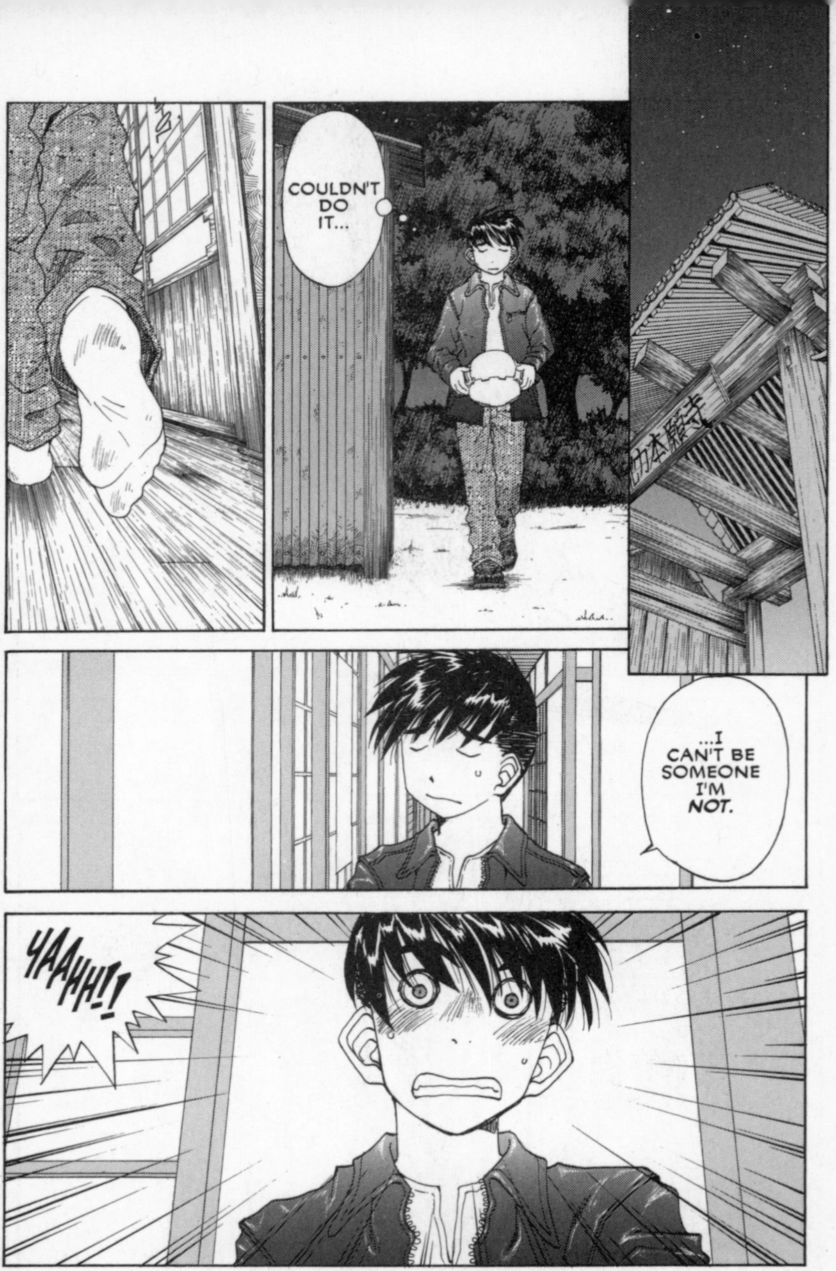
COULDN'T DO IT...
...I CAN'T BE SOMEONE I'M *NOT.*
YAAHH!!

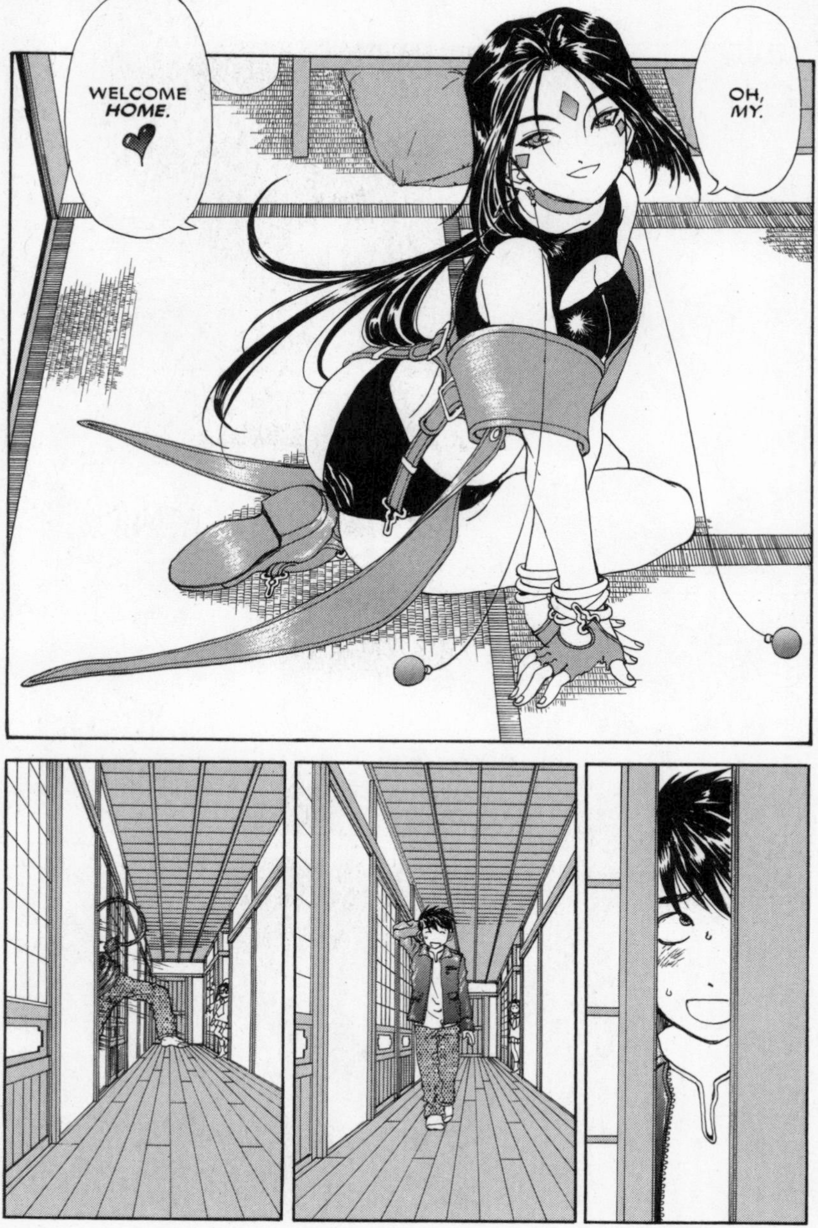
OH, MY.
WELCOME HOME.

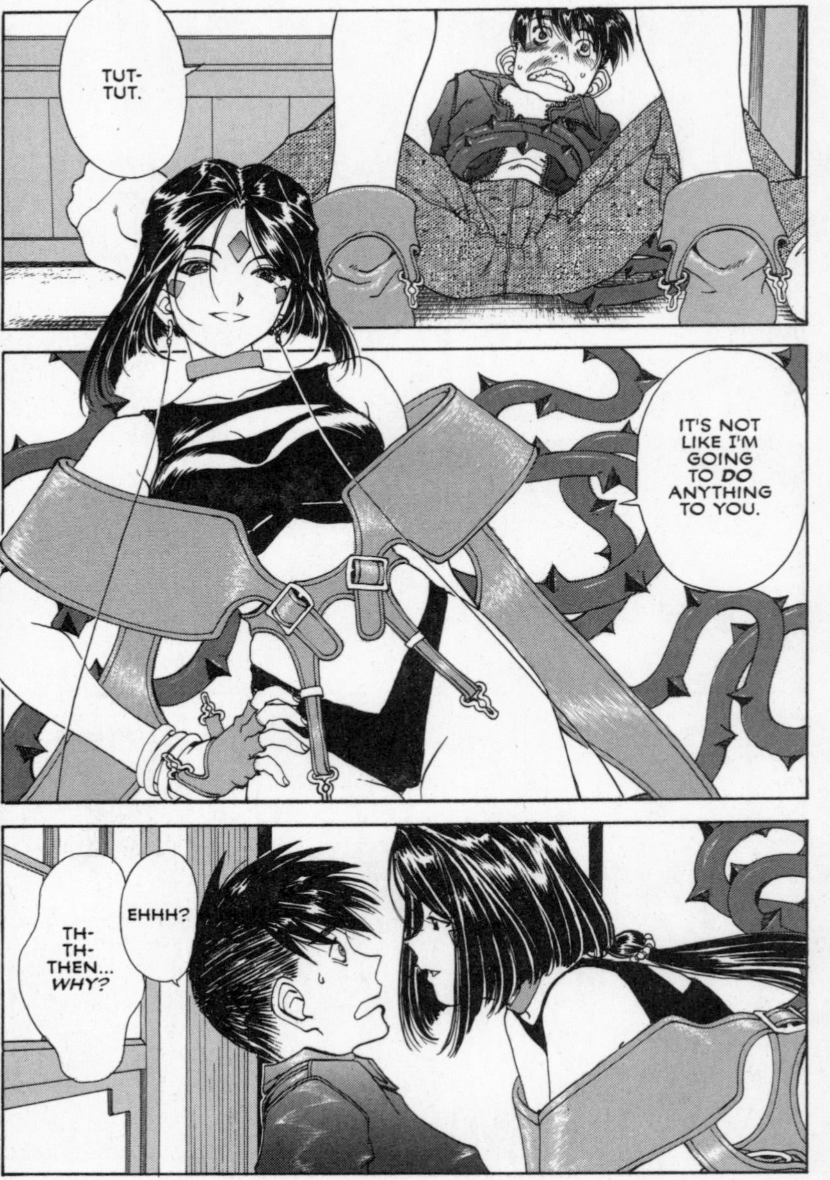
TUT-TUT.
IT'S NOT LIKE I'M GOING TO *DO* ANYTHING TO YOU.
EHHH?
TH-TH-THEN... *WHY?*

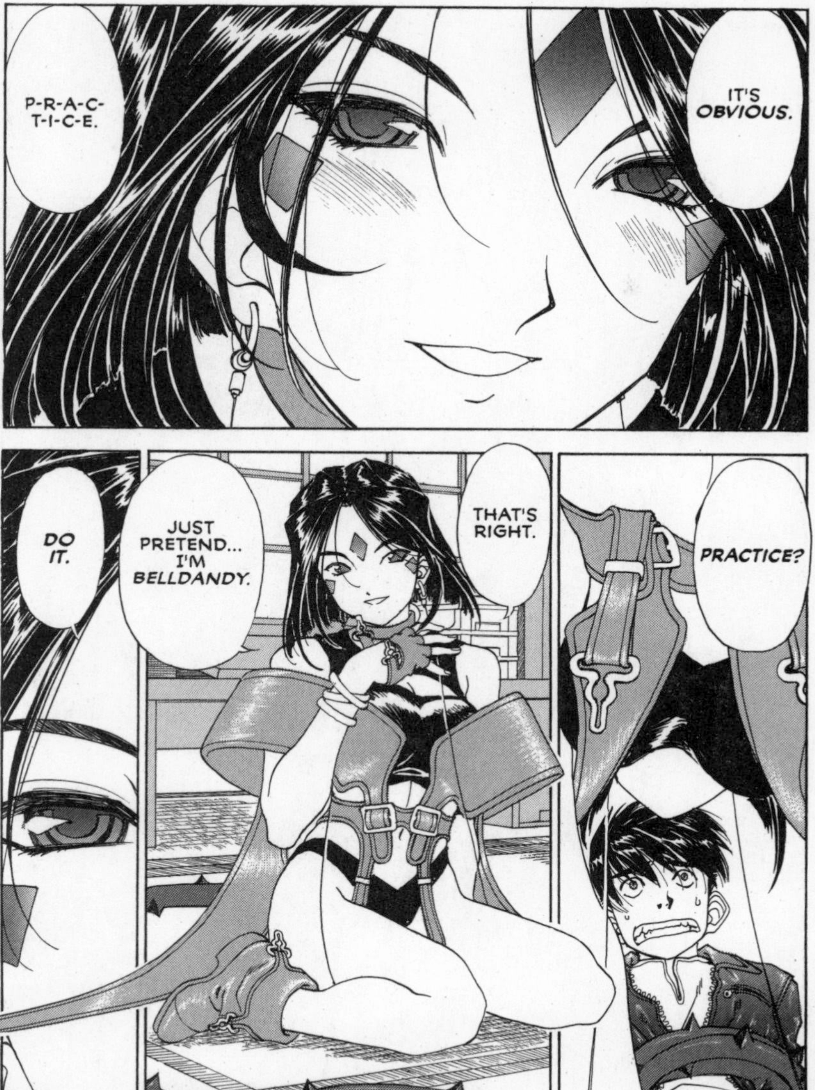
IT'S *OBVIOUS*.
P-R-A-C-T-I-C-E.
PRACTICE?
THAT'S RIGHT.
JUST PRETEND... I'M *BELLDANDY*.
DO IT.

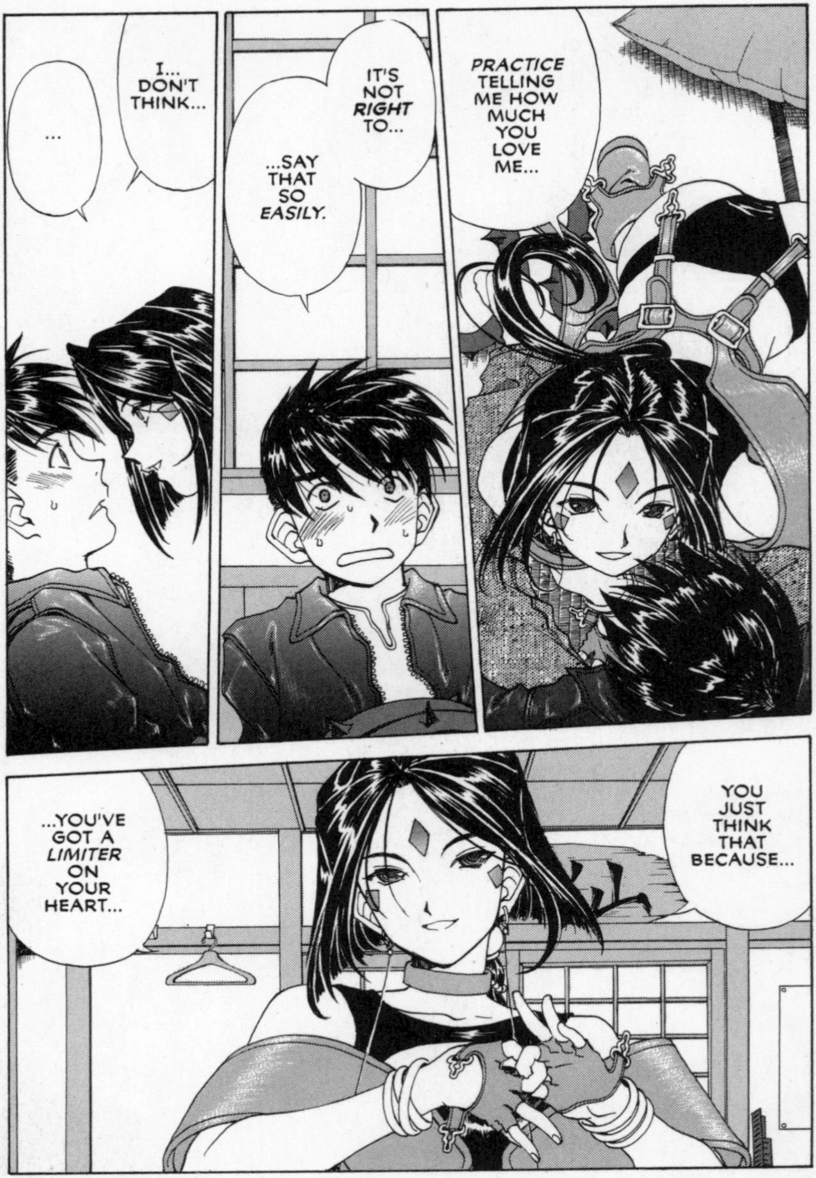
PRACTICE TELLING ME HOW MUCH YOU LOVE ME...
IT'S NOT RIGHT TO...
...SAY THAT SO EASILY.
I... DON'T THINK...
...
YOU JUST THINK THAT BECAUSE...
...YOU'VE GOT A LIMITER ON YOUR HEART...

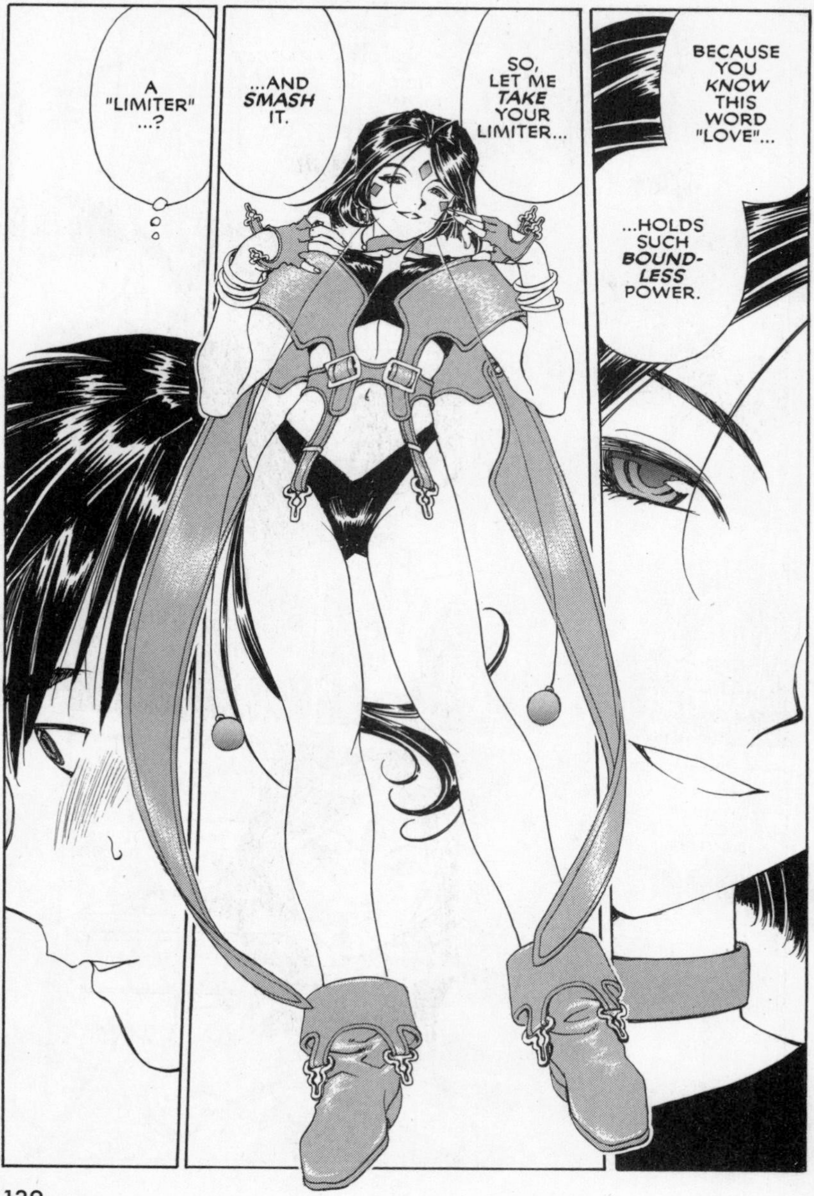
BECAUSE YOU KNOW THIS WORD "LOVE"...
...HOLDS SUCH BOUNDLESS POWER.
SO, LET ME TAKE YOUR LIMITER...
...AND SMASH IT.
A "LIMITER" ...?

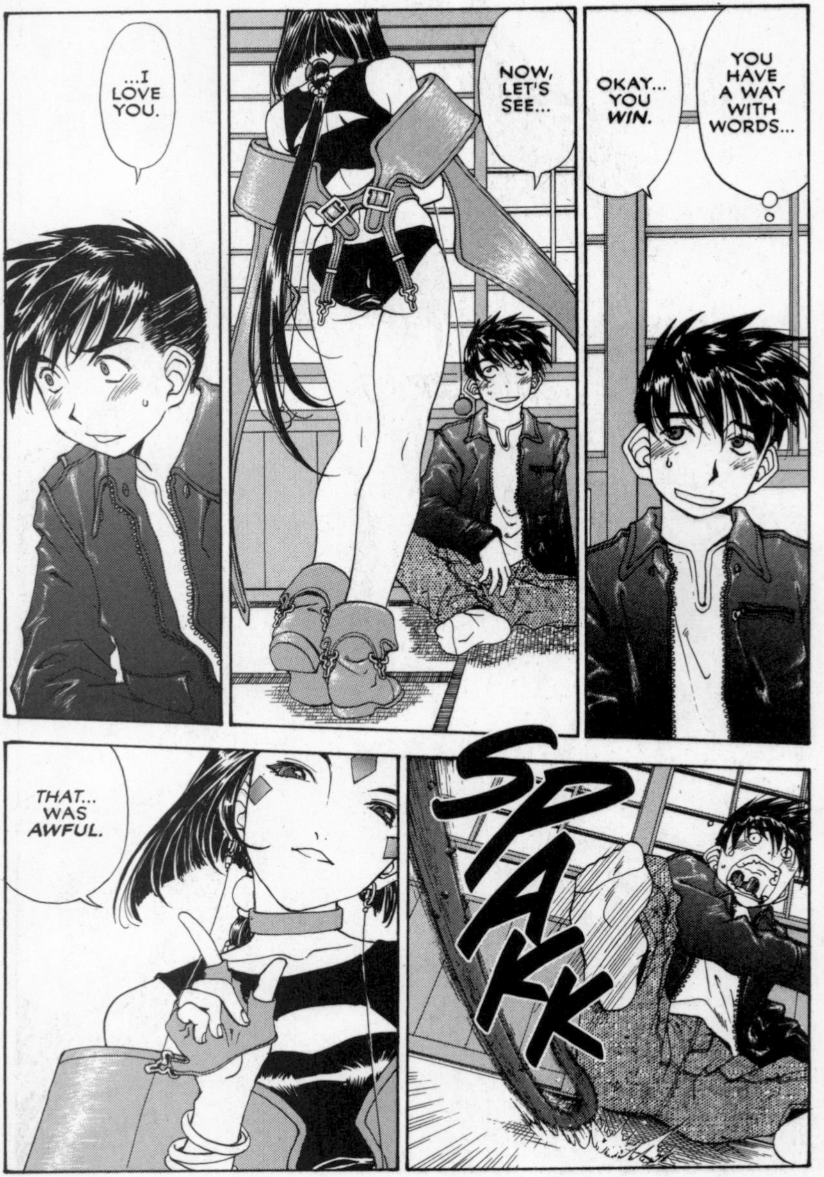
YOU HAVE A WAY WITH WORDS...
OKAY... YOU *WIN.*
NOW, LET'S SEE...
...I LOVE YOU.
SPAKK
THAT... WAS AWFUL.

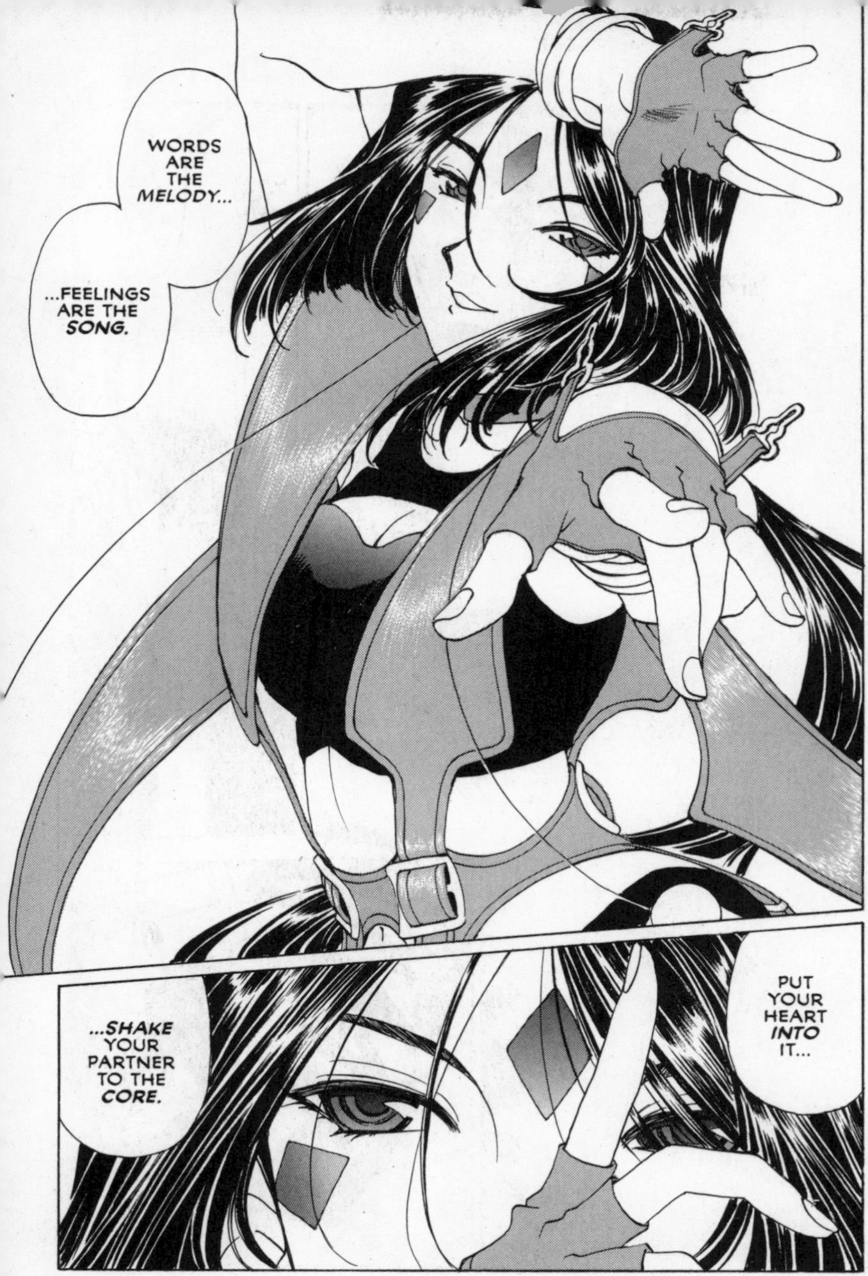
WORDS ARE THE *MELODY...*
...FEELINGS ARE THE *SONG.*
PUT YOUR HEART *INTO* IT...
...*SHAKE* YOUR PARTNER TO THE *CORE.*

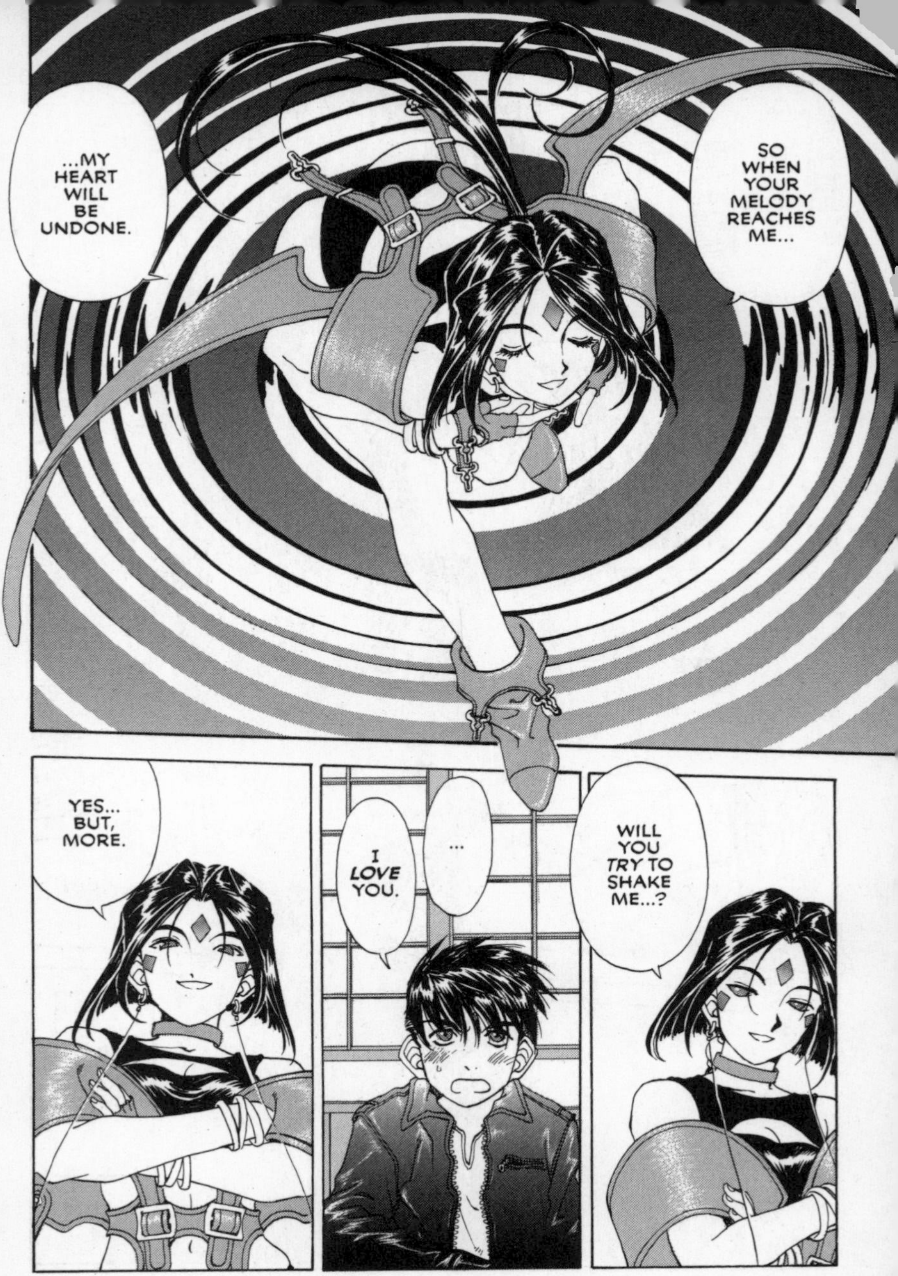
SO WHEN YOUR MELODY REACHES ME...
...MY HEART WILL BE UNDONE.
WILL YOU *TRY* TO SHAKE ME...?
...
I *LOVE* YOU.
YES... BUT, MORE.

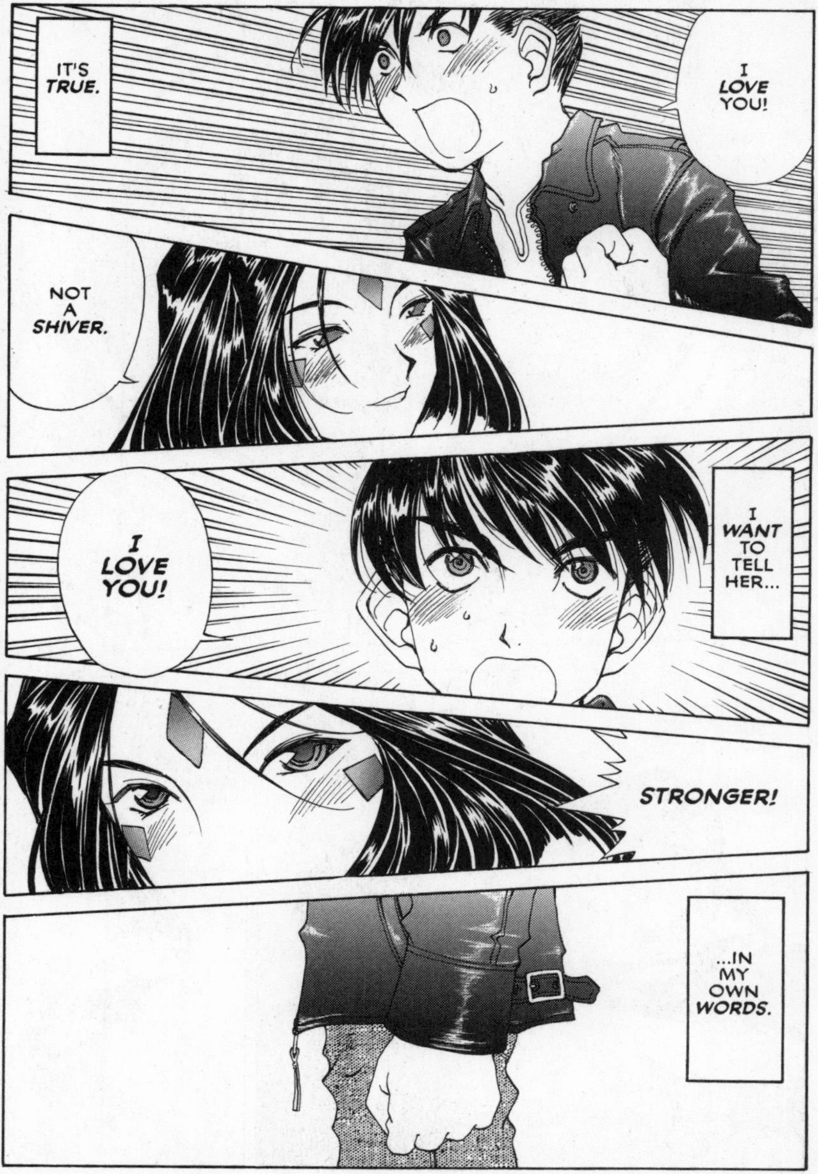

I LOVE YOU!
IT'S TRUE.
NOT A SHIVER.
I WANT TO TELL HER...
I LOVE YOU!
STRONGER!
...IN MY OWN WORDS.

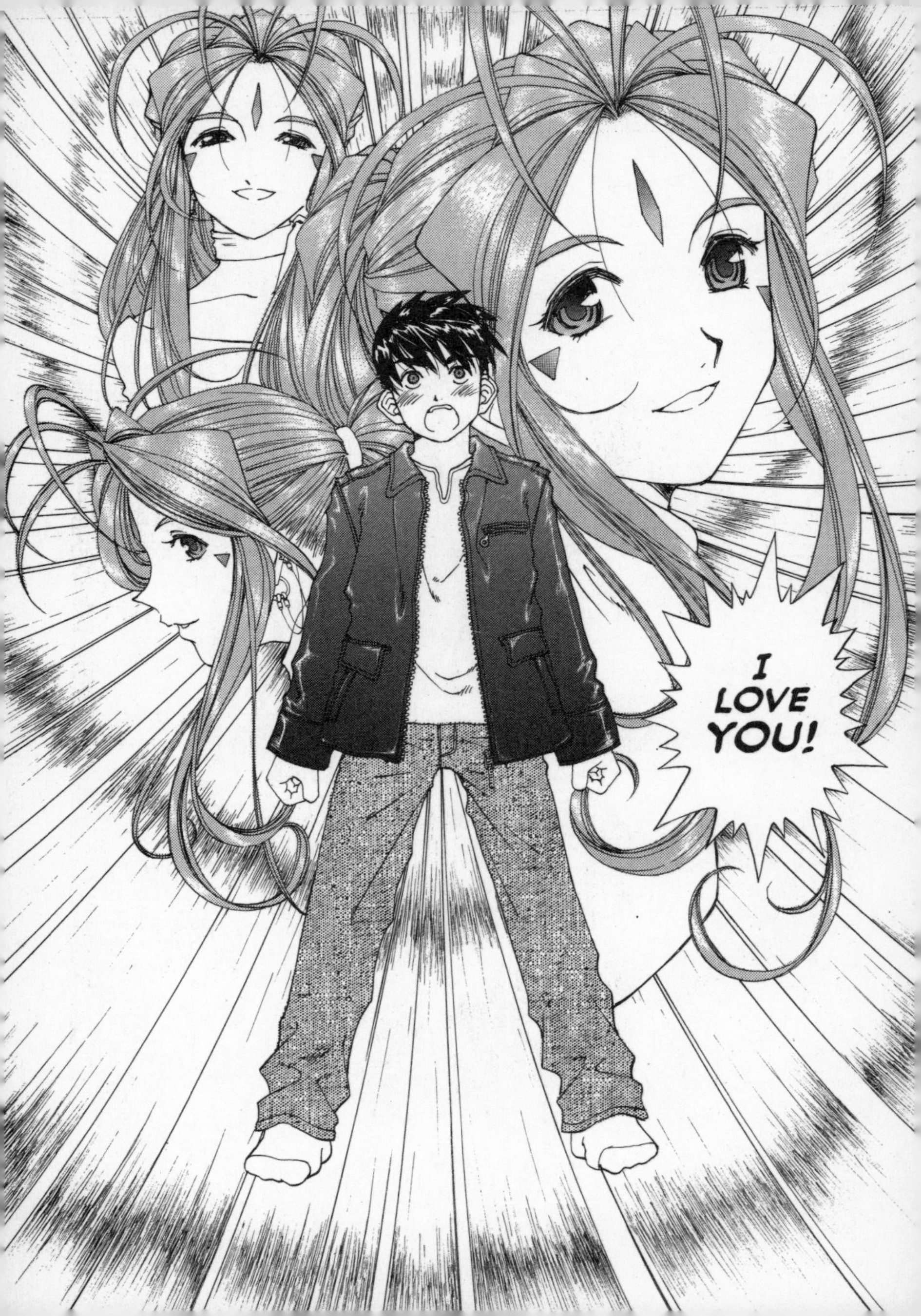
I LOVE YOU!

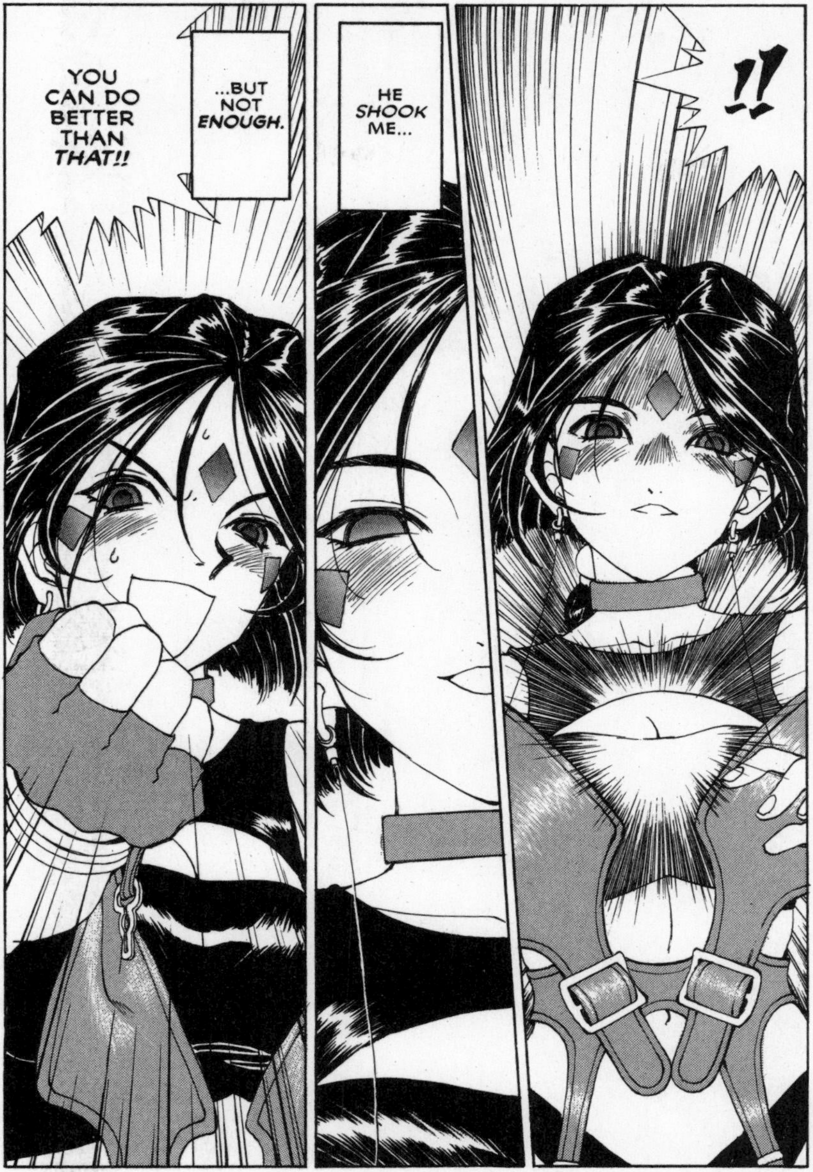
!!
HE SHOOK ME...
...BUT NOT ENOUGH.
YOU CAN DO BETTER THAN THAT!!

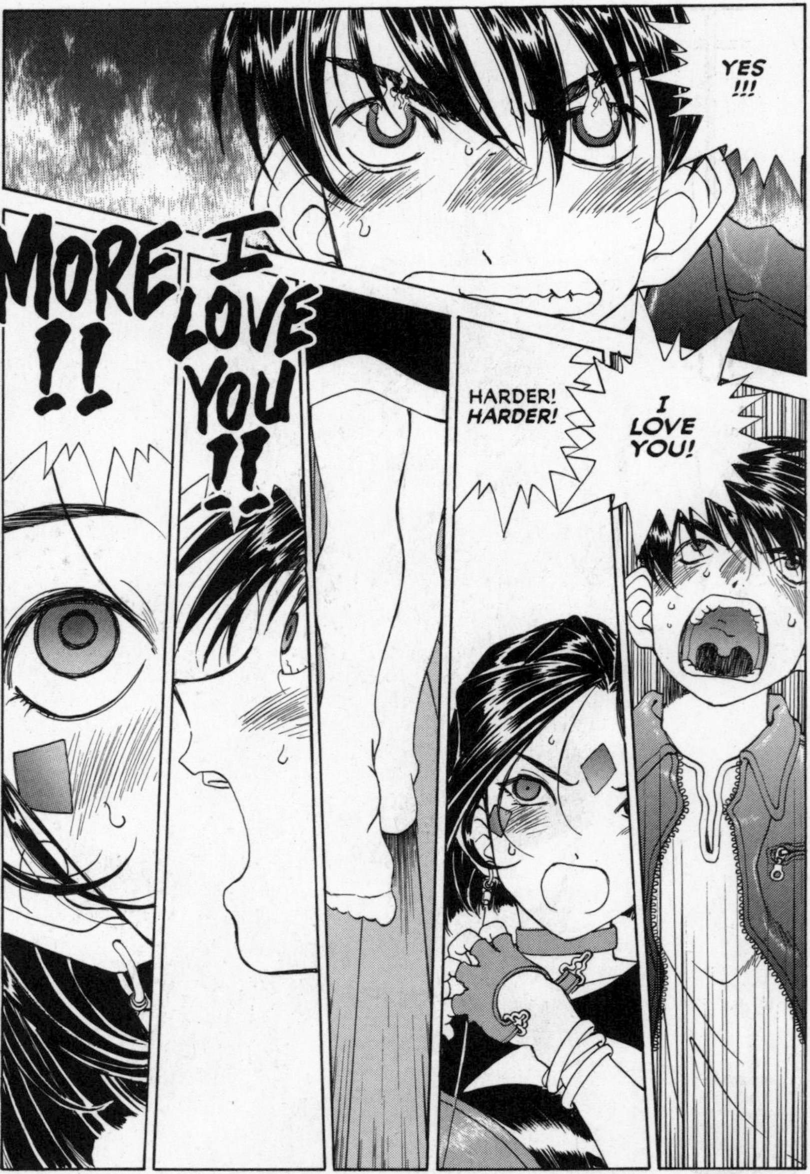
YES !!!
I LOVE YOU!
HARDER! HARDER!
I LOVE YOU !!
MORE !!

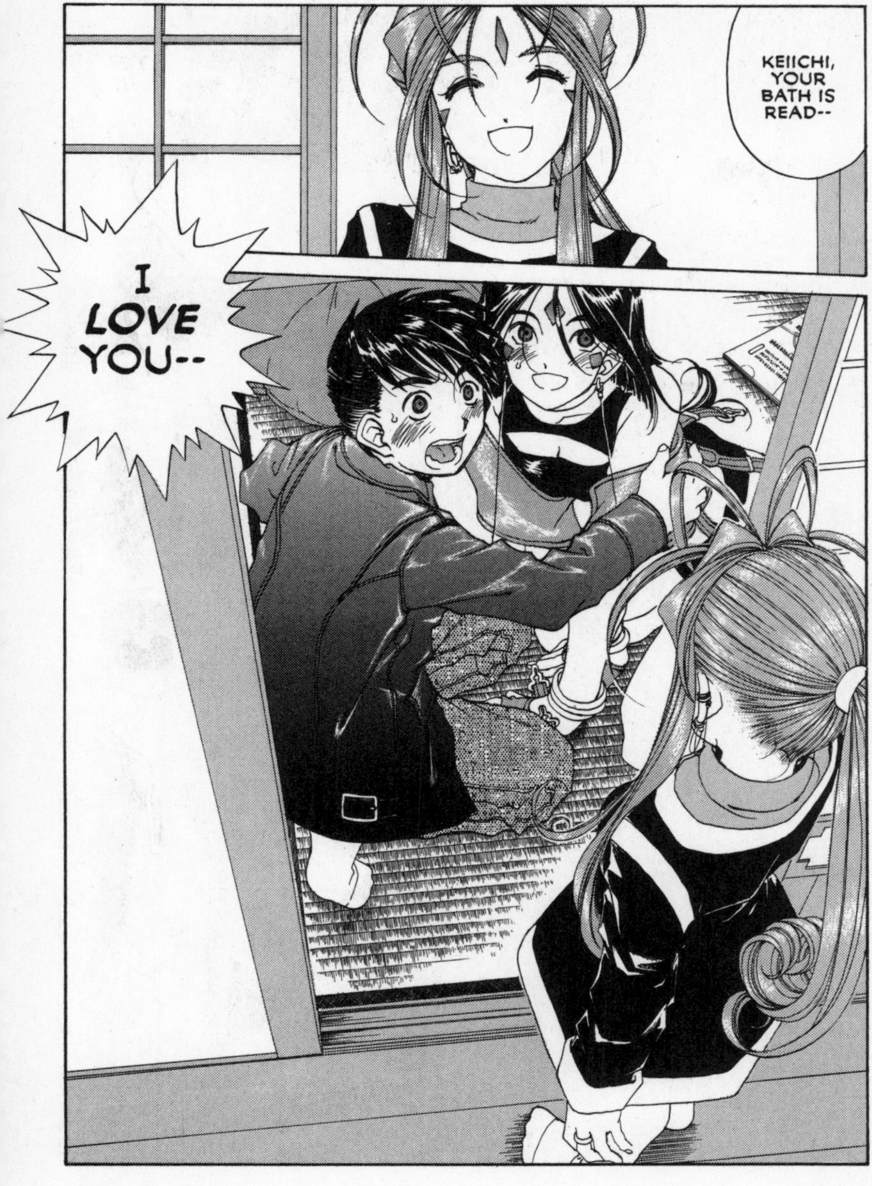
KEIICHI, YOUR BATH IS READ--
I LOVE YOU--

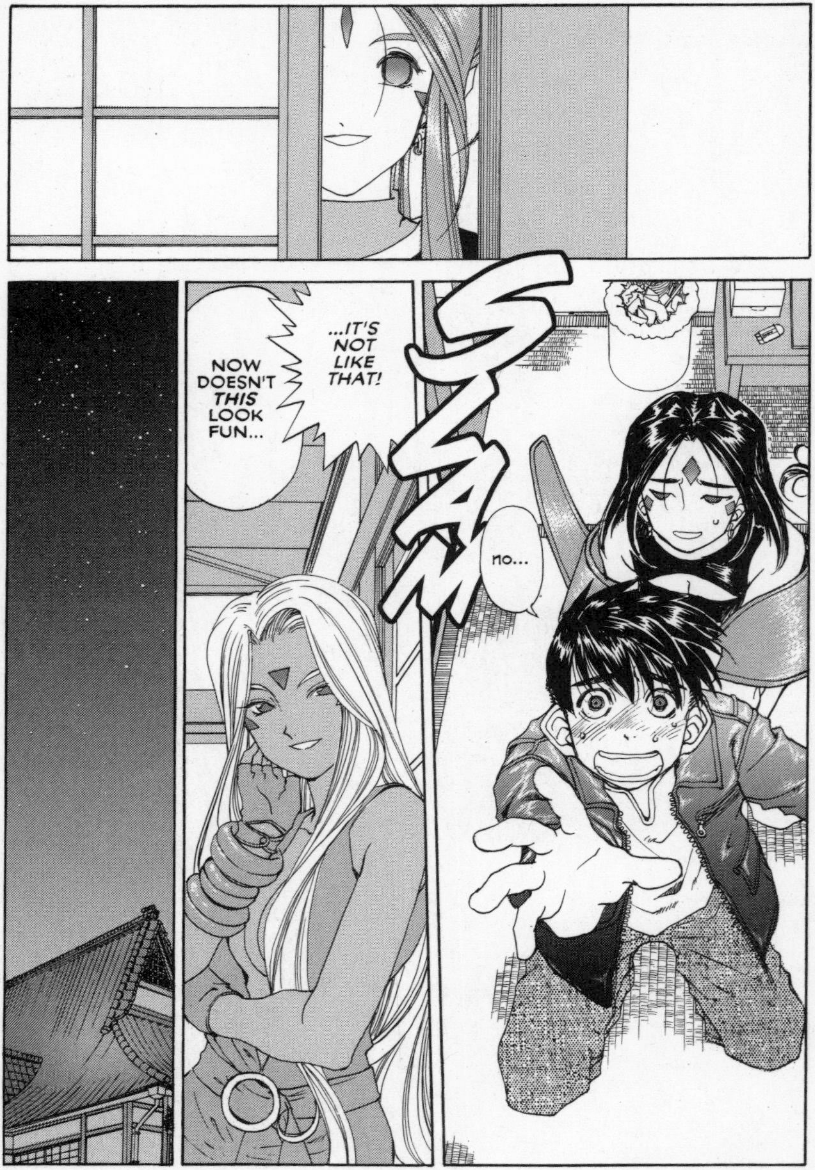
SLAM
no...
...IT'S NOT LIKE THAT!
NOW DOESN'T *THIS* LOOK FUN...

EDITOR
Carl Gustav Horn

DESIGNER
Scott Cook

ART DIRECTOR
Lia Ribacchi

PUBLISHER
Mike Richardson

English-language version
produced by Dark Horse Comics

OH MY GODDESS! Vol. 30
©2008 Kosuke Fujishima. All rights reserved. First published
in Japan in 2004 by Kodansha Ltd., Tokyo. Publication rights for this
English edition arranged through Kodansha Ltd. This English-
language edition ©2008 by Dark Horse Comics, Inc. All other material
©2008 by Dark Horse Comics, Inc. All rights reserved. No portion of this
publication may be reproduced or transmitted, in any form or by any
means, without the express written permission of the copyright holders.
Names, characters, places, and incidents featured in this publication either
are the product of the author's imagination or are used fictitiously. Any re-
semblance to actual persons (living or dead), events, institutions, or
locales, without satiric intent, is coincidental. Dark Horse Manga™
is a trademark of Dark Horse Comics, Inc. All rights reserved.

Published by Dark Horse Manga
a division of Dark Horse Comics, Inc.
10956 SE Main Street
Milwaukie, OR 97222
www.darkhorse.com

To find a comics shop in your area,
call the Comic Shop Locator Service
toll-free at 1-888-266-4226

First edition: August 2008
ISBN 978-1-59307-979-6

1 3 5 7 9 10 8 6 4 2

Printed in Canada

letters to the
ENCHANTRESS

10956 SE Main Street, Milwaukie, Oregon 97222
omg@darkhorse.com • www.darkhorse.com

NOTE: Full addresses and e-mail addresses will not be printed, unless you ask! All fan art-work, letters, and e-mails submitted become the property of Dark Horse Comics.

In Vol. 29, we printed a letter about how *OMG!* made a friendship closer. But this manga can do even more than that . . .

Dear Letters to the Enchantress:

It's that time again when I must update my commitment to *Ah!*, or *Oh!*, *My Goddess*. I appreciate Dark Horse and their staff for continuing the long-running series in these pages, and I really appreciate the new manga-style format while keeping the editor comments and letters section intact.

I love how the series has developed, and even Kosuke has put on a proper display of change in his manga. I really hope and wish I can thank him someday for his devotion to the series, but for now I will continue to thank the staff and every one of you at Dark Horse for publishing the work.

I have purchased the series since it was in comic book format (even from the first issue) and ironically, it's how I found my husband from Canada, Arnold. We've been married seven years now, and I remember during our INS interview showing them the issues with the "Letters to the Enchantress" that said how we met, and the progress of our relationship.

I will never forget how fate worked out. It was even along the same lines as the manga. We were looking for pals, and almost as if by a simple phone call, we found each other. If it wasn't for *Oh My Goddess!* or Dark Horse, I would not continue to be happily married. I truly want to continue to thank you for this fact and always will be a fan.

I did some fan art recently, as I have always done before both for my husband, and to share with you. Please continue your success, and always hope to get more. Some way, some how, thank Kosuke most of all.

Sincerely,
Martha Schwartz
http://www.bamcomics.com/

"Kosuke," is it? Even the editor doesn't get to call him by his first name. ^_^ Well, as usual, I must apologize for the delay between your sending in your letter, and the time it took for it to appear in these pages. How long ago was it? It was so long ago, that the envelope had a 41-cent stamp.

As some of you may know, whenever someone in America wants to bring another person into the U.S. for marriage or family reasons, the INS (Immigration & Naturalization Service) wants to see some evidence of the relationship. So we're glad "Letters to the Enchantress" is considered one of the acceptable forms of documentation! Who knew? There must be a government list somewhere that says, *"Please bring one of the following: baptismal certificates, drivers' licenses, military discharges, your fan art in 'Letters to the Enchantress'. . ."*

Fan art by Martha Schwartz

But it's hard to imagine a more appropriate story for "Enchantress" than that of you and your husband. First of all, the person who brought *Oh My Goddess!* into English in the first place is also a Canadian who came to America, Studio Proteus founder Toren Smith—and it was through his love of manga that he met *his* wife, letterer and retouch genius Tomoko Saito (check out her yaoi parody work in *Empowered* Vol. 3!). Gainax cofounder Yasuhiro Takeda, by the way, mentions a bit about how it happened in his *The Notenki Memoirs*, available in English from ADV.

As a matter of fact, I'll go further, and say that I hope your story encourages Keiichi and Belldandy that they, too, should tie the knot at last. ^_^

Martha's fan art can be seen right above! I love the floral motifs in the background, and on Belldandy's dress, which, of course, are in keeping with the inside covers of the manga itself. Thank you once again, and everybody, please keep writing in!

GUNSMITH CATS

REVISED EDITIONS!

Kenichi Sonoda's original *Gunsmith Cats* stories are back, revised and repackaged as deluxe omnibus editions!

Rally Vincent and Minnie-May Hopkins are experts in their respective fields of marksmanship and explosives, but they're so cute you'd never know! Neither would the perps unlucky enough to be hunted by these two bounty-hunting girls on the dangerous streets of Chicago.

Presented for the first time in their authentic Japanese format, these giant-sized volumes are action-packed, unretouched, unflopped, and sure to please.

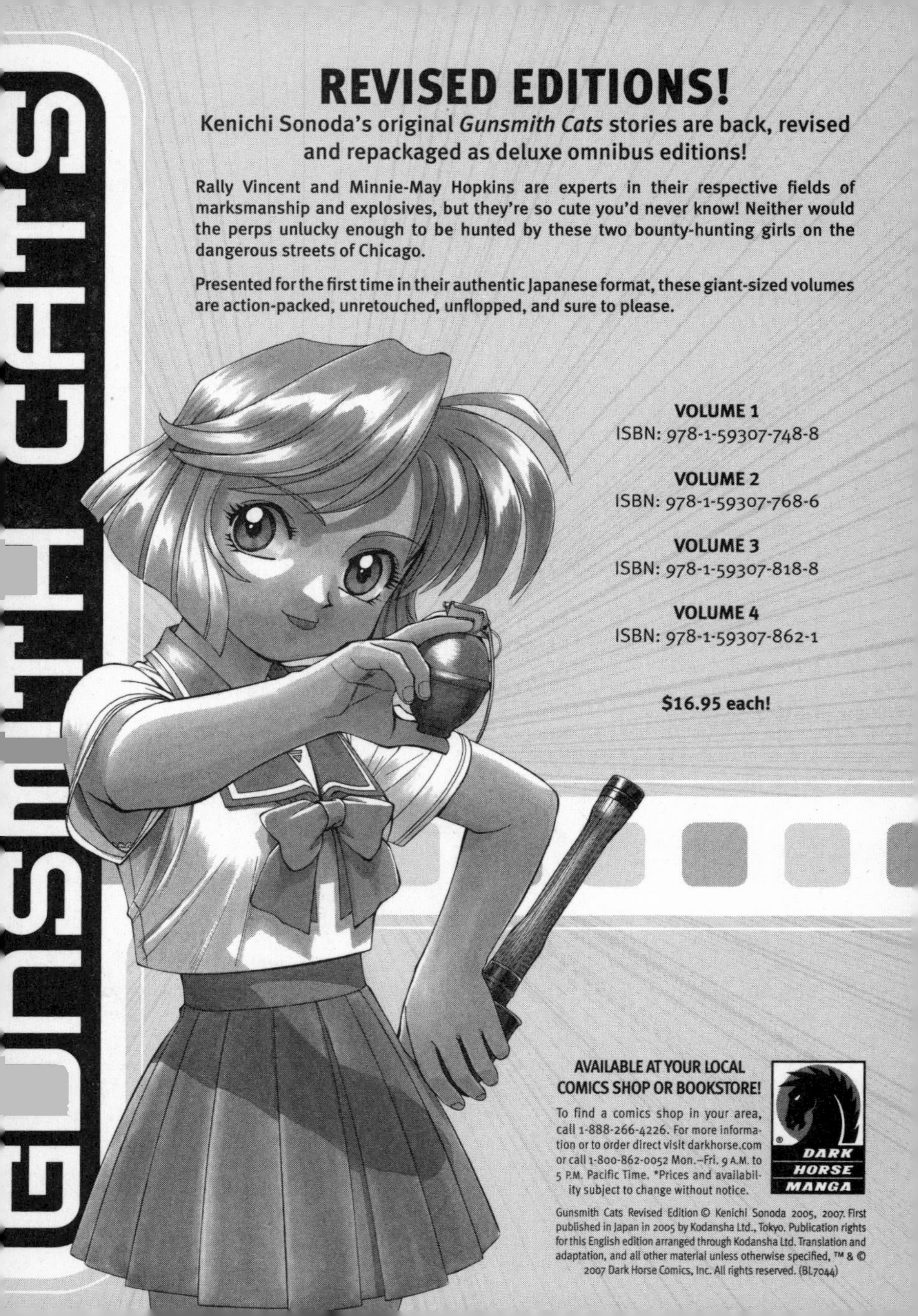

VOLUME 1
ISBN: 978-1-59307-748-8

VOLUME 2
ISBN: 978-1-59307-768-6

VOLUME 3
ISBN: 978-1-59307-818-8

VOLUME 4
ISBN: 978-1-59307-862-1

$16.95 each!

AVAILABLE AT YOUR LOCAL COMICS SHOP OR BOOKSTORE!

To find a comics shop in your area, call 1-888-266-4226. For more information or to order direct visit darkhorse.com or call 1-800-862-0052 Mon.–Fri. 9 A.M. to 5 P.M. Pacific Time. *Prices and availability subject to change without notice.

DARK HORSE MANGA

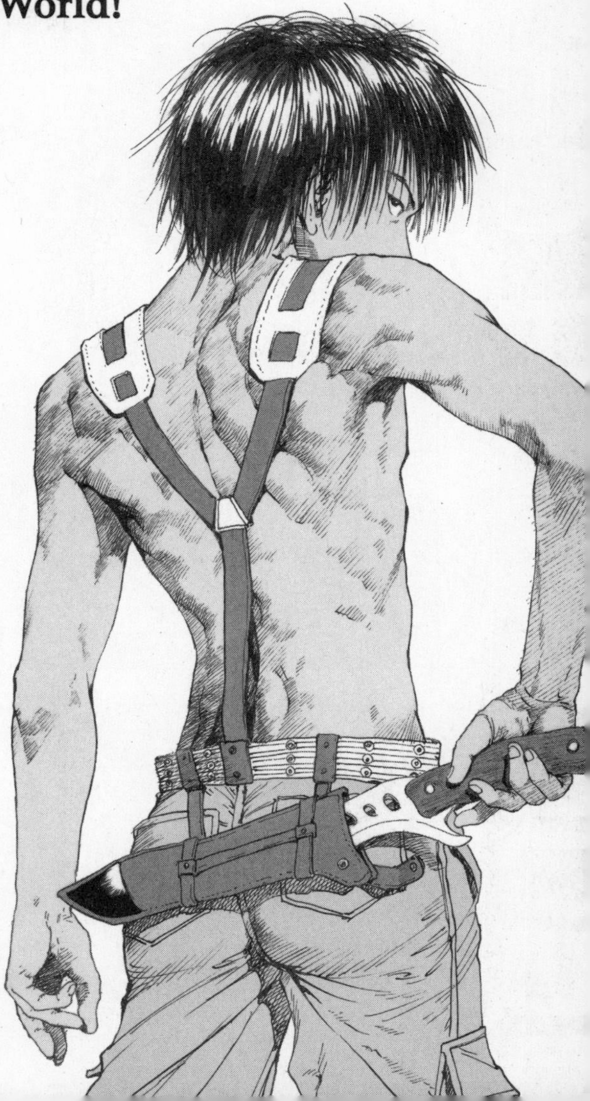

AN ALL-NEW NOVEL BASED ON THE HIT MANGA AND ANIME!

OH MY GODDESS!

— F I R S T   E N D —

WRITTEN BY

YUMI TOHMA

WITH ILLUSTRATIONS BY

KOSUKE FUJISHIMA and HIDENORI MATSUBARA

Keiichi Morisato was a typical college student—a failure with women, he was struggling to get through his classes and in general living a pretty nondescript life. That is, until he dialed a wrong number and accidentally summoned the goddess Belldandy. Not believing Belldandy was a goddess and that she could grant his every wish, Keiichi wished for her to stay with him forever. As they say, be careful what you wish for! Now bound to Earth and at Keiichi's side for life, the lives of this goddess and human will never be the same again!

ISBN 978-1-59582-137-9 | $14.95

DARK
HORSE
BOOKS

darkhorse.com

AVAILABLE AT YOUR LOCAL COMICS SHOP OR BOOKSTORE
To find a comics shop in your area, call 1.888.266.4226. For more information or to order direct: •On the web: darkhorse.com •E-mail: mailorder@darkhorse.com •Phone: 1.800.862.0052 Mon.–Fri. 9 AM to 5 PM Pacific Time.

Kosuke Fujishima's

Oh My Goddess!

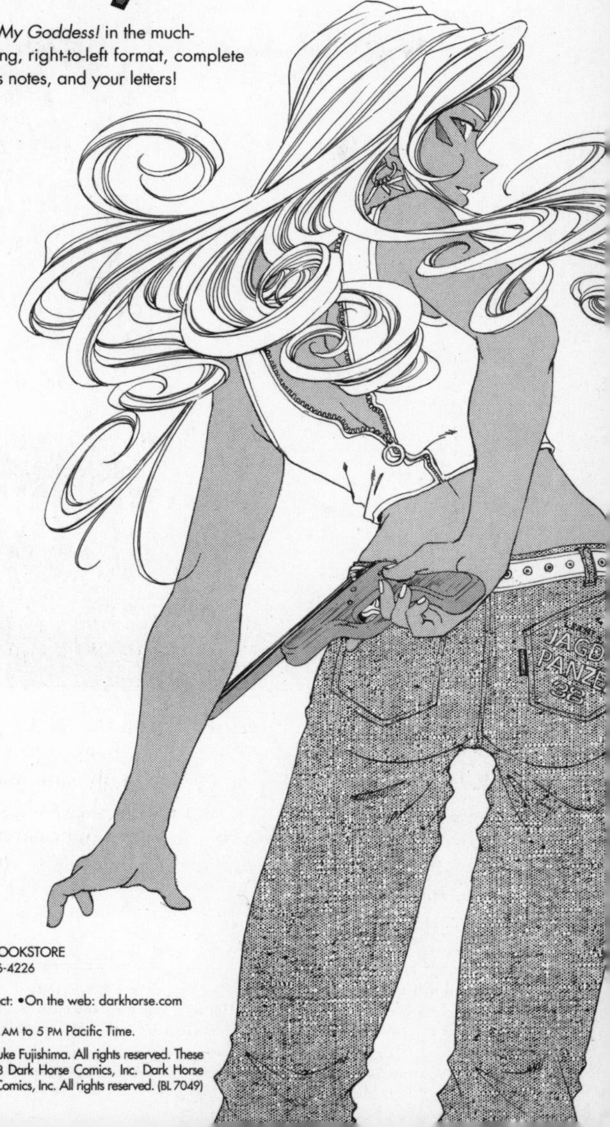

Dark Horse is proud to re-present *Oh My Goddess!* in the much-requested, affordable, Japanese-reading, right-to-left format, complete with color sections, informative bonus notes, and your letters!

Volume 1
ISBN 978-1-59307-387-9

Volume 2
ISBN 978-1-59307-457-9

Volume 3
ISBN 978-1-59307-539-2

Volume 4
ISBN 978-1-59307-623-8

Volume 5
ISBN 978-1-59307-708-2

Volume 6
ISBN 978-1-59307-772-3

Volume 7
ISBN 978-1-59307-850-8

Volume 8
ISBN 978-1-59307-889-8

Volume 22
ISBN 978-1-59307-400-5

Volume 23
ISBN 978-1-59307-463-0

Volume 24
ISBN 978-1-59307-545-3

Volume 25
ISBN 978-1-59307-644-3

Volume 26
ISBN 978-1-59307-715-0

Volume 27
ISBN 978-1-59307-788-4

Volume 28
ISBN 978-1-59307-857-7

Volume 29
ISBN 978-1-59307-912-3

$10.95 each!

AVAILABLE AT YOUR LOCAL COMICS SHOP OR BOOKSTORE
*To find a comics shop in your area, call 1-888-266-4226

For more information or to order direct: •On the web: darkhorse.com
•E-mail: mailorder@darkhorse.com
•Phone: 1-800-862-0052 Mon.–Fri. 9 AM to 5 PM Pacific Time.

Kosuke Fujishima's

Oh My Goddess!

Can't wait on the Goddesses? Change directions!

Just gotten into the new unflopped editions of *Oh My Goddess!*, and found you can't wait to see what happens next? Have no fear! The first **20 volumes** of *Oh My Goddess!* are available ***right now*** in Western-style editions! Released between 1994 and 2005, our *OMG!* Western-style volumes feature premium paper, and pages 40% larger than those of the unflopped editions! If you've already got some of the unflopped volumes and want to know which Western-style ones to get to catch up, check out darkhorse.com's "Manga Zone" for a complete breakdown of how the editions compare!

Vol. 1: Wrong Number
ISBN: 1-56971-669-2 / $13.95

Vol. 2: Leader of the Pack
ISBN: 1-56971-764-8 / $13.95

Vol. 3: Final Exam
ISBN: 1-56971-765-6 / $13.95

Vol. 4: Love Potion No. 9
ISBN: 1-56971-252-2 / $14.95

Vol. 5: Sympathy for the Devil
ISBN: 1-56971-329-4 / $13.95

Vol. 6: Terrible Master Urd
ISBN: 1-56971-369-3 / $14.95

Vol. 7: The Queen of Vengeance
ISBN: 1-56971-431-2 / $13.95

Vol. 8: Mara Strikes Back!
ISBN: 1-56971-449-5 / $14.95

Vol. 9: Ninja Master
ISBN: 1-56971-474-6 / $13.95

Vol. 10: Miss Keiichi
ISBN: 1-56971-522-X / $16.95

Vol. 11: The Devil in Miss Urd
ISBN: 1-56971-540-8 / $14.95

Vol. 12: The Fourth Goddess
ISBN: 1-56971-551-3 / $18.95

Vol. 13: Childhood's End
ISBN: 1-56971-685-4/ $15.95

Vol. 14: Queen Sayoko
ISBN: 1-56971-766-4 / $16.95

Vol. 15: Hand in Hand
ISBN: 1-56971-921-7 / $17.95

Vol. 16: Mystery Child
ISBN: 1-56971-950-0 / $18.95

Vol. 17: Traveler
ISBN: 1-56971-986-1 / $17.95

Vol. 18: The Phantom Racer
ISBN: 1-59307-217-1 / $17.95

Vol. 19/20: Sora Unchained
ISBN: 1-59307-316-X / $18.95

Adventures of the Mini-Goddesses
ISBN: 1-56971-421-5 / $9.95

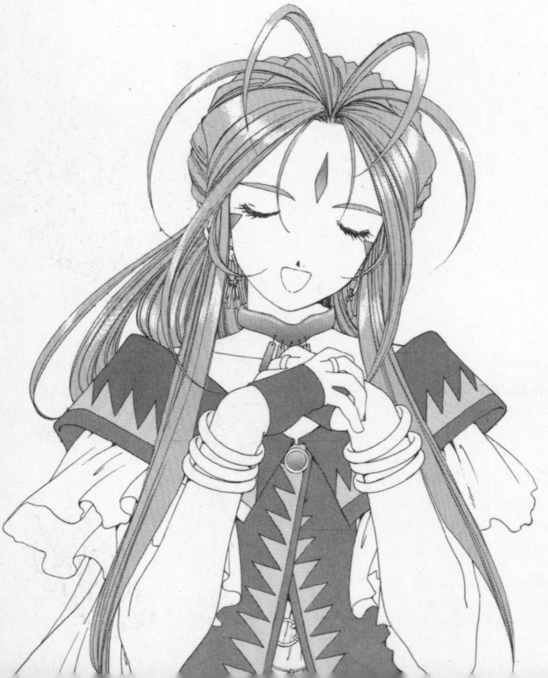

AVAILABLE AT YOUR LOCAL COMICS SHOP OR BOOKSTORE
*To find a comics shop in your area, call 1-888-266-4226

For more information or to order direct:
- On the web: darkhorse.com
- E-mail: mailorder@darkhorse.com
- Phone: 1-800-862-0052 Mon.-Fri. 9 A.M. to 5 P.M. Pacific Time.

Red String

Volume 1
ISBN 978-1-59307-624-5

Volume 2
ISBN 978-1-59307-884-3

Volume 3
ISBN 978-1-59307-958-1

$9.95 each!

When first-year high-school student Miharu Ogawa gets a call from her parents, telling her to come straight home from school, she prepares herself for the worst, but nothing she could ever have imagined could have prepared her for their "great news" . . . Miharu is getting married! How's a spirited and independent teenager who has never even kissed a boy supposed to deal with suddenly having a fiancé she's never even met? And how will her feelings change when she finds out that there are other boys out there vying for her affection, and other girls ready and willing to take away the man she's not even sure she's ready for?

Check out the collected volumes of this hit webcomic by Gina Biggs, which deals with all forms of love: parental, romantic, heterosexual, homosexual, platonic, unrequited, heartbreaking, dishonest, and all stops in between!

B U R S T

Don't miss the latest adventures of the most fun-loving, well-armed bounty hunters in Chicago! Rally Vincent and Minnie-May Hopkins return with Kenichi Sonoda's *Gunsmith Cats: Burst*, back in action and back in trouble!

Presented in the authentic right-to-left reading format, and packed full of bounty-hunting, gun-slinging, property-damaging action, *Gunsmith Cats: Burst* aims to please.

VOLUME 1
ISBN 978-59307-750-1

VOLUME 2
ISBN 978-1-59307-767-9

VOLUME 3
ISBN 978-1-59307-803-4

$10.95 EACH!

DARK HORSE MANGA

AVAILABLE AT YOUR LOCAL COMICS SHOP OR BOOKSTORE!

To find a comics shop in your area, call 1-888-266-4226. For more information or to order direct visit darkhorse.com or call 1-800-862-0052 Mon.–Fri. 9 AM to 5 PM Pacific Time. *Prices and availability subject to change without notice.

STOP! This is the back of the book!

This manga collection is translated into English, but arranged in right-to-left reading format to maintain the artwork's visual orientation as originally drawn and published in Japan. If you've never read comics this way before, take a look at the diagram below to give yourself an idea of how to go about it. Basically, you'll be starting in the upper right-hand corner, and will read each word balloon and panel moving right-to-left. It may take a little getting used to, but you should get the hang of it very quickly. Have fun! If this is the millionth manga you've read this way, never mind. ^_^

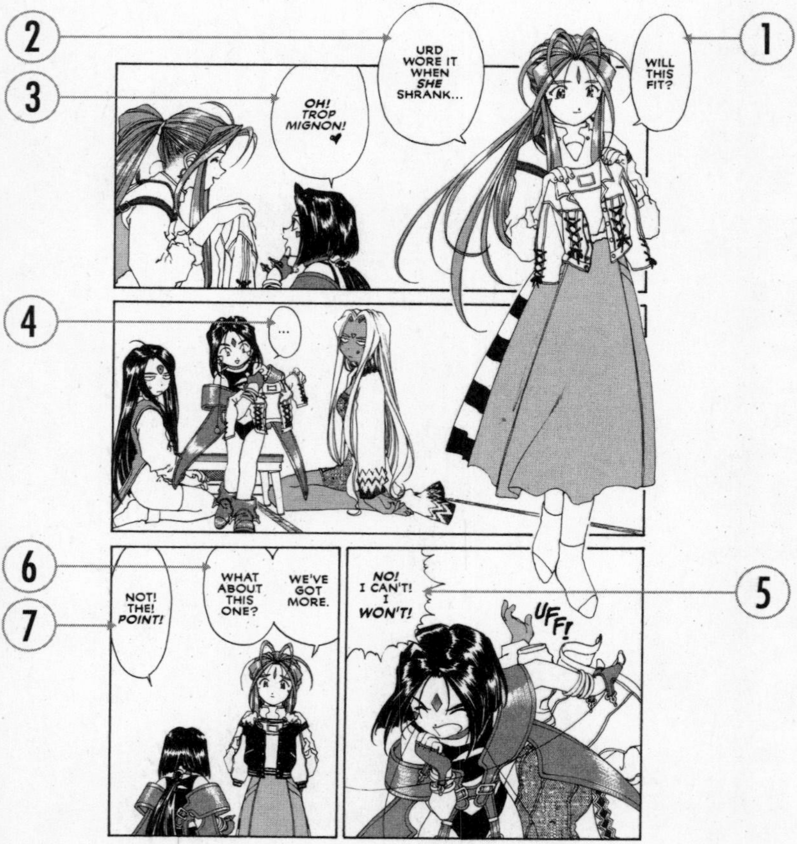

1
WILL THIS FIT?
2
URD WORE IT WHEN *SHE* SHRANK...
3
OH! TROP MIGNON!
4
...
5
NO! I CAN'T! I *WON'T!*
UFF!
6
WE'VE GOT MORE.
WHAT ABOUT THIS ONE?
7
NOT! THE! *POINT!*